The Taste of Sweet

The Taste of Sweet

Our Complicated Love Affair with Our Favorite Treats

Joanne Chen

Crown Publishers

New York

Published in the United States by Crown Publishers, an imprint of the
Crown Publishing Group, a division of Random House, Inc., New York.
www.crownpublishing.com

CROWN is a trademark and the Crown colophon is a registered trademark
of Random House, Inc.

Library of Congress Cataloging-in-Publication Data

Chen, Joanne.
   The Taste of sweet: our complicated love affair with our favorite treats /
Joanne Chen.
      p.   cm.
   Includes bibliographical references and index.
   1. Sweetness (Taste).   2. Food—Sensory evaluation.   3. Senses and sensation.
   4. Sugar.   5. Sugar—History.   I. Title.

   QP456.C475 2007
   641—dc22   2007035500

ISBN 978-0-307-35190-6

Printed in the United States of America

Design by Lauren Dong

10 9 8 7 6 5 4 3 2 1

First Edition

For my mother and father

Contents

Introduction

WHEN PEOPLE HEARD THAT I WAS WORKING ON a book about sweets, they assumed one of two things: I was either producing an exposé on junk food or creating one of those beautifully photographed dessert books. Neither could be further from the truth, since I am a firm believer in consuming king-sized chocolate bars and hardly a gourmet. What fascinates me, rather, is our relationship with sweets. The truth is, the sweets we enjoy are rarely the immaculate cakes gracing glossy magazines or the shrink-wrapped stuff of vending machines. For most of us, sweets consist of a little of both and plenty in between. They permeate every aspect of our lives and, in doing so, raise a litany of questions: Why are some of us cookie snackers and others potato chip eaters? Why are certain sweets denigrated as garbage while others, with equal amounts of sugar and fat, are cherished as luxurious treats? And why do I always have room for dessert?

As all these questions accumulated, I began to collect clues that shed some light on these topics—notes from interviews I've conducted as a magazine editor, articles ripped from newspapers, insights from books, random theories scribbled on the back of a press release. It all started as a lone folder marked "sweets," which then grew to fill out my filing cabinets and shelves. Eventually I decided to give this collection of factoids and ideas some semblance of organization. This is how the book came to be.

I'VE ALWAYS HAD a fixation with sweetness—not simply the taste itself but also how we perceive and react to it. Chapters 1 and 2 explore the nature of those reactions: Why are some of us able to refuse a tray of fresh-baked chocolate chip cookies, just because we're not hungry, while the rest of us can't say no? Why are certain chocolates relegated to the drugstore shelves, next to the AA batteries and plastic sunglasses, while others are worthy of beautiful boxes and welcomed as gifts? It used to surprise me that the same sweetness in seemingly similar contexts can trigger such different responses, but after visiting sensory specialists, professional food tasters, and trend researchers, I realized that taste isn't simply about the tongue at all. Each taste experience is an elegant orchestration of all the sensory organs working together, with our brain guiding the whole affair. It's a complicated enterprise, loving the foods we love.

When it comes to sweets, we don't dole out our affections indiscriminately. We can be very selective. Nuances are important, so much so that even the humblest of restaurants might offer two or three or more different types of sweeteners, all recognizable by their white, pink, blue, yellow, and brown packets. In contrast, it's a rare spot that offers an army of vinegars on the table, though different brands also have subtle differences in flavor. Sweet condiments are among the few things we request by their brand name, as in "Please pass the Equal." This is not the same as "Please pass the Kleenex," a case where a brand name has morphed into a generic term. When we ask for Equal, we are being very specific about what we want our "sweet" to taste like—something we almost never have the opportunity to do with our mustard, barbecue sauce, and olive oil.

But then again, in the grand scheme of things (and by this I mean not simply the food industry or the restaurant scene, but the planet itself), the taste of sweet is special. If I gathered as much as I could in the thick forest behind my old house and sampled everything that sprouted from the ground or on trees, most of it would taste bitter or sour; the non-plants, like stones and soil, would probably be salty. I can only imagine, then, what a happy surprise an early hunter-gatherer would have had when she stumbled across the taste of sweet after a long search for edible food—a look of sheer joy, I would expect, like the look my friend's daughter gave when she took her first bite of chocolate cake on her first birthday. That look, her pastry chef father explained to me, was as if she were thinking, "I can't believe something this good was kept secret from me for so long!"

For hundreds of centuries, sugar, the current gold standard of what sweetness should taste like, was kept secret from most of the world too. Its crystals lie hidden in simple foods that taste sweet, such as honey, maple and palm syrup, fruit, and other plants, including sugar beets and sugarcane. Going by the scientific name *sucrose,* a sugar molecule is in fact two simple sugars, glucose and fructose, linked together. Simple sugars are compounds of carbon, hydrogen, and oxygen, with the latter two always in the same two-to-one ratio as water. They are sweet in and of themselves; but linked together, they produce an entirely different, more complex, sweet nirvana. Sucrose is sweeter than glucose but milder than fructose. It gives food moisture and texture while it enhances quietly, invisibly, leaving the fundamental flavors of that food intact.

The sucrose we enjoy today is taken from the juice of sugarcane and sugar beets. The older source—and the source that constitutes 70 percent of the world's sugar production—is sugarcane, of which *Saccharum officinarum* is the most important.

An unexpectedly oversized member of the grass family, it can grow as tall as twenty feet and as thick as two inches in diameter. As sturdy as it sounds, it's also sensitive about its surroundings. Sugarcane demands nutrient-rich soil, brilliant sunshine, and decent moisture. In order to experience its sweetness, one cannot simply pluck or pull, as one would a fruit. The cane must be cut with blades, and you must extract the sucrose-containing liquid quickly and carefully because the cane is fragile and, when cracked, is prone to spoilage. You then boil the juices to produce the syrup, which is, in turn, cooled and boiled several more times until finally you are left with a yield of sweet white crystals. Molasses is the syrup that's extracted from boiling, and with each successive round of the refinement process, its color gets darker as the sugar gets whiter. Brown sugar is sugar that has undergone an abbreviated refining process. Although these days, with an eye for consistency, the beige tabletop crystals are sometimes refined completely, and molasses is added back in. Either way, for the perfect, purest sweetener, timing and temperature are of the essence. It must be hot enough to allow the impurities to evaporate, but not too hot so as to burn the whole concoction.

Understandably, it took some time before humans looked beyond obvious appearances and discovered the taste inside. The first sugar eaters simply sucked and chewed on the cane plant, letting the sweet juices wash over the palate. The juice is 15 percent sucrose—four to five times less sweet than dried dates or honey, but undeniably purer, giving no hint of fruitiness or waxiness or woodiness.

Historians suspect that sugarcane was cultivated in New Guinea before 8000 B.C. and spread in several directions in the millennia that followed, perhaps arriving in the Philippines and India around 6000 B.C., and then later in Indonesia, though it may have been cultivated independently there as well. The plant seems to have stayed put for a long while, until probably the third century B.C., when it was brought to southern China from either Southeast Asia or eastern India.

Back in those very early years, it was the sweet juice that was savored. The *Ramayana,* a Sanskrit epic dating to about the third century B.C., describes the city of Ayodhyā. The water there "was sweet as the juice of the sugarcane," we're told. A southern Chinese poem, written about the same time, lists a number of remedies for nursing a dying king to health; among them was "roast kid with sugarcane sauce." Sailing along the Indus River through India in 327 B.C., Nearchus is believed to have noticed "a reed . . . [that] brings forth honey without the help of bees." Little did he know that the real prize had yet to be discovered.

Exactly when crystals were first isolated from the juice is a point of contention among historians because sweet substances also come from other plants. It's likely that the discovery occurred in the first century in India, if notes from Dioscorides are to be believed. While visiting the subcontinent, the Greek physician and botanist described a "concreted honey" that comes from reeds and is "like in consistence to salt." Better evidence of the existence of sugar in its crystallized form doesn't appear until A.D. 500, in a Hindu religious text. Whatever the truth may be, there's no doubt that the labor involved in securing decent amounts of table sugar required a clever mind and an able body. I can't help but think that this is nature's way of protecting the sweet precious crystals—or of protecting us from ourselves.

After all, once we discover a favorite sugar fix—and we all have one, whether it's a piece of fruit or a candy bar—we grow very attached to it. Sweets have always had a special place in our minds and in our hearts. And for Americans, it is the only taste that we imbue with all that is good. Bitter, salty, and sour suggest surly characters; umami registers no personality at all. But with "sweet" as a descriptor, the person in question glimmers with goodness and possesses instant appeal. *Sugar,* from the Sanskrit *sakara,* or gravel, has been turned into a term of affection, as have *honey, sweet pea, sweetheart,* and *sweetie pie.* Marketers have taken advantage of sugar's sweet tug on our emotions. We have a beauty line named Sugar, a cell phone known as Chocolate, a magazine called *Cookie.* At the fanciest restaurants, we have smoked salmon and cream cheese balls parading as lollipops. When food makers deliver healthy ingredients, their concoctions often take on candy shapes and textures, as is the case with granola bars, cough drops, and nicotine gum. Sweet-natured creations tend to have a built-in allure. Chapters 4 and 5 explore the reasons behind this.

Physiologically, the taste of sweet is so appealing that some suspect it may even be addictive. Emotionally, the pull may be just as persistent, or even more so. Certain sweets, after all, offer us a taste of lost youth. In my particular case, my childhood home brimmed with blue tins of Danish biscuits and fat jars of crystalline rock candy sticks. From Sunday breakfast to the afternoon snack to dessert, sweets were a reason to take a breath and linger a while. One of my favorites was a pancake my mother would fashion out of the dough left over from making dumplings. She'd stuff it with peanut butter and serve it hot from the pan, chewy inside and crispy outside, with a sprinkling of sugar. It was delicious—but more than that, it extended the pleasures of the family dinner.

Not surprisingly, I now can't help having a special affection for sweets and the people who love them. By this I do not mean the "I'll just have a small bite of yours" types, the sharers, or the fruit plate eaters. I'm referring specifically to the intrepid ones, those who take the lead and say, "Let's order dessert!" and those who insist on a plate each, if not more. To me, dessert is flush with symbol and meaning, and to embrace dessert is to embrace the child within.

Not everyone agrees, of course, and health-obsessed eaters have spent years trying to eliminate sweetness in their daily routines. It hasn't worked. The lure of sweet seems to have the nine lives of a cat—every time it comes close to being snuffed out, it tiptoes back into our routine when we least expect it. We might hunt down an ice cream with less sugar for an afternoon snack, but we end up taking it in, naively, the next morning for breakfast in the form of newfangled yogurt flavors like caramel and vanilla crème. We might avoid sugar in our breakfast cereal, only to give in to it, unwittingly, with a dessertified morning latte. We might choose sugar-free sodas, but caloric sweeteners slip right back into the bottle as flavored waters, sports drinks, iced green teas, and fruity martinis. Despite our ever-growing efforts to diet, the average American consumed more candy in 2006 than he or she had in the past seven years: 25.5 pounds of it. And as our total consumption of caloric sweeteners has leveled off a little, we're each still consuming 99.2 pounds of sugar and other caloric sweeteners such as high-fructose corn syrup every year, and spending about $12 billion annually on packaged sweet baked goods. A few years ago, at the height of the low-carb Atkins diet craze, lines were still snaking out of the best chocolate shops and bakeries.

Chapters 6, 7, and 8 examine our collective response to this incredible force of nature: Do we, as members of a nation, economic class, or social group, embrace it or fear it? On this side of the Atlantic, sweets don't make us feel so good sometimes, and I've always been astonished by the way sweets can render us out of control and sick with remorse. Though I'm always ready to forgive that brick of a chocolate cake for my transgressions, I've also become suspicious; matters have only worsened in recent years, as head-lines continue to implicate something so cherished in history and in my childhood as the culprit behind a litany of social ills, from bad behavior in the classroom to belly fat. I miss the all-out enjoy-ment of sweets, but more so, I miss the rituals and flavors that are made possible by them—and that are slowly disappearing because of our attempts to push sweets away.

In the past couple of years, well-meaning skinny people, alarmed at the plumpness of our cupcakes, among other things, have taken the liberty of offering diet advice from faraway lands. Mireille Guiliano, CEO of Cliquot and author of *French Women Don't Get Fat,* revealed to the *Today* show audience that she does in-deed eat chocolate, but only one piece (or maybe it was two—in any case, it was not the entire bar, as I am accustomed to) per day. Naomi Moriyama, author of *Japanese Women Don't Get Old or Fat* and a marketing consultant in luxury goods, quotes her mother, who in-structs: "Food should be eaten with the eyes as well as the mouth. Serving food is like painting a picture. Food should be arranged like exquisite jewelry." These are both admirable notions, to be sure. But for people like me, who count the massive mess of a cin-namon roll at the airport Cinnabon as one of the joys of traveling, any advice concerning small portions or satiation-by-sight does not work. I prefer my helpings large and sloppy, so I can fill my mouth, so it's hard to speak, so I can taste it better. If the sweet is small, like a petit four, then I would like at least a few on hand, please, so the pleasure is sustained, and so I can make sure it's as good as I thought it was the first time.

IT'S HARD TO comprehend living in a world without sugar, but somehow our ancestors managed. It wasn't until around the sixth century that the Persians discovered sugarcane in the Bengal region of India. With the help of irrigation systems, the cane flourished in their homeland both in Makran, near India, and the Euphrates-Tigris delta, before farmers carried it inland and northward. In the hundreds of centuries that followed, the taste for sweetness became inextricably linked to a quest for power. In 632, when Mohammad and his Arab devotees launched their pursuit of a global Islamic state, they also spread a taste for sugar. They encountered sugar for the first time when they invaded neighboring Persia and liked it so much that they brought it along with them, disseminating it throughout the population with each subsequent victory, just as they did with the teachings of the Koran. Between the seventh and twelfth centuries, Islamic rule expanded to Palestine, Syria, Baghdad, Egypt, Morocco, Sicily, Spain, Cyprus, Crete, and Malta—and so did the taste for sugar and the business of growing and producing it. When the conquest came to a halt and the local cane manufacturing eventually faltered, the people's penchant for sweetness remained.

Sweetness spread throughout the rest of western Europe with the Crusades in the eleventh century, as Christian soldiers became more exposed to the white crystals in the lands occupied by their Turkish enemies. They liked this unusual "spice" so much that they sought out a direct route to the eastern spice kingdoms and eventually created a powerful sugar empire of their own in the New World.

The English may be famous for their sweet tooth, but it was the Spanish who brought sugar to America. In 1493, upon the request of King Ferdinand and Queen Isabella, Christopher Columbus hauled cane from the Spanish-ruled Canary Islands to Santo Domingo, where the plant was then cultivated. It wasn't long before the English, Dutch, and French established their own sweet-producing colonies. But with large plantations in Barbados (settled in 1627) and Jamaica (established in 1655), an enormous influx of slave labor from Africa, and a voracious appetite for sugar to match, the British ultimately dominated the trade. Sugar had turned into a kitchen staple in England by the middle of the eighteenth century, and in America a century later.

Upon getting their hands on the same sweet white crystals, people from different parts of the globe chose to do very different things with them, depending on their particular historical, political, and geographical circumstances. This book explores the consequences of some of these decisions. For instance, when the French vanquished the royals, the royal help, too, lost their jobs. Among the newly unemployed were chefs, who subsequently turned their attention to creating complicated pastries for an already established aristocratic class. Certain parts of China had their share of urban elites, too, but not many cows. The consequent lack of dairy products (milk and butter) essential to rich European pastries led the Chinese to lighter buns and cakes that were delicately steamed over the stove, since ovens, too, were rare. For the nomadic Turks in the eleventh century, the absence of ovens meant a steady diet of flatbread, cooked on a griddle; to add some variety, not to mention thickness, someone ingeniously came up with the idea of a layered pastry.

And so, this is, in part, why we enjoy a dessert of crème brûlée in our neighborhood French bistro, why we see light-as-air sponge cakes through the glass showcases of Chinatown bake shops, and why we pick up baklava from our favorite falafel joint. Sweets provide a window into the lives of those who created them, and they're our connection to the past.

OUR SWEETS ARE still evolving, faster than I had anticipated and fueled by more factors than I had imagined. I soon realized that what I've ended up recording is a mere moment in time—a compendium of my personal musings and a record of the discoveries that resonated most for me. The final two chapters of the book explore two of what I think are the most intriguing areas of that evolution-in-progress. These are areas where experts, prompted by the health-consciousness of the times, are asking: How can the taste of sweet be healthier? How can healthy foods taste sweeter? Chapter 9 explores the ever-increasing varieties of artificial sweeteners and why we're still uneasy about them. Chapter 10 looks at how at least one nutritionist hopes to use sweetness to our advantage. A shift in attitude can be swift. In the case of chocolate, a compound found by scientists to impart health can cast a new and wholesome light on an entire category of sweets. But as answers are found, new concerns arise: If, say, we make our vegetables sweeter, will an appreciation for bitterness be lost in future generations? And will the appreciation for the pure taste of sugar—whose intensity is some six hundred times less sweet than the leading high-intensity sweetener—follow? Even the best intentions leave us fraught with questions.

Sweets, I've come to conclude, are the ultimate feel-good, feel-bad food, and as such they're as beguiling as they're exasperating. They inspire stories as rich and deep as an intoxicating love affair. A better understanding of this relationship provides some insight into the meanings we instill in our food and the reasons why we consume it the way we do; it uncovers our pasts, our unspoken beliefs, fears, and desires. It sheds light on the way we view others.

You must think I exaggerate. I once would have thought the same; tasting sweet seems an intimate, isolated act. But as my pet project progressed, I quickly understood that sweetness hardly exists in a vacuum. It influences and is influenced by more things than

I could have ever expected. It's modified by smell; it's shaped by sight, sound, and touch. It's transformed by time, place, science, culture, and money. By looking at the world through the lens of sweet, I learned about the vulnerabilities and desires that color human nature and came to discover how the quest for the perfect sweet reflects our endless search for happiness without compromise.

Chapter One

Sweet Enough for You?

THERE ARE CERTAIN THINGS IN LIFE THAT ARE NOT open to debate, or so I thought. Freshly laundered cotton sheets feel nice. Lilacs smell lovely. The sun, when it sets, looks glorious. The fact that cookies-and-cream ice cream tastes delicious I would surely file into this category, as I would the virtues of thick, warm chocolate chip cookies, Red Velvet cake frosted with buttercream, and fried dough flecked with confectioners' sugar. All wonderful things—as wonderful and, to me, as necessary as clothing, shelter, and the air we breathe.

For the longest time, I met no naysayers; no one scoffed or raised an eyebrow when I enthusiastically consumed copious amounts of these foods. I may be wary of unfamiliar things on the savory menu, but add a sweetener, call it a dessert, and I will happily put it in my mouth. I also enjoy a Dunkin' Donuts Bow Tie for breakfast from time to time, not to mention a brownie for a snack on a bad day and banana bread pudding on a good one, or vice versa. And so I was able to cling to the notion that sweets taste good as fiercely as I did when I was a small child, even after I moved from rural New England to the food capital of the world, New York City.

My sugar-centric universe crashed when I turned thirty. I had just begun working in an office where we often ate lunch at our desks—and where a dessert was as likely a sight as a gerbil in a cage. I had also begun meeting with—and subsequently eating with—people who had quibbles about my opinions on sweets and no hesitation in voicing them: "Oh no," they would say, hands raised as if for protection, when I'd offer to share. "It's too sweet." Being a rather judgmental sort, I couldn't help but secretly think less of them. I knew it was silly, but I couldn't stop myself. My irritation sometimes seeped through in my words and actions, affecting my friendships. Why *not* pick up a Krispy Kreme when the red "HOT NOW" light is on? How could they not see the goodness of a fresh-baked pie as surely as they would the light of day?

I met Marlene, who turned down my offer of a new carton of ice cream—chock-full of brownie bits, pretzels, and other chunky forms of wholesome goodness. I met Nori, who found chocolate cake unpleasant on the palate. I met Bari, who had a mystifying preference for Jolly Ranchers, lollipops, and gummy bears over a Snickers bar. I met Carolina and Loree, who would order a second or third glass of wine instead of dessert. I met Victoria, who had no qualms about the taste of sweetness delivered in those pink packets of sugar substitute.

And then I met Linda Bartoshuk, a psychologist who ultimately changed my attitudes about the taste of sweet and, unwittingly, my suspicions about other people.

Bartoshuk is a tall, gregarious South Dakotan with salt-and-pepper hair and a clear, sharp voice that can be heard down a long hall. She likes pecan pie and peanut butter fudge. She has a recipe for marshmallows. "If I weren't so worried about getting so much sugar, I'd take four packets in my coffee," she says unapologetically. "I can't get sweet strong enough."

I liked her instantly. She's a food lover of the best and rarest kind—comfortable with her likes and dislikes, yet open to everyone else's. Scrunch up your nose in disgust, if you like, as she tells you about her Fruit Roll-Up snacks; but confess your love for Twinkies, and she won't judge you. As a psychologist and a taste scientist, she knows better; she realizes that people's taste realities can be starkly and profoundly different. And so while I grumble, "I can't believe that person doesn't like ice cream as much I do," Bartoshuk might actually find herself wondering, "I wonder why she *does.*"

WE MEET FOR the first time at a wine event in New York City. Her co-panelist, an elegantly dressed woman who has just jetted in from her vineyard in France, has brought the booze, but it is Bartoshuk, whose wardrobe tends toward sensible shoes and monochromatic outfits, who really gets people talking. Her little demonstration, something I've seen several times now, never ceases to enthrall me, like a magic trick that never gets old.

She is a presence on stage, her language lay-friendly and her movements quick and efficient. Raising the energy level of the room before her lecture even begins, she starts by passing out disk-shaped filter paper in mysterious small envelopes, along with butterscotch candy in bright yellow wrappers.

"Did everyone get PROP paper and a piece of hard candy?" she asks the audience, who by now are murmuring to one another like kids on the first day of school.

PROP stands for 6-n-propylthiouracil, a compound used to treat hyperthyroidism. The filter paper has been dipped in a minuscule amount of PROP, she assures the audience, so it's perfectly safe to taste. At this point, she tosses the whole disk into her mouth. "I can get it good and wet like this," she says, making smacking sounds. "And I taste nothing. Just paper." She then invites everyone to take a taste of theirs, but warns them to approach it slowly. Gradually, the room realizes why. Part of the audience is making faces of disgust. Others, with the disks still in their mouths, are wondering what the fuss is about. PROP, it turns out, is a chemical that for some people tastes like bitter medicine, and for others, like nothing at all.

The first paper on taste blindness was published in *Science News Letter* in 1931. The researcher, Arthur L. Fox, from E.I. du Pont de Nemours and Company, reported on the serendipitous discovery that took place in his lab when a poof of a compound related to PROP, phenylthiocarbamide (or PTC), was accidentally released into the air. His colleague, who unintentionally inhaled it, presumably with his mouth open, was struck by how bitter it was. Fox tried it, too—maybe not the most careful methodology on his part, but then, in the old days people were always putting things in their mouths in the name of science. In any case, in doing so, he realized that he, curiously, tasted nothing at all. This led him to coin the term "tasteblindness," which eventually gave rise to the terms "taster" and "non-taster." Magnified images of the tongue later revealed that the difference is a matter of anatomy: tasters have more taste buds than non-tasters.

Decades later, Bartoshuk has found that the differences in people's ability to taste PROP are only part of the story. She and other researchers realized that sweet tastes sweeter to PROP tasters, and salt tastes saltier. And because the presence of more taste buds is linked with the presence of more texture- and pain-detecting nerve fibers, fats also feel fattier on the tongue of PROP tasters and hot peppers feel more fiery.

PROP tasters fall into two categories: medium tasters and super-tasters. The super-tasters are those who treat the pink sweetener packet as if it were poison, Bartoshuk explains, and they prefer a little milk or sugar, or both, to take the edge off the bitterness of black coffee. (My friend Victoria, therefore, might be a non-taster, and entirely undeserving of my snide remarks about her use of the pink stuff.) With many more taste buds on the tongue, super-tasters are even more sensitive to the taste and texture of food than a typical taster. "They live in a neon taste world, while non-tasters live in a pastel taste world," says Bartoshuk.

Exactly how profound the difference between a non-taster and a super-taster can be is not readily evident in the typical nine-point category scale, like the kind used in pain assessments, with 0 being not sweet at all and 9 being extremely sweet. The problem is that my definition of strong may not be the same as yours or the next person's. In a conversation such as "Does this lemonade taste very sweet to you?" "Yes, it tastes very sweet to me," no useful information is actually exchanged. "Absolutely none," Bartoshuk insists. You're assuming that labels like "very sweet" denote the same perceived intensities to everyone. In other words, if people are asked to rate pain on a scale from 0 (no pain) to 100 (most intense pain ever experienced), everyone will say his or her most intense pain will be 100. But of course that's not really the case: it's just not logical to think that everyone has personally experienced the same level of pain. And so Bartoshuk has devised a better way to ask the question. She asks people to compare their most intense pain with the brightest light they have ever seen—usually the sun. Lo and behold, the differences come through in the responses. Women who select childbirth as their worst pain will rate that pain about 20 percent higher than the brightest light they've ever seen. The average man will rate his worst pain about *equal* to it.

That's why, in order to evaluate what her test subjects are truly tasting, Bartoshuk insists on using a system where people can rate sensations of different kinds on the same scale. With this method, something described as "the strongest taste imaginable" is often more intense for a super-taster than for a non-taster by a factor of three.

It's a rather abstract concept, as difficult to grasp as it is to fathom what it's like to be in another person's shoes. A few years ago, Bartoshuk came up with a method for explaining these intangible ideas to a group of medical students. Think of it this way, she said: If everyone were given a series of progressively sweeter sugar solutions and asked to pick out the solution they deemed "very sweet," they would all pick the same solution— somewhere three-quarters of the way up the range (the natural tendency is to leave the very top for "extremely sweet"). But then, if you were to give everyone a set of headphones and ask them to turn up the volume so that the level equals the intensity of the sweetness of that "very sweet" solution, you'd find that the loudness would vary remarkably. The tasters would adjust the knob louder, perhaps to the level that you might hear at a trendy clothing boutique; the super-tasters would turn the volume way up, to the uncomfortable noise level of a dance club. We all might call the same thing "very sweet," she says, but in fact we're not sharing in the same experience at all.

WITH THE DISCOVERY of new categories, scientists couldn't help but begin putting people in their proper place. About 25 percent of Americans are non-tasters; about 25 percent, super-tasters; and about half, medium tasters. More women than men are super-tasters. More white men tend to be non-tasters than tasters. Asians and thin women of any race are apt to be super-tasters. Alcohol drinkers are often (much to my surprise) non-tasters, as are those who take their coffee black.

Taste sensitivity seems to be genetic. If your mother and father are tasters, then you are likely to be one too; the same idea goes for those with parents of the non-tasting persuasion. Oddly, people with the same taster status tend to be an unlikely romantic match. According to a small but intriguing University of California, Berkeley, study that appeared in the *Annals of Human Biology* in 1989, taster women tend to marry non-taster men. The authors' logic is as follows: The most stable relationships often arise not from shared food preferences, but from shared values and personality traits (such as how independent they are or how well they get along with parents). These criteria, at least in part, seem to depend on the age at which a person reaches puberty. There's a very small but significant tendency for late-maturing women to have more in common with late-maturing men because late maturers of both sexes tend to have similar characteristics: they both have slightly more strained relationships with their parents, according to the study's authors, and they tend to have more dependency and confidence issues compared to early maturers. It just so happens, curiously, that this puberty gene is linked to the taster gene, but in opposite ways for men and women: early-maturing women tend to be tasters and early-maturing men tend to be non-tasters. Since couples who marry often have similar emotional (not taste-bud) dispositions, you have the unexpected partnership of two people with different tasting intensities. Happily, though, most couples eventually work out their disagreements about taste over time. The more meals they share together, the more they adapt to each other's likes and dislikes and ultimately reach a common ground.

Of course, genes aren't the only reason why people experience food the way they do. Taste experts, including Bartoshuk, believe that by far the biggest factors as to why we appreciate certain items over others are culture and habit. For instance, a non-taster child can be raised to think that carob is an acceptable sweet alternative to chocolate. A determined super-taster dieter can muster up all her willpower and teach herself that vegetables and black coffee don't

taste so unbearably bitter after all. Still, there's something irresistible about a simple physical explanation that's literally on the
tip of our tongues. See-it-and-believe-it physiology lends credibil-
ity to abstract theories about tasting, just as brain scans do for addiction, anxiety, and other human experiences deemed a figment
of our imagination until technology came along.

When I take that first cautious lick of PROP paper at the wine
event, I can't decide what I want the outcome to be. Tasting nothing would explain, at least in part, my enthusiasm for intensely
sweet "everything but the kitchen sink" sundaes. But then again,
tasting PROP and earning super-taster status would be a nice little
victory—it always feels pretty good to be a super-anything—though
it wouldn't really explain my boundless love for cakes and cookies
and doughnuts and ice cream.

I taste. Immediately I am caught off guard by the strength of
its bitterness, the sort of aggressive bitter that seems to coat the entire tongue, change its texture, and take over all your senses. This
must mean I'm a super-taster, I think, and as I leave the event
later that morning, I'm feeling inexplicably proud.

THE SECOND TIME I meet Linda Bartoshuk, she is building up a
taste lab with her colleague and old friend Frank Catalanotto, a
professor at the College of Dentistry at the University of Florida,
Gainesville. Since the PROP tasting at the wine panel, I have relished the idea of being a super-taster but secretly feel like a fraud,
since my tasting sprees for sweet baked goods and chocolate bars
are as unstoppable as other women's penchants for expensive
handbags and shoes. When Bartoshuk and I speak one bright
weekend in April, she is in the midst of putting together a presentation for a sensory meeting later that spring. Scientific articles
are piled high behind her desk in her cramped office. Dozens of

business cards and scrawled-on Post-it notes are taped onto the computer and file cabinets.

When I tell her about my inconsistent taste preferences, she is quick to explain that just because PROP tastes intensely bitter to me, it doesn't necessarily mean I'm a super-taster. While not tasting PROP confirms that you're a non-taster, tasting it means that chances are you're a taster or a super-taster, but to know which for sure, you have to count the taste buds in the tongue. "The physiology never lies," her doctoral student tells me.

And so, the next day, I'm led into a room equipped with a large reclining examining chair, computer screens, and cameras that take images of the mouth. It looks like a dentist's office, except that the room is filled with sweets. There are boxes and boxes of strawberry Fruit Roll-Ups, squirt bottles of Hershey's Syrup, and bags of coffee jelly beans. "That's for the taste exams," explains Catalanotto.

By the time a patient visits, he or she is generally at the end of his or her rope. For instance, in the coming week Bartoshuk and Catalanotto would meet a former truck driver haunted by strange scents and no longer able to appreciate the taste of his wife's apple pie. They'd also see a sixty-something woman from Tallahassee, who explains calmly and clearly, her hands folded on her lap, that she has had a burning sensation in her mouth for the past twelve years. The patients are given a tongue examination as well as a battery of taste tests. Sometimes strange sensations, like burning, can be relieved, says Bartoshuk. "But a cure for the absolute disappearance of tastes is still out of reach." (Super-tasters, by the way, are more prone to burning mouth syndrome, and knowing this, I decide that being simply a taster wouldn't be so bad after all.)

My appointment starts with a snapshot of the tongue in order to determine taster status. My tongue is efficiently swabbed with a blue dye, the deep blue of M&M's, which colors everything except the tiny mushroom-like protrusions that have a name that is fun to say: fungiform papillae. These stay pink. (For kicks, you get the same effect by drinking milk and then examining your own tongue in the mirror.)

From the top, the fungiform papillae look like rings. Nestled inside these rings are taste buds, each of which is made up of 50 to 100 taste cells. You also have taste buds on structures called circumvallate papillae (arranged in a V in the back of the tongue) and foliate papillae (on the sides of the tongue, in trenches at the rear). But the fungiform are the easiest for doctors to see, so they are the ones that are dyed.

Super-tasters have smaller fungiform papillae compared to everyone else's, but a lot *more* of them. Some will have so many scrunched up together that hardly any space appears in between. Bartoshuk has seen super-tasters with as many as 60 within a 6 mm area as well as non-tasters with as few as 5. Each taste bud within these papillae is surrounded by nerve cells, so the more taste buds that a bite of food excites, the more nerves that are activated.

Contrary to popular belief, the taste map of the tongue is pure myth. The front of the tongue is not the only place you can taste sweet, and the back isn't relegated to bitter. The misunderstanding, explains Bartoshuk, stems from a poor English translation of a paper written in German in 1901. In fact, tastes are not region-specific. Sweet, sour, bitter, salty—they all can be tasted wherever taste buds exist, and taste buds are in more places than I had ever imagined. They are on the top of the tongue, on the ridge, on the back, and close to the throat where you're about to swallow. Taste buds are even on the pharynx and larynx, and the epiglottis, uvula, and esophagus. Believe it or not, there are also taste-bud-like cells in the stomach; scientists are still in midst of finding out what function they serve exactly, but they seem to have something to do with how full we feel.

"The original article was trying to show that there are different thresholds for taste in the various part of the tongue—which is true. But those differences are extremely small," says Bartoshuk, who plowed through the original article in German. "I've tried to kill off the idea of a taste map for years! I've written about it, made fun of it. Nothing helps."

By now, I am holding my blue tongue still against a microscope slide, which sends the image onto a screen. Bartoshuk scrutinizes it, directing the shot as if it were a centerpiece at a photo shoot for a magazine. "Try to go over on the other side, too," she says to Catalanotto, as he makes adjustments. "That's beautiful. Let's just take a whole bunch of them. Very nice."

IN THE FOURTH century B.C., Aristotle began the task of categorizing taste and was partial to the idea of opposites: sweet and bitter, succulent and salty. He also considered astringent, acid, pungent, and rough as rightful candidates for tastes. What we know now (though science may revise this later) is that there are five tastes: sweet, sour, bitter, salty, and umami. When we talk about the taste of something, however, we're usually talking about flavor. Flavor is many tastes combined, embellished, and fine-tuned with aroma and texture. It's not merely, say, the spare sensation of sugar or vinegar on the tongue, but the full-blast gustatory experience of lemon pound cake, apple pie, or candied oranges. It's the sense of taste made gorgeous with the senses of smell and touch.

A person's gustatory world becomes whole thanks to a vast network of nerves and receptors on the tongue, in the mouth, up the nose, and in the brain, all assiduously doing their part. When one is not up to snuff, the brightness of a food's flavor dims a little.

Seventy to 80 percent of what we taste relies on smell; some suspect that as much as 90 percent does. In any case, the collaboration of the two is seamless—until some pernicious virus wreaks havoc on our breathing passages, causing our noses to be unceremoniously stuffed up. I never minded so much if, for a few miserable sick days, a steak shed its fabulous, savory succulence to morph into a brick, all brown and bland. But rob me of the pleasures of a warm buttery cake, and gloom sets in.

A piece of cake, once in the mouth, is a moving target, causing conditions that are difficult to re-create in the lab and making taste especially tricky for scientists to study. The temperature of the food rises or falls until it finds its equilibrium in your warm mouth; its viscosity changes. As you chew, you're not only breaking down the food but also stirring up the air around it; aromatic components rise up as the solids move toward the back of the tongue and are eventually swallowed. The back of the nose catches a whiff, a process known as retronasal olfaction. When it's blocked by congestion from a cold, the flavor of a food becomes muffled and the pleasure is lost. (In contrast, orthonasal olfaction is what you breathe in through the front of the nose. It's what allows success for bakeries, spas, and fragrances in crystal bottles; it's what woos. Retronasal olfaction is quiet and hidden, but it's what makes food worth savoring.) Without the scent of the food's components, you're left with only the stimulation you get on the tongue.

Here, saliva plays an important role. It not only breaks the food down into smaller pieces made for swallowing, but in doing so, it also releases molecules that stimulate the taste buds, called tastants. The tastants interact with taste receptors on the taste buds—and depending on whether you're a non-taster or a super-taster, you'll have fewer or more taste receptors to receive those tastants and register intensity. The nerves clustered around the taste buds then transmit impulses to the brain, telling it what tastants have been encountered, so that you ultimately register the thought: this tastes *this* much sweet, or salty, or sour, or bitter, as the case may be.

Each taste bud contains a variety of receptors, so it has the ability to sense all tastes. The sweet receptors are two protein molecules, T1R2 and T1R3, entwined together on a taste bud cell's membrane. We taste sweet when sweet molecules in our food bind to the cell, thereby stimulating a series of chemical reactions. These reactions ultimately set off the release of neurotransmitters through a series of nerve cells, and thus bring the message from taste bud to brain.

Scientists agree that the sweet receptor cell has many different binding sites, and that sweet molecules bind to certain ones depending on their structure—but the effect of this variation is unclear. Molecular geneticists believe that despite the multiple binding pockets, there is only one taste of sweet. And so, even though saccharin binds to a certain set of sites and sucrose to another, the nature of the sweet effect is the same. What accounts for the difference in overall taste is that saccharin might also bind onto bitter receptors while sucrose doesn't. Bartoshuk is skeptical. "As a non-taster, I don't taste the saccharin as bitter, but I think its sweet taste is very different from that of sucrose."

I agree. The experience I get from Splenda in my iced coffee is very different from the one I get with NutraSweet or sucrose. Could there be some unacknowledged or undiscovered tastes at play? (The taste of metallic comes to mind.) Or are there in fact different nuances of sweet? The mystery remains to be solved.

What scientists do know is that taste is carried by two sets of cranial nerves, a set of three on each side of the head. The chorda tympani (which is actually a branch of the facial cranial nerve) runs through the middle ear, just behind the eardrum, and senses taste inputs from the front two-thirds of the tongue; the glossopharyngeal nerve, located near the tonsils, does the same for the back third; and the vagus nerve covers the territory way in the back of the throat. Also important to the enjoyment of eating is the trigeminal nerve, which doesn't influence taste per se, but makes chewing possible. And of course, the olfactory nerve allows us to smell.

The chorda tympani seems to be the alpha nerve of the bunch. Under normal circumstances, it not only detects what's on the tongue but also mellows out the taste effects of the other two taste nerves and the trigeminal. When the chorda tympani is damaged—from an ear infection, for instance—the impact of the other nerves on the injured side become more pronounced; curious circumstances may result. Some people experience inexplicable bouts of bitter, while others, like Bartoshuk (who has tested the effect by temporarily knocking out one of her own chorda tympani nerves with an injection of a numbing agent into her ear), perceive a fleeting taste of sweet. Bartoshuk calls these mysterious experiences "phantom tastes," a counterpart to visual hallucinations.

Taste is robust, however. It usually takes a disease or a head injury to erode taste, or it may be a side effect from a medication. More than 250 drugs might hamper the way we smell and taste, and some of them are widely used—drugs such as hydrocortisone, loratadine (an antihistamine), and lovastatin (a lipid-lowering drug). In rare cases, tonsillectomies could be suspect; damage to the glossopharyngeal nerves—the ones that lie close to the tonsils—has been known to lessen the intensity of the taste of sweet. Upper respiratory viral infections, too, can wreak havoc on our chemical senses, especially in the elderly. The viruses are believed to migrate through the Eustachian tube, which connects the pharynx to the middle ear. From there, the viruses tamper with the chorda tympani and rob the sense of taste from the front part of the tongue on the same side as the infection. Chorda tympani damage can also occur with ear infections. If the infection on one side of the head is mild or moderate, then it may cause the other (healthy) side to compensate, says Bartoshuk, or even to overcompensate by producing more taste cells. If the condition is severe, then the ability to sense taste and texture becomes muffled. Those patients end up preferring foods with more intense tastes and textures, which often means foods high in sugar, salt, and fat. So far, her research suggests that these subjects tend to weigh more than those who never had a bad ear infection.

Medical conditions aside, our ability to taste remains pretty constant over time. Not so with smell. There we're sharpest in our twenties and thirties. Around age sixty, we begin to notice that our favorite soup needs more salt and that its aroma has lost its strength. Scientists report that the decrease in smell is probably a result of the disappearance of olfactory cells and changes to the surface cells inside the nose. They also suspect it's perhaps the aging effect on smell that's really to blame for the rare instances in which taste seems to have eroded with advanced age. One experiment found that a group of elderly subjects rated the taste of a salt solution as less intense than did a group of young adults. But when both groups wore nose clips, the elderly group's new intensity ratings were not too far from their initial scores; the younger group's fell sharply and resembled those of the elderly.

Compared to other tastes, sweet is a bit of a trickster. Bite into a spoonful of miracle fruit, the small red berry from West Africa, and everything you eat a half hour or so afterward will suddenly taste sweet. Take a taste of artichoke and, if you're genetically inclined, your glass of milk or water will take on a dash of sweet. Have a sip of diluted saltwater, and the molecules will leave the taste of sweet on your palate too. Sweet snacks taste even sweeter with a puff of marijuana. The structure of our sweet receptors, it seems, allows for all sorts of taste shenanigans to occur on the tongue.

BACK AT the taste lab, an image of my tongue emerges on the screen, resembling the cratered terrain of a blue planet. Bartoshuk takes a hard look. "This is interesting," she says. "It's not the tongue of a classic super-taster." I see white circles here and there, filling in a surface of blue, but it still is, I admit, almost sparse compared with the patient with burning mouth syndrome—hers had taste buds packed so closely that it was hard to discern the blue space between them.

Bartoshuk then has me taste a series of supermarket snacks: a strawberry Fruit Roll-Up, chocolate syrup, a coffee jelly bean. I swish them on my tongue and concentrate, trying to assess the sweet taste independently from the sour or bitter tastes, as well as from the flavors. The sweetness, I decide, is pretty considerable, and so is the flavor. (My affection is for baked goods and confections, sweets with salty and sour notes and rich textures on the tongue, not for one-note fruit candies. I never understood my friends' enthusiasm for Jolly Ranchers or gummy bears, which come on too strong for me.) On a scale of 0 to 100, 0 being a dim room and 100 being the brightest light I've ever seen, I rate the snacks' sweetness somewhere between 30 and 55. Repeating the taste test with my taste buds numbed, the scores plunge 20 points. "I would say you're a taster, borderline super-taster," concludes Bartoshuk.

A middle-of-the-road verdict. Not super, but satisfying nevertheless. It explains my broad acceptance for the taste of sweet, as well as my relative self-control when it comes to savories, thick with the texture of fat. Physiology can be destiny, at least when it comes to our favorite foods. I've since tried to imagine what life would be like as a non-taster, relishing in the sting of hot chile peppers and the heft of a juicy steak, or appreciating the intense* sweetness of a toffee chew more than the taste of a shortbread cookie. But I can't. The nuances of experiences just can't be the same for two people, no matter how much we try to put ourselves in another's shoes, whether it's a night at the theater or a simple meal; we can only accept our differences. "It's really underappreciated how differently people perceive food," Bartoshuk says. "We understand how people don't see the same or hear the same—as in the case of color blindness or deafness—but we have a hard time understanding how people can taste differently."

Before I return home, Bartoshuk and I go out for a barbecue dinner. "It's the best part about living in the South," she says. She loves collard greens and pulled pork, while to me it's all about the dense layer cakes and warm crusty cobblers and pies. And so we savor our dinners in our own way—she, digging enthusiastically into her main course; I, picking at my chicken but devouring my mound of peach crumble at the end of the meal. Let the Francophile cake connoisseurs turn up their noses and the Atkins purists gasp. As far as my borderline taster buds could tell, big-hearted southern desserts are heaven.

Chapter Two

The Myth of the Refined Palate

L EGEND HAS IT THAT RED VELVET CAKE, MY FAVOR-
ite, was not invented down south but rather at the Waldorf-
Astoria, the hotel in midtown Manhattan with the grand
staircase and glittering chandeliers. How the chef dreamed up the
wacky notion of dyeing a chocolate cake with red food coloring
and dressing it up with waves of pristine white frosting is not
known. As the rumor goes, a customer at the restaurant took a bite
and fell madly in love with it. When she asked the chef for the
recipe, the chef graciously obliged—and then tacked a hundred-
dollar charge onto her bill. (That's why it also goes by "$100 cake.")
To get back at the Waldorf, she dispersed the recipe, far and wide,
for free.

The hotel has no record of the heated exchange and common
wisdom is that Red Velvet cake is, in fact, a southern confection. It
probably started out as plain old chocolate layer cake, which appeared in cookbooks in 1880 but decades later acquired the more
provocative name of "devil's food" because of the cocoa powder's
naturally reddish tinge. The story turns fuzzy after this, but it has

been suggested that by the early 1900s, food coloring was added to turn the shade a more sensuous ruby. In any case, the Waldorf does acknowledge that the cake was a signature dessert from the 1920s on, and even though it's not on the restaurant menu today, they'll make it for you if you ask. And so I do.

I've always been a tad obsessed with Red Velvet cake. When I noticed it sometime back in smart bakeshops across the city, I began to read up on it, taste it whenever I could, and take notes. I couldn't get enough of it. It partly has to do with taste and texture—that delectable marriage of dense cake and smooth cream-cheese frosting—but it mostly has to do with its lowbrow/highbrow appeal, how the cake is as well loved at a county fair as it is at a white-tablecloth restaurant. In straddling the two universes, Red Velvet calls into question whether there's such a thing as a so-phisticated or refined palate, a notion that I, being an equal-opportunity lover of all things sweet, have tried to quash for a very long time.

After all, there seems to be a perceived inverse relationship these days between the level of sweetness and the level of sophisti-cation of the person enjoying it. Dark chocolate seems more dis-tinctive than milk chocolate, as the former has a higher percentage of cocoa and contains less sugar. A cabernet sauvignon is generally considered more sophisticated than a merlot, given that the latter is sweeter and less tannic. Other tastes are not judged the same way. Something can be too salty or sour, but only extreme sweet has the dubious honor of having a special term: cloying. If we like something very spicy or very bitter or sour, we're adventurous eaters. But if we like something very sweet, whether it's wine or chocolate or the icing on our cake, we, and our palate, are often deemed less than refined.

I wanted to find out why. Why, for instance, do we think it's "better" to choose a chocolate chip cookie from a trendy bakeshop over a Pepperidge Farm soft-baked variety warmed in the toaster oven? Why is cake from the Waldorf a more sophisticated choice than the supermarket variety? The whole affair is upsetting. Sweets are supposed to bring people together—just think of birthday cakes and Valentine chocolates and bake sales—but here's an instance where an elite category of sweets turned into a tool to keep the masses at a distance.

Distance can be defined on many levels. It can be measured in miles or felt from the other side of an emotional barrier. It can be a language gap or a breach in understanding. In distancing ourselves from a crowd, we reveal our secret desire to be special, noticed, and respected, but in doing so, we also shut people out. In the world of food, the notion of a sophisticated palate creates distance on all those levels, and on every level there is very little room for sweetness.

That's because sweetness, for the most part, is the opposite of distance; it's about letting people feel welcomed, whether it's the distribution of candy at Halloween or the offering of a home-baked pie to a new neighbor. While distance is hard, sweetness is easy; the pleasure, direct and instantaneous. Anyone can understand it, including children, people who live in the middle of nowhere, those with little education and little money. As a result, sweetness has become "devalued," as Jeffery Sobal, a sociologist at Cornell University, describes it. "This is so straightforward a thrill that only somebody with no taste and no culturally learned palate would eat sweets exclusively." Not so with slimy seafood delicacies or stinky cheeses; these you need to spend time with before you can appreciate them. Like a classic opera or a passage of Shakespeare, they're difficult. "They require an investment before you reap the rewards," says Sobal.

Perhaps it can be thought of as the culinary parallel to "aesthetic distancing," a term Pierre Bourdieu uses in his book *Distinction: A*

Social Critique of the Judgement of Taste. As he tells it, a group of subjects was given a series of objects and asked which would make a great photograph. The least educated chose those that fit into the typical notions of something we'd frame and hang over the couch— sunsets, landscapes, and such. The most educated dismissed those choices as "vulgar" or "trivial" and preferred images that were more obscure, such as the bark of a tree or a metal frame, objects that were less obvious and less inviting. In explaining this behavior, Bourdieu, a sociologist at the Collège de France in Paris, wrote that there seems to be a tendency for an aesthete to "introduce a distance, a gap—the measure of his distant distinction." An aesthete puts up a front, snubbing his most instinctive emotions and basic thoughts (those he shares with the masses) in favor of the unusual and unexpected.

I suspect that this is precisely what so-called sophisticated palates are up to when they pass over the sweetly frosted layer cake on the menu in favor of some concoction involving a topping of olive oil sorbet. The latter isn't an obvious source of pleasure. In choosing it they demonstrate that they have the luxury (of money, time, and education) to make this choice. The cake, in contrast, is self-explanatory and provides no intellectual brownie points for its eater. Choosing it tells others nothing about yourself except that you are just like everyone else.

Or worse, like a child. Knowing that children embrace sweetness across the board, food manufacturers, of course, often differentiate the kid's from the adult's version of a product with extra helpings of sugar. Recent research out of Danielle Reed's lab at Monell Chemical Senses Center in Philadelphia suggests that the early sweet tooth serves a physiological purpose—we crave sweets most when our bones are growing fastest, and we need those extra calories. Still, we can't seem to shake off the link between sweet and infantile taste.

Anecdotal evidence suggests that when people are given an unfamiliar food they tend to pick the sweetest variety available. When a novice wine drinker is choosing a bottle, "they'll reach for a Riesling," says Jordan LeBel, an associate professor of Food & Beverage Management at Cornell University. "People make decisions based on their memory bank of flavors. When their repertoire expands, then they'll have the option to make different decisions." But in the meantime, they choose what is easy, safe, familiar—and sweet.

Sweetness is easy because it's hardwired. Before humans began farming some 11,000 years ago, foods picked from the wilderness either offered sustenance or caused death. Sight couldn't be relied on. One bunch of bright red berries could safely provide a good dose of vitamins, but the next could be poisonous. Taste, however, provided pretty reliable guidance. Sweetness signaled safe eating and an infusion of valuable calories; bitterness, found in toxic wild almonds, for instance, was a warning that snackers had best spit the thing out. Leslie Stein, a physiological psychologist also at Monell Chemical Senses Center, believes taste was a part of how life itself evolved. "Taste and smell were our first ways of interacting with the world around us, back when we were primordial blobs," she says. "So they're very ancient. From an evolutionary perspective, they have very ingrained influences on how we interact with the world today. Taste is the last bastion of defense before we put something in our body."

Our mothers' milk has elements of sweet, salty, and fat in it, which might explain why fatty snacks paired with either of the two tastes are so delicious to us. It may also explain why the liberal use of common condiments, namely table salt and sugar, have, in the eyes of some judgmental types, become shorthand for a person's lack of sophistication. Giving in to that innate love of salt and

sugar betrays a lack of awareness of exotic spices; it belies an inat-
tention to the subtleties of flavor; it suggests a taste more attuned
to processed than fresh whole foods; and it hints that, from a
health standpoint, you're letting yourself go.

Potent levels of salty, bitter, or sour may make us gag or run for
water, but the taste of sweet rarely triggers such violent eruptions.
It goes down easy. Even in cultures less sugar-laden than ours, such
as China and Japan, the taste of sweet isn't outright rejected. Liking the taste of sweet is universal; it bridges the differences among
people from every sphere, and therefore it is rarely the darling of
sophisticated palates.

BUT IS THERE truly such a thing as a sophisticated palate, a super-
palate that's structured and wired differently from the typical
human variety? The answer depends on what we mean by sophisticated. If we mean having a palate that can detect intensities that
others can't, the answer is yes: some of us are super-tasters and
tasters; others are non-tasters. If we mean being equipped with
one that's wired to tell upscale from downscale, then the answer is
no, at least not objectively.

We all start out in the same way from a physiological standpoint.
Beginning around our sixth week in the womb, a primitive form of
papillae breaks through the surface, clusters appearing in the front
of the tongue first, then slowly making their way back, until finally
during our fifteenth week, the first full-grown taste buds appear. By
the time we're born, we're outfitted with a sufficient number of
them to enjoy the foods that life has to offer—though tasters end up
with more taste buds than non-tasters.

The discovery of this difference has left certain individuals in
culinary circles feeling insecure, if not defensive. At a wine panel
Linda Bartoshuk hosted, one food writer became especially agi-

tated about being labeled a non-taster. "[People] interpret it as a value judgment," says Bartoshuk with a trace of disbelief. She tells me about a writer who gave a group of famous chefs a PROP test, and then needed to pull the article from publication because the chefs didn't want their status known. "Apparently the non-tasters thought that they were being described as insensitive, and the super-tasters thought they were being described as overly fussy."

For years, Bartoshuk has been approached by gourmets curious about their status. One nervous food critic took the test and, unhappy with the results, swore her to secrecy. A winemaker in California asked for PROP paper so that he could administer the test to his employees and fire the non-tasters. "I launched into a lecture on the value of having people from all three groups since his consumers were also from all three groups. Just in case," says Bartoshuk, "I did not send the papers."

The fact is, Bartoshuk says, super-tasters don't taste "better," they just taste "louder," so to speak. In other words, flavors are more intense for super-tasters than for non-tasters—which may explain why chefs tend to fall in the former category. But the ability to detect a flavor, no matter how faint, isn't the same as having impeccable culinary taste, just as having above-average hearing won't make you an aficionado in jazz or classical music. In fact, at the wine event where I first met Bartoshuk years ago, the room, filled with food editors and wine connoisseurs (presumably people who have some appreciation for the nuances of taste), reflected the general population: roughly half were tasters, and the rest were super-tasters or non-tasters.

Moreover, all the wine and food classes in Paris won't change the nature of your taste buds. You're stuck with what you're born with, and once you've hit adulthood their sensory capabilities won't get any better. Gary Beauchamp, the director at Monell, explains that the subtle nuances we appreciate in food are learned. The process occurs in the brain, not on the tongue. And it starts early in life, even well before we're born. Infants whose mothers drank carrot juice while pregnant or breast-feeding fussed less than their nonexposed counterparts when presented carrot-flavored cereal upon weaning. Babies fed a bitter- and sour-tasting infant formula for six months appeared to enjoy it afterward, and they continued to consume it even when a sweeter option was offered. Experience shapes expectations, and our expectations can often affect our preferences in a certain context.

The process continues into adulthood. We may not like the bitter aftertaste in a sweetener, but we might enjoy bitterness in a cup of coffee because we learn that's what coffee should taste like. New sensations and experiences create new neural connections, and we grow accustomed to these experiences, whether by habit or by peer pressure. Over time, we arrive at conclusions as to what's good or bad based on our culture and environment.

What's "good" to so-called sophisticated palates these days, of course, is a complexity in flavors. To train my brain how to decipher it, I seek out Gail Civille, the director of Sensory Spectrum, in New Providence, New Jersey. Civille might nibble on dozens of chocolate bars one day to make sure they hit the same sweet note, and chew scores of bubble gum to make sure there's no gum-wrapper taste the next; if anyone can explain complexity, she can.

The trick, she says, is to avoid being fixated by price or hype and to realize that it's not so much the degree of sweet that determines quality, but the flavor context that surrounds it. A sweet at any price point can, in reality, taste richly complex or cheaply flat. "If it's sweet and balanced and refined, and the flavor character works well together, then sweet can be sophisticated." With cheaper sweets, you don't get the aromatics; you don't get the balance of tastes. "All you get is sweet, sweet, sweet," she says.

She offers a lesson over the phone, and tells me to try it myself at home. What you notice first when you take a sweet into your mouth, she says, are the top notes. These are the ones you can smell: the fruity or floral characters—the sweet aromatics, as she calls them—like maple sugar or vanilla. "Pay attention before they fly away," she says. She suggests that I try some Häagen-Dazs vanilla ice cream, and roll it on my tongue. "Notice the vanilla," she instructs, "how fat and round and floral and raisiny it is." With lesser ice creams, she says, what you get is synthetic vanillin, and it disappears quickly. A learned palate notices the staying power and fullness of a pure product—liking it or not is another matter.

The next step is to focus on the actual tastes: the salty, sweet, sour, and bitter notes. "All of this is happening at once," says Civille. "The trick is to sort it out and not go insane. . . . It's like listening to music. Music critics don't have better ears. They just have the capacity to sort."

"Now feel the texture," she says. "See the smoothness?" If you were tasting a solid, like cake, you would also take note of the hardness, she explains—how it responds to the force of your bite. Ask yourself: Is it crumbling or rupturing? Is it crispy or chewy? How is it responding to your teeth? How wet is it, or is it still pretty dry? "Are the pieces coming together so it's a chewy adventure," she says, "or is it all over my mouth?" She tells me that some sweets can burn. That's because a sweetener can function as a preservative and will draw moisture. A high concentration of sugar can actually suck the saliva from your tongue and leave it feeling parched.

Besides chewing (which you must do quite a bit of because you can't taste without breaking the food up and sending those aromatic molecules up through the back of your nose), she also suggests slurping. This way, you'll get a bigger "hit," so to speak.

Civille offers a considerable roster of downmarket items with upmarket tastes (to none of which she has any financial ties, she assures me). Besides the Häagen-Dazs vanilla ice cream, she likes Sara Lee All Butter Pound Cake, Tropicana Pure Premium orange juice, and the Snickers bar ("Beautiful," she declares. "The nuts are never stale").

By the time we finish our session, I realize that a sophisticated palate is simply a knowledgeable one—a matter of knowing what you like and being able to explain why. Peter Dea, for instance, admits it: he likes milk chocolate. Gourmets, who say the pure cocoa taste in dark chocolate is much more profound, may be aghast. Dea is, after all, a taster by trade. A manager at Mattson, the largest independent food innovation company in the country, he is commissioned by the likes of Starbucks and Kraft to come up with the next big thing. But to hear him talk about milk chocolate, one cannot doubt that he is sophisticated about his tastes. "It's sweeter," he explains, "but it also has more caramel notes. It's creamier."

Complexity might be fun to analyze, but why do food snobs think it is better? After all, even as we value complexity in flavor, we often embrace simplicity in poetry and fashion. This is precisely why Beauchamp himself is a little wary of the ways of wine connoisseurs. "[They] will hate me for saying this," he says, "but the idea of some wines being better than others comes largely from learning. Is a great wine truly great, or is it great because we learned it's supposed to be that way?" In wine and chocolates, as in life, what's "good" is all in the mind, and sophistication simply comes with speaking the language—and convincing others you're right.

AT THE WALDORF, where dignitaries and presumably sophisticated palates might dine, the Red Velvet cake is concocted out of ingredients one wouldn't expect. The typical box variety contains oil and red dye. But the morning I am there, I witness the use of mascarpone cheese, butter, and beets. As I arrive, Mary Ellen Miller, an amiable longtime member of the pastry team, is adding confectioners' sugar to her mix—it does a better job than table sugar of drawing out the moisture in a frosting and softening it, she explains. She also adds a slightly salty mascarpone cheese to the cream cheese frosting to mellow the sweetness, and whipping cream to smooth out the texture. As for the cake batter, she adds enough unsweetened cocoa powder to give it flavor and colors it with beet juice, along with a single teaspoon of red dye (other recipies may call for as much as one ounce). The whole process is a lot more "sophisticated" than my usual protocol of dumping cake mix, water, and eggs into a metal mixing bowl.

I begin to wonder about the motivations behind going that extra mile for such a cake, especially when there are other recipes that are quite serviceable. It turns out, we Americans, the middle and upper classes in particular, have always been picky about what we eat, in the sense that we care about what our food says about us. Depending on what we choose, we're either savvy or clueless; we're fussy or authentic; we have class or no class; we're cheap or generous. Depending on how *much* we eat, we're either gluttonous or anorexic. As Sidney Mintz, an anthropoligist at Johns Hopkins University, put it to me one day: "Food is a medium for meaning. We have a lot of human foibles tied into food."

Perhaps we take our taste preferences so personally because what we taste is swallowed and becomes a part of us. An unkind word about our food is in essence an unkind word about *us*. In the past, regional foods have been employed as racial insults. Before ethnic cuisines were part of the American food culture, Italians were denigrated as garlic eaters, and I still hear derisive comments about the Chinese and dog-eating. Our language, too, encourages this association between food and sophistication. "Taste" refers to our personal style as well as what we sense with our tongue, and we can't help but apply comments about our food preferences to our very being. "When you say a word, it lights up a whole universe of other words and feelings connected to it," explains Jean Berko Gleason, professor emeritus of psychology at Boston University. "When you say, 'He has good taste' and 'This tastes good,' they don't mean the same thing, but because they sound the same, they are linked in your brain. When you think of one word, you can't help but think of the other." And so good taste in food has come to suggest good taste in general. If we recognize good food, then surely we must appreciate good art, good music, fine fabrics and fragrances. At least this is the assumption.

Immanuel Kant, the eighteenth-century philosopher, explored the dual meanings of taste and meditated on the notion of a dinner party. "The aesthetic taste of the host shows itself in his skill in choosing [the menu] with universal validity," he reasons in *Anthropology from a Pragmatic Point of View*. This, he says, is "something which [the host] cannot bring about through his own sense of taste, because his guests might choose other foods or drinks, each according to his own private sense. Therefore he sets up his meeting with variety, so that everyone will find something that suits his sense; which yields a comparatively universal validity." And we all like to feel validated, don't we? It's human nature, and food has long been a way to seek that validation, long after the guests have gone home.

I wonder if the personal nature of food is so strong because, in America, our food tradition is not. In countries like China or Italy or France, where the culinary heritage is rich and deep and defines the nation's people, rich and poor share essentially the same food. Royalty may have had a lot more, especially at banquets, where abundance is a sign of wealth, and they may have had access to rare delicacies. But for the most part, fellow countrymen delight in the same flavors and staples; they miss the same foods when they move away from home—the burn of chile peppers or the tang of toma-toes, garlic, and onions or the taste of curry spices. It's this cultural bond with food—not the fat content and calories—that served as the original basis behind the idea "You are what you eat."

But who are we when our culinary history is young and mixed, and our food choices run the gamut? Those of us whose parents are not recent immigrants don't have foods we automatically reach for at any given time of day. We might have huevos rancheros or a bagel for breakfast—because we feel like it, not because they define the morning meal for us. As Americans, we live in a land of plenty, with wide-ranging options and the freedom to choose from them. It's a unique set of circumstances that leaves us especially exposed to the judgment of others. After all, if we all ate the same foods, or if someone else determined what we ate, food would no longer be a means of self-expression or a feasible measure of our worth—just as a dress no longer defines a schoolgirl's personality when there's a school uniform. The fact that our palates are being judged at all is testament to our living in a young and food-rich melting pot of a democracy. Without a deep tradition of flavors and tastes to define us as a nation, we use our food choices as a way to define us as individuals.

It's not surprising, then, that the foods we choose to label "so-phisticated" are those from places we deem desirable, the more far-flung the better. Of course, there's also cachet, in these envi-ronmentally correct times, in buying local and investing in made-in-America products; nevertheless, given two choices at the same price, there's an innate value placed on the one that comes from a distance. To Americans, inexpensive French chocolates have a cer-tain appealing je ne sais quoi compared to their domestic counter-parts. Ordinary packaged biscuits from Argentina are more of a curiosity than their American equivalent at Wal-Mart. At the same time, the gloppy scoops from Cold Stone Creamery, the you-call-it-we'll-mix-it ice-cream chain, may be a weekend ritual in American suburbia, but there's a gloss of hipness about the Scottsdale, Arizona–based company in Tokyo, where the first branch opened in the swish Roppongi Hills complex. For the most part, eating exotically has more often than not been a way to distance yourself from the locals and to demonstrate that you're in the know.

There are, of course, regional differences. While Los Angeles and New York experience a southern-baked-goods moment, a pastry-shop owner in an Atlanta suburb has reason to fear their extinction at home. "I'm kind of sad you can't go out and get a great, simple chocolate cake anymore," says Angie Mosier, a member of the Southern Foodways Alliance, a group interested in preserving traditional foods south of the Mason–Dixon line. "Bakeries in Atlanta serve all kinds of European baked goods, and things are messed with, and they're delicious. But there's nowhere to get pineapple upside-down cake. There's not a great place for coconut cake anymore." She misses the days when you could get a cake without pretense, when it was "packed up in a white cardboard box and some string." Like simple supermarket sweets, southern treats seem to have been deemed by some of her southern cohorts as too accessible to be fine.

MORE THAN a thousand years ago, though, when sugar had to be fetched from the other side of the globe, the people doing the fetching thought that sugar was among the finest foods on Earth. There was high glamour before the mediocrity. As we saw earlier, it was someone in Asia, most likely in India, who first figured out how to extract the sweet crystals from the tall, sturdy reeds. Subsequently, the sugar habit spread westward. Until it arrived, only honey and fruits sweetened the meal—none of which offered the clean taste that sugar did. Apparently the Ancient Greeks, for all their fancy feasting, had to make do without it and instead, relied on sugar-rich fruits such as dried figs and date syrup. Honey, enjoyed by the Egyptians by the latter half of the third millennium B.C. and the Greeks perhaps a thousand or so years after that, was the luxury sweetener of its day. By medieval times Europeans were still dispensing honey sparingly, as one would a spice, and often into savory dishes.

Sugar outshone honey, however, wherever and whenever it made its debut, and the farther sugar had to travel, the more precious it was considered. At the turn of the eighteenth century in China, where sugarcane grew domestically, delicacies such as bird's nests and bear paws were rarer and therefore were a display of far greater opulence than sweets. As Sucheta Mazumdar puts it in *Sugar and Society in China,* sugar was used "in comfortable but not extraordinarily wealthy households." It was more prized back in the seventh century, when serviceable canals first began shipping sugar from the southern parts of the country, where it was grown, to an elite few farther north. During the eighth century (when sweet-eating habits were just beginning to percolate in urban parts of China), sweets enjoyed by foreign merchants, such as the Persians and Arabs, exuded an exotic cachet and, in turn, inspired the Chinese to create sweet treats of their own. In the cosmopolitan hot spots of the Song dynasty, early thirteenth-century night markets sold an array of cakes, confections, and candied fruits, but according to Mazumdar, sugar probably took off at the time not simply because of its taste but because it was an effective way to ship and preserve the trendy fruit recently made available from faraway provinces.

Enthusiasm grew as sugar headed west. The Persians, gourmets of the Middle East, already had a cherished tradition of sweet treats: early pastry chefs had been concocting quince jams and almond-stuffed dates by the sixth century, but with the introduction of sugar a couple of centuries later, their repertoire bloomed, and white dustings of sugar fell onto fruit compotes, macaroons, and flaky breads. When the Arabs overtook Persia, they decided they quite liked their new subjects' sweet traditions and picked them up for themselves, setting up a primitive industrialized sugar refinery around A.D. 1000, in what is now the island of Crete (which the Arabs called Qandi, meaning "candied," or made from the crystallized juice of sugarcane). Between the seventh and twelfth centuries, the Arabs' conquests continued, eventually spanning parts of three continents. As Arab rule expanded, so did the fascination with sugar around the globe. In northern Africa, the nobility honed the art of sugar sculpture—mixing sugar, water, and nuts to form marzipan clay. This would then be molded into mosques, palaces, animals, and other impressively large sculptures, including a tree at the banquet of an eleventh-century sultan, in Egypt, who, during Ramadan, used more than 33,300 pounds of sugar.

Still, as beloved as sweets were in the region, sugar wasn't pursued to the extent it was farther west. Europeans became increasingly aware of sugar when crusading Christian soldiers swept into the Middle East. As they waged battles in the name of God, they also took the opportunity to look around and check out what people were eating. By then, the Seljuk Turks, a clan from north-central Asia, had seized control of Jerusalem, Persia, and the surrounding sweet-eating areas, and so they were already well acquainted with sugar, sprinkling it onto their fruits and pastries and mixing it into their savories. Subsequently the Europeans picked up the habit and brought the expensive white crystals home, where they used them more sparingly than honey, and consumed them with a bit of a swagger. Eating and serving sugar wasn't simply a luxury, but a powerful symbol of wealth. Few things were sweet enough, it seemed, as they combined sugar with fish, vegetables, and even honey. One preparation of boiled pike was cooked inside a sugar-topped tart. The whole dish weighed five pounds upon completion, and a fifth of that heft consisted of sugar and raisins.

Meanwhile, the royal courts (and eventually lower nobility and the Church) adopted the Islamic art form of sugar sculpture, calling their creations "subtleties." So meticulous and serious were the masters of this craft that the great French chef Antonin Carême considered confectionery to be the most important branch of architecture, and he delighted dinner guests with spectacular renderings of castles, animals, people, flowers, and images from classical mythology. The more elaborate the structures, the wealthier and more powerful the host.

By the seventeenth century, the wealthiest Europeans weren't sweetening only their foods with sugar, but also the trendiest new drinks at the time: tea from Asia, coffee from the Middle East, and chocolate from the Americas. With the taste of sweet in such high demand, the Western powers began staking out their claims in the New World. In cultivating a domestic sugar industry, they tried to break free from their dependence on foreign lands and changed the course of sugar consumption, and history, forever.

As Sidney Mintz recounts in his book *Sweetness and Power,* sugar production and consumption soared, and with it, English power. At the same time, prices plummeted. Between 1700 and 1809, the consumption of sugar per person per year in England skyrocketed by 400 percent. In colonial America, where culinary trends tended to lag after those of the British, sugar consumption rose in the latter half of the nineteenth century. (As British colonists, Americans required permission from the Crown to manufacture products for themselves; without the means to refine sugar, they depended on the British to supply it, and paid high prices for it, even after the Revolution.)

A number of developments bolstered sugar production and sent the prices spiraling downward. In continental Europe, sugar extracted from sugar beets, a technique discovered by a German scientist in 1747, grew more prominent: the Napoleonic Wars had blocked trade from the West Indies, and sugar beet factories arose in the decades that followed to feed the market's demand. In 1855, the invention of the vacuum steam pan decreased the temperature and centrifugal force (and therefore the fuss) required to isolate sugar crystals from the cane juice. Further improvements to sugar refining and advancements in transportation also helped to make the white crystals more accessible.

Eventually, a wide assortment of inexpensive sweets, made possible by inexpensive sugar, slowly but surely saturated Western markets. Among the early sweet treats, popular by the 1830s, was a hard candy made from sugar and boiled water. These penny candies, as they were called, came in a rainbow of colors, many molded into the shapes of animals, dolls, and flowers. Unlike the sugar sculptures worthy of royal wedding feasts more than half a century earlier, the penny candies appealed almost exclusively to children, a far cry from the luxe sweets of old.

NOT SURPRISINGLY, the so-called sophisticated palates of the world soon decided that maybe the taste of sweet was not so sophisticated after all. And so they abandoned their old the-more-the-better attitude concerning sugary treats, now manufactured close to home, and set up new parameters as to which sweets were considered desirable and which weren't. The line drawn between sophistication and mass was no longer a matter of geographic distance only, but one based on informational currency: being in the know about what you're eating and having exceptional access. It's not simply the ingredients themselves, but what you do with them and, later, where you got them and who else is consuming them.

Consider, for instance, the layer cake in the nineteenth century.

These treats, considered so humble today, counted as a status symbol back then. At the time, Americans typically had fruit for dessert, or they might whip up a simple pie or pudding. But when important company was expected, these lovely home-baked cakes were in order. Baking powder, which cut down on time spent beating the batter, wasn't invented until 1856, and the electric mixer didn't exist until the next century. Therefore, one had to be a woman of some wealth with servants and leisure time to bake these cakes. There was a sense that in fact all plated desserts required a level of sophistication and refinement on the part of the chef to be made right. As Isabella Beeton, whose books made her the Martha Stewart of the Victorian era, wrote: "If there be any poetry at all in meals, or the process of feeding, there is poetry in the dessert."

Moreover, these cakes, as with other fine desserts, required precision and skill. Sugar, when it was still precious and sold in solid cones, had to be cut carefully and sparingly. Mixing the batter took patience and intuition, and unreliable ovens required constant checking. All this had to be done flawlessly because dessert wasn't about satisfying the appetite but about adorning the table and impressing the guest. Like the elaborate European and Egyptian sugar structures of centuries past, these cakes demonstrated one's social status, though now the currency concerned not the amount of sugar used but how and where it was used. At the time of Beeton's writing, the ranks of the middle class were swelling, sending its upper echelons into a frenzy to distinguish themselves from the lower, less established rungs, flaunting what skills, talents, and knowledge they had to mark their status. "Active snobbery" is how Nicola Humble, a senior lecturer at the University of Surrey, Roehampton, put it—something to be expected when one realizes that in a young capitalist economy one can lose his wealth and position in an instant. Cake, like art, music, and clothing, happened to be a convenient way to keep up appearances. Even if families had to eat modestly most days to make ends meet, they pulled out all the stops for important guests.

These cakes were made with meticulous attention to recipes from the trendy women's magazines and cookbooks of the day, like *Mrs. Beeton's Book of Household Management* (first published in book form in 1861). It's not unfair to say that the husband's status lay in how successfully his wife could pull off her cake. "They proved her husband's wealth in the big city," says Alice Ross, a professor of culinary history at New York Universtiy. "They baked to show they were fashionable."

While the savory dishes were handled by the maid, it was the grand-finale course that showcased the wife's talents. The cake recipes in the *Centennial Buckeye Cookbook,* originally published in 1876 and the best-selling cookbook in the nineteenth century, instructed women to make sure their hands, apron, and table are spick-and-span before mixing the cake batter. It requires "a knack," the cookbook cautions: "Don't stir, but beat thoroughly."

As for Beeton, she reminds her readers in *Household Management* that "the beauty of the dessert services at the tables of the wealthy tends to enhance the splendour of the plate." Thus she instructs women to serve "choice and delicately-flavored" cakes, along with biscuits and seasonal fruits of all kinds, for which she offers no fewer than eight sketches of how they should be presented. Her readers (there were 2 million by 1868) took careful note, for the whole affair bolstered their husbands' reputation in business—and theirs at home.

WITH ALL THE painstaking attention to presentation, one can only presume that taste—the kind sensed on the tongue—wasn't all that mattered. Taste of the stylistic sort did too. The same goes for the cakes of today, though with the wide availability of flour, not to mention KitchenAid mixers and high-tech convection ovens, the bar is higher. Cake bought from the shop of a notable chef or carefully made from his cookbook (after hours of laboring in the kitchen) is the de rigueur hostess gift in certain circles; cake mixes (which incidentally can contain 40 percent more sugar than flour) are sacrilege to sophisticated palates. Now, as then, the allure comes from not just the sweet itself but the buzz surrounding it. This explains, for instance, the sudden enthusiasm for Chupa Chups lollipops after their appearance in New York City's fashion shows. This also explains the mania for Cake Man Raven's Red Velvet cake after Oprah and Robert De Niro ordered it. Funny enough, our environmentally minded climate may inspire us to embrace local produce today, but in the 1930s, farmers sold their fresh-from-the-earth products in order to afford canned foods— then touted as "urban" foods.

"Desserts," says Tim Zagat, who founded the restaurant guides with his wife, Nina, "have a tendency to come and go. There are now people who do plays on doughnuts and blueberry pie. But it takes just one person to say, 'I want a cherries jubilee,' and the *Times* will write about it and soon everyone will be eating a cherries jubilee."

Perceptions of place work into the equation as well, as Brian Wansink, at Cornell University, demonstrated with an experiment with wine. With his coaching, waiters at a restaurant on campus offered diners a glass of a "new" cabernet sauvignon, on the house. Half the diners were told that it was from North Dakota; the others were told it was from California. When asked to assess the wine and the meal—both of which were in fact exactly the same for everyone—the North Dakota group rated their glass and their entire dinner much more poorly than the California group. (The wine was a cheap $2 bottle of Charles Shaw from the grocery store.) The findings suggest that we make choices that distance ourselves from what's perceived as not particularly sophisticated, while closing in on the gap between us and the "hot" person, destination, or thing of the moment. The more quickly we catch on, the farther ahead of everyone else we can be.

BACK AT the Waldorf, I am working my way through a plate of petits fours, chewing with great purpose, when Mary Ellen Miller finally emerges with several round cakes on a giant baking tray. They're not so much cakes as they are cakes-in-waiting, each no more than an inch thick, their height and beauty not yet fully realized. Worse, they aren't the jubilant cherry-red-lipstick color I imagined for this Red Velvet cake, but a serious rusty brown. I have to admit, they are kind of a letdown at this stage.

But when Miller begins to frost the layers, my interest perks up. She takes the closest cake and starts at the center, her wrist quick and agile, the frosting knife swirling gracefully as she works outward. Miller knows not to overdo it; she stops a good half inch or so before she hits the edge, lest the frosting ooze out the sides and overpower the cocoa flavor of the cake itself. She places one layer on top of the first, and then another, and then another. She finishes off by creating continuous waves of frosting on the side of the cake, thereby sealing the four disks into one beautiful dessert.

I taste and take care to chew well. I detect the aromatic chocolate note and a bit of earthiness from the beets, something you don't get from simple bakeshop varieties. The sweetness is subtle and balanced by the frosting's slight tangy note. There is substance, a nice bite, to each forkful. I move the cake around my tongue, as Gail Civille instructed, and thanks to the generous layers of frosting between the tiers of cake, each mouthful feels dense and smooth at the same time. It's complex, as sophisticated palates might say, and I appreciate that, though I'm determined to continue to embrace its lowbrow cousins as well. After all, there is plenty of room in my world for delicious cakes, especially when there's no pretension—which is why I like this cake even more when Miller lowers it into a big cardboard box and ties it up with some string and a smile.

Chapter Three

The *Real* Taste of Strawberry

EATING OUT CAN BE UNPREDICTABLE, BUT NO MATter what, one thing is for sure: whether we are at an ice-cream parlor or a cream puff shop or a small French pâtisserie, my mother will have the strawberry. It doesn't matter if there are cream puff fillings in all colors of the rainbow, including the limited-edition pumpkin orange. It doesn't even matter if we're at an ice-cream shop featuring thirty-one flavors. My mother will stay the course. She will have the strawberry.

How can strawberry not get tedious after a while? I ask her, always baffled but never surprised. Here, look at this—this could be exciting! Banana and cashews! How about oatmeal cookie ice cream with dark chocolate chunks? Occasionally, if there is a raspberry option, she can be persuaded. But more often than not, the answer will be no, the strawberry, please.

For those of us easily persuaded to try the next new thing, sticking with the same flavor seems unadventurous and boring. But for others who know the secrets of how flavor comes to be—people like Marie Wright, for instance, a flavorist at International

Flavors & Fragrances, a flavor manufacturer based in New York City—single-flavor devotion is not unexciting at all. In fact, if you've tasted strawberries and strawberry-flavored confections consistently for the past few decades, you've experienced an enormous variety of flavors. Some flavors, like vanilla or chocolate or strawberry, might seem immortal, and they are, in a sense. But like the simple white T-shirt that changes its silhouette season after season, flavors evolve over the years, too, though sometimes so gradually we hardly notice.

That's because the flavor components used in the recipes of our favorite sweets, whether they're bought in the grocery store or made from scratch, are, in fact, composed of recipes themselves. These little recipes may include more sugar, as in the case of a particular varietal of strawberries harvested in a field; or they might include a new compound that has a subtle floral note, as in the case of a strawberry flavoring composed in the lab. In effect, both the fresh strawberry and the strawberry-flavored supermarket treats reflect our shifting tastes—and the food industry's attempt to satisfy them. The best ones strike the perfect balance between the reality of what strawberries actually taste like and the fantasy of what we *want* them to taste like. And because both are in a constant state of flux, flavors have a dynamic life of their own.

AT MARIE WRIGHT'S lab butterfly mobiles fly overhead, and the sign by her window, LE JARDIN DES ARÔMES, channels the fragrances of the garden her mother tended to in England. Creating a flavor, it seems, requires some inspiration. "When I go into my creative mode, I don't want to feel as if I'm in a chemistry lab," she says. "I'd like it to be more stimulating. I like having paintings and color."

Before a flavor is made into a real, live substance to be mass-

produced and packaged, it's simply an idea. Flavorists, like paint-
ers, need to be able to take that idea—say, of a healthy oatmeal or a
champagne-worthy strawberry or a "sexy" vanilla—and build it up
from components that might seem nothing like it. As an artist
painting a garden or a sunset would, the flavorist must decide what
sort of palette she'd like to use, which hues to make more intense,
which to make more subtle; the finished interpretation ends up to
be very personal and unique.

Consider strawberry, which, even in this day of "exotic" flavors
from Brazil and Southeast Asia, still leads the fruit category in
popularity. If two people are asked to create a strawberry flavor for
a yogurt, she says, they won't be exactly alike. About three hundred
chemical components collaboratively give a fresh strawberry its
scent and flavor. Depending on which she chooses to emphasize,
and what else she'd like to toss into the mix (for instance, notes of
chocolate or kiwi), the resulting flavor can be very different. Some
of them are jammy; some of them have candy notes; others have a
hint of grassiness.

Strawberry flavor is also dependent on real time. It might reflect
the taste and scent of a strawberry off the plant that is still in the
process of ripening, in which case it would taste simple and fresh. Or
it might reflect the flavor when the fruit is crushed, in which case it
might have a juicier aroma, reflecting the enzymatic reactions triggered right after it's plucked from the plant. "There are endless iterations of strawberries," she says. "It's as if different artists were asked
to paint the same rose; there will be numerous interpretations.
There's always room for another strawberry." With the tricks of the
trade, the flavors we can choose from seem as limitless as our imagi-
nations.

Wright demonstrates how she composes a flavor by taking out
four brown opaque glass bottles and dipping a scent strip in each for
me to sniff. (Flavors, as you might recall, are made from substances

that are sensed as much as 90 percent by your nose, so smelling them gives us a good approximation of how they will taste.) The contents in one bottle smell like guava juice; another, labeled "grass," like a fresh-cut lawn; another like cotton candy; and still another generally juicy, like grape or apple. None smelled anything like strawberries. But then she asks that I fan them all at once in front of my nose. When I do, the four scents blend together to become one—and slowly, mysteriously, the scent of strawberry creeps into the air.

After twisting the caps back on tight, Wright reaches for a fifth bottle. She dips in another scent strip and gives it a little wave. Instantly a scent I haven't smelled for a long time materializes in the room, like a ghost, invisible but unmistakably present. "It's the old strawberry, from the fifties and sixties," she reveals. "The products at the time were all based on this note, and in the United States, it stayed around much later."

The scent is thick and sugary. Some might remember it fondly as the strawberry of their youth, with all the accompanying scents and memories of strawberry bubble gum and lip glosses. It's unclear which came first, our naïve preference for the fantasy flavor or the creation of it. But whatever the case may be, it suited us just fine, and miles apart as it is from true strawberries, the flavor become our reality.

TO UNDERSTAND Wright's work, it's useful to know a little about the history of the flavor industry. The first flavors were natural, of course—herbs and spices from the plants themselves. By the turn of the seventeenth century, British flavorists had found ways to extract or distill oils and essences from fruits, vegetables, and other plants, and the technique eventually made its way across the Atlantic. At first, flavors were primarily blended into medical lozenges and syrups to mask bitterness; aromatic oils were made into perfumes. Lozenge-makers eventually realized that they'd sell more if the medicine were taken out and the flavor left in. Additional techniques were borrowed from fragrance makers, and with the advent of inexpensive cane sugar, as we've seen, penny candies were born. The art of flavoring went commercial by the 1850s, and the first crop of flavored foods included gelatin, soft drinks, and ice cream. New varieties emerged in the years that followed and Americans embraced them as unique and sophisticated—bubble gum, cola, tutti-frutti.

By the middle of the next century, gas-liquid chromatography enabled scientists to break down flavors into separate components. Rather than re-creating a particular type of strawberry flavor by trial and error with ingredients in the lab (or using the actual strawberries—which can be expensive and tricky from a consistency standpoint), flavorists could now sniff the isolated elements and compose a flavor more accurately. If we consider Wright's analogy of a painting, it's as if the machine dissected the components of a sunset into reds, oranges, and yellows.

In the 1970s the technique was combined with another analytical tool: mass spectroscopy. The coupling—called the GC-MS system—modernized the industry: Once dissected into its various parts, a mixture could now be analyzed and labeled with its exact chemical components rather than being identified by a scientist's nose. In other words, it detected the fingerprint of the flavor. "It was as if, all of a sudden, artists had new colors," says Wright. And so we now know that bananas smell and taste like bananas in part because of a compound called amyl acetate, that lemons taste like lemons thanks to the compound limonene, and that strawberries can taste like strawberries with as little as five compounds, but for a more complex flavor, you might use as many as thirty. Scientists could also now track down substances that had escaped them all those years—including those like furaneol, for instance, the elusive key to creating a more natural-tasting pineapple flavor.

Early incarnations of the GC-MS system were the size of industrial freezers. It wasn't until the past decade or so that the machine shrank to the size of a mini fridge (thanks in part to more precise engineering) and found its way into flavor houses around the world.

As a result, the creation of flavors and foods has become a lot more efficient. Somewhere in nature or in a kitchen, a flavor can now be noticed and captured.

"Making flavors is a tedious process," explains Robert Sobel, director of technology and innovation at FONA (Flavors of North America) International, a flavor house in Geneva, Illinois. "Twenty years ago, analyzing a flavor took about a month. Now we do it two or three times a day." As a result, Sobel is on the receiving end of strange packages from faraway places. Sometimes he discovers a whole fruit at his doorstep—durian, mangosteen, açai—shipped in inert gases. Sometimes he gets sent a headspace vial that contains the gaseous chemicals with the sought-after scent.

A headspace vial is a sensory snapshot. Let's say, for instance, you love the smell of your mother's strawberry pie at precisely the moment she takes it out of the oven, and you want to create a cookie that tastes like it. To do this, you can't just throw the whole pie into the GC-MS system. No. You must do a headspace analysis. This means you take a sample of the pie as soon as it comes out of the oven and place it in a headspace vial, a glass container that can be as small as a test tube or as big as a canning jar with a cap made of rubber and a metal ring. Then, with the cap crimped on securely, you send it off to a flavor house. There someone like Sobel will puncture the cap with a special syringe needle containing a silica fiber. That fiber absorbs the volatiles, as your hair does when it's exposed to cigarette smoke. After about fifteen minutes, he'll retract the syringe from the jar and release the volatiles into his GC-MS system, which finally breaks the scent down into its components and reveals the molecular compositions that make the pie smell so good.

As Sobel sees it, he's the "geeky analytical guy." He takes the natural scents and tastes that we fantasize about and gives us the reality—what it really consists of, what it really tastes like. We may not like what he discovers—açai, he says as an example, doesn't actually taste very good in nature, even though it has gained a following among healthy eaters—but that's why the information is sent to a flavorist like Wright. She tames the wild parts (like sourness), polishes up the positive points (like hints of chocolate and berry), and delivers the flavor the way we like it. She's the facilitator of fantasies.

THE WEEK I meet Marie Wright, she has been hired by a major food company to update the flavor of its new-and-improved oatmeal cookie. In the far corner of the room, a heap of foil bags have already been piled onto a cart: cookies (baked up at IFF's kitchen using the recipe provided by the food manufacturer) that didn't make the cut from the day before. But today is a new day, and six shiny pouches lie expectantly on the counter before her, the contents of each slightly tweaked to emphasize a different aspect of what people like about the taste of oatmeal. Her mission: to deliver an oatmeal cookie that would give consumers a Heightened Oatmeal Experience—in other words, a flavor of oats so big that it tastes as healthy as it does down-home delicious.

Never mind that oatmeal by itself tastes pretty bland. She knows, as we know, that when we say oatmeal in the context of cookies, we don't mean the white porridge in a breakfast bowl. We mean a multisensory experience of something brown and grainy, cinnamony and sweet; in other words, our oatmeal fantasy, chock-full of crunchy walnuts and oats, chewy raisins, and the texture of brown sugar.

Wright's job is to match the mood of her client's specs. She might start anew and create a version of oatmeal flavor no one has ever tasted before, or she might browse the white shelves along the wall, lined with hundreds of neatly labeled bottles, and reach for an old favorite to get the process started.

Wright's client wanted a revamped oatmeal flavor to comple-ment its new and improved "healthy" version of the cookie. Fla-vors that communicate "healthy" while still tasting good are, not surprisingly, among the most popular requests in recent years, says Wright. The American population is aging while its waistline is expanding, and we've wised up to the dangers of trans fats as well as the benefits of whole grains. So while sales of cookies have de-clined overall, the calorie-conscious variety (like the 100-calorie packs), the organics, and the low-sugar sorts have been gaining ground—with sales up 9 percent since 2004. And even as 10 per-cent fewer consumers report buying standard packaged cookies in the past month than was the case in 2005, they're now more apt to consider the thick, chewy, premium sort so prevalent today on the menus of high-end restaurants. Apparently we avoid the urge to spoil our diets, but when we do indulge, we expect our cookies to be scrumptious.

Putting ourselves in another's shoes may be near impossible, as we discovered in Linda Bartoshuk's lab, but Wright's success, in large part, depends on exactly that. Wright may be a mother of two and a native of England, but when she is concocting an energy drink, for instance, she must tap in to her inner American teenager. She must ask herself, what sorts of flavors would inspire rock-star-caliber energy? What would taste like stamina on a soccer field? Sometimes the answer is simply a different spin on something she's already created; other times, she researches local markets and bakeries to get a read on the trends. For the oatmeal project, not being an avid eater of cookies, she did a little of both.

But what does a "better" oatmeal cookie taste like? From a flavor standpoint, the possibilities are many. It could mean recapturing the essence of a childhood oatmeal cookie, something sweet and rich that goes well with milk. It could also mean having a more "natural" taste, which in and of itself is open to a whole host of interpretations, such as tasting oatier or nuttier or more raisiny, among many other things.

"Sometimes we don't know what we like until we taste it because it's hard to describe," she says. That's the case with many clients. They give her a sketch in what is called a brief: whom they're targeting, what they want to achieve. In this case, they wanted to enhance an existing flavor to push their new health angle. But the rest they've left to her. "It's hard sometimes," she says. "You have to get it exactly right. They won't say 'This is perfect; we just have to add a little more sweetener.' It's either right or wrong. They may not explain what it is, but they'll know it when they taste it."

Wright begins with bag number one, which is sort of the skeleton of the potential cookie; that is to say, it has the texture and color of the regular oatmeal cookie, but with no flavor added. "It's very bland," she declares. (I, on the other hand, perhaps fooled by the look and feel of the cookie, rather like it.) Bag number two, the first in the series with an added flavor, she considers more seriously. She chews for what seems like many minutes before she spits the macerated cookie into a small plastic cup (which is how she keeps her weight in check, she says) and cleans her palate with water.

Meantime, I take a few more bites and swallow. Olive oil, I venture carefully, to which she and her assistant respond with a confused look. "That's interesting," everyone says, pretending to take it into consideration. The third tastes to me like pistachio. The fourth, for reasons I cannot explain, I like best, though it isn't apparent whether Wright agrees. And the fifth, which is the client's own interpretation of an oatmealy oatmeal, doesn't quite impress either. There is no love at first bite this time around, but Wright still has a few more days to keep tweaking.

Weeks later, after several in-house tastings, it becomes apparent that even though her client produces mass-market cookies, this new version should have the flavor of one made by hand. Indeed, sales of premium cakes and pies from bakeries in grocery stores grew 5.5 percent between 2003 and 2005 while the packaged variety stagnated; trend watchers expect so-called premium varieties to take hold of the cookie business as well. That is to say, the cookie should be of substantial size. It should be crispy on the outside and moist on the inside. It should be sweet, but it should also communicate the taste of toasted oats, which *isn't* actually sweet and is in fact a little dry. Meeting a customer's demands has become quite daunting. We have come to have so many expectations as to what our sweets should taste like (and the flavor industry has been so exacting at giving us what our taste buds want) that we've lost touch with reality a little.

THE DISCOVERY of mass spectroscopy meant that we could re-create flavors in the lab exactly as they appear in nature. But that didn't actually happen, not all the time, because we had our own ideas of what flavors should taste like. To sell a mango-flavored product twenty years ago, food manufacturers did better to ask consumers what they wanted rather than to mimic what mangos really tasted like. The mango is said to be among the sweetest, most popular fruit in the world, but the notion of mango flavor to ice-cream lovers in, say, Detroit is very different from the flavor people living in the tropics grew up with.

Thirty years ago, when I was child, a mango was a rarity. Once in a while my mother would spot one in the Stop & Shop and add it to her cart of groceries. Chances were the cashier would ask "What is it?" and once told it was a mango, she would simply shrug and call the manager for a price check.

Outside the produce section, the sweet, tangy taste of mango could be found only in the odd jelly bean in a novelty store or in the rare sorbet at a white-tablecloth restaurant. But neither snack would really taste like the luscious fruit we'd cut up at the dinner table; the sweetness wasn't the same, though I couldn't put a finger on why.

It is only during my visit with Wright that I find the answer. As is the case with many packaged fruits, exotic flavors become friendlier if there's a hint of the familiar. That is why when Snapple created a red-tea drink containing açai, the product development team paired it with mixed berries; and why some of the earlier pomegranate juices were coupled with orange or grape. The mango may have originated in India around four thousand years ago, but the first successful crop wasn't harvested in the United States until the nineteenth century in Florida. In the 1970s it was still a new, unusual sensory experience. Mangos inspired visions of exotic islands and seaside cocktails, and while Americans wanted a taste of that world, they wanted just a small taste. When International Flavors & Fragrances tried out a flavor reflecting the true taste of mango, the food testers thought it too weird. What they really wanted was pineapple and orange with a *hint* of mango—the American fantasy of the mango.

Times have changed, of course. In the past thirty years, we've grown more global in the way we communicate, shop, make our money, and live. More than 38 million Americans crossed borders in 2005 (almost 12 million more than in 1996), and that's only those whose took nonstop flights. Meanwhile, armchair travelers and gourmets can rely on a steady diet of travel magazines and television shows. And more than 35 million U.S. residents, or 12.4 percent, are foreign born—twice the number in 1970, a time when even pineapples still seemed exotic.

As we begin to see the world through a broader lens, we taste it that way too. Whereas once we had the French cooking of Julia Child on PBS and a few books on foreign cuisine, there are now at least a dozen high-profile celebrity chefs, an entire Food Network, and more than 50,000 cookbooks to choose from on amazon.com, many of which feature cuisines from far-flung places. Catherine Hogan, marketing manager for sweet goods at IFF, believes that consumers don't necessarily want the Americanized version of trop-ical fruits anymore. "As more Americans have tried real mangos," she says, "mango-flavored products can taste more like real mango."

Still, differences remain, even in today's jet-set population. Vanilla flavors sent to China have a stronger egglike note than those shipped to purveyors in America, explains Mariano Gas-con, chairman of the Society of Flavor Chemists. And soy ingre-dients in smoothies have a stronger beanlike note in the east than here. Likewise, the chocolate candies I bought in England seem to have more of a caramel note than those I buy in the States. Flavors are forever shifting, says Gascon, especially when you cross oceans.

COMFORT FOODS are as much about remembered flavors as they are about the true flavors themselves. The Red Velvet cake at the Waldorf was delicious, but the taste of sweet didn't ring out as shamelessly as in the box-mix varieties my mother sometimes made. I was excited to try a peanut-butter-and-jelly cupcake from a popular bakeshop, but was disappointed to find that it consisted purely of chopped nuts and raisins—all good ingredients, but not when I was expecting the unique flavors you can only get from the jar.

Food aficionados may embrace the whole-foods movement, but there's something to be said about the heightened eating experience of a thoughtfully made flavor, artificial or not. I remember the hard watermelon candy, rosy and translucent like stained glass; it didn't refresh the way the actual fruit did, but in fact coated the tongue with a flavor as sweet and thick as honey. I remember the just-baked, jammy smell of frosted Pop-Tarts shooting up with an urgent *click!* from the old springboard toaster (blueberries never tasted so sweet or looked so purple). Sure, I might order a salad of fresh berries at some greenmarket restaurant, but when I'm anticipating an evening alone and a whole pint of something sweet is in order, I might go for the carton of black raspberry ice cream that tastes more like vanilla than the actual fruit but is perfect for the occasion nonetheless. I go for the fantasy.

Flavor is part taste, part smell, and part expectation. A few years ago, a food-science consultant to the Wild Blueberry Commission of Maine concocted a low-sugar natural blueberry smoothie. The timing seemed right. Researchers at Tufts University had found blueberries to be high in antioxidants, which, as anyone who has ever watched a moisturizer commercial knows, can help prevent the free-radical damage that comes with age. In doing so, antioxidants are thought to help prevent wrinkles, cancer, and even memory loss. With a growing number of consumers buying foods for health reasons, blueberries were au courant, and the project seemed a sure thing. It wasn't. The resulting smoothie was loaded with blueberries, but when consumers tried the product, they rejected it. It didn't taste like blueberry, they said. It wasn't sweet enough. They wanted something closer to the fantasy, despite their best intentions.

THE RIGHT SWEETENER is as important to the allure of a dessert or smoothie as the flavors themselves. Some bring the flavors out; others obscure them. New flavors aren't ready until a food company adds the right amount and type of sweetener to suit the needs of its customers. Kris Mains, a product development manager at Snapple, considered at least four sweeteners when creating the brand's white green tea line: cane sugar (sucrose), organic sucrose, crystalline fructose, and high-fructose corn syrup. Cane sugar, or sucrose, is the granulated sugar you have at home; as we learned earlier, it's extracted from the sugarcane plant and composed of the two simple sugar molecules, glucose and fructose. Organic sugar is made from organically grown cane plants and skips a second refining process. Fructose, the simple sugar found in fruits, is 30 percent sweeter than glucose, the other simple sugar in cane sugar. High-fructose corn syrup consists of fructose and glucose, like cane sugar, but the two molecules exist in a liquid solution as separate entities, no longer linked by a chemical bond. It's cheaper than sugar and tastes almost the same.

Mixed into a beverage, however, the effect can be noticeably different, as Mains demonstrated with her colleague Gino Olcese, the ingredient technology manager for sweeteners at Snapple. Like Marie Wright, they sample in small portions and use spit cups, since a full stomach does not make for accurate tasting. Food scientists must consider prices as well as flavor when choosing sweeteners for a new product. Because this particular product is aimed at men and women seeking health and balance, they also have to consider whether the sweetener, like the fruit ingredients selected for these teas, fits into the overall "message" of the beverage.

With this in mind, they worried that high-fructose corn syrup may carry too much baggage according to public perception, having been widely cited by health experts as a culprit in the obesity epidemic. But from a taste standpoint, it may not be the perfect choice anyway. When mixed into a sample of white green tea, it gave a more "local sweet" taste, said Mains—hitting the middle of the tongue instead of exploding with the taste of tea all over the mouth. Crystalline fructose normally works nicely with acidic juices by coming on strong at first and disappearing quickly to highlight the tartness. But it wasn't quite right either, she explained. "It still lacked fullness."

Organic cane sugar, while in theory a nice fit with the wellness notion, tasted a bit off. It gave her a feeling of "cooked juice" or baked apple—not exactly right when "clean and crisp" was the desired profile.

They ended up going with the cane sugar. After all, now that artificial sweeteners are both popular and demonized, sugar seems virtuous again. The unnecessary but desirable descriptor "cane" offers an added halo effect: it sounds more natural—you can't help but think of big sky and vast fields when you hear the word. Cane sugar works well tastewise too. The sweetness arrives clean and dissipates quickly, allowing the green-tea taste to come on strong. They figured that a modest 6 grams of sugar per 100 grams of solution, or 6 Brix, would satisfy the sweet tooth of their target audience—men and women wanting something that tastes as "healthy" as the lifestyle they aspire to. Snapple's regular iced tea line hovers around 11 Brix in the United States. If the product is exported, the sweetness, as we saw with flavors like vanilla, is often adjusted to local tastes: somewhere around 14 in the Philippines, for instance, 12 in Mexico, and 9 in Japan. The British prefer their Brix like ours, around 11, but also prefer their tartness turned up— so their drinks offer a different sweet experience. These parameters are important because the level of sweetness helps nudge an unfamiliar flavor into the range of the consumer's comfort zone. It's the difference between a flavor that's too far out and one that fits the local fantasy.

PURISTS MAY BE appalled by the efforts used to make foods more palatable, but these days, we rarely eat *anything* plain or straight from nature. The truth is, the flavor of strawberries, blueberries, oatmeal, and many other foods is in reality difficult to accept. Oatmeal tastes bland without the bells and whistles. Strawberries, to many, taste better when they're sprinkled with sugar, laced with honey, or dipped in cream or chocolate. When we say we like chocolate, we're actually saying we like chocolate heavily doctored with sugar and oftentimes milk. Manipulating the taste of food by adding ingredients is a uniquely human habit, save for a group of monkeys on Koshima Island in Japan, who apparently have quite the sweet tooth as well: they like dipping sweet potatoes in salty water before eating them, and as any smart monkey knows, salt enhances the taste of sweet.

Fruit and sugar have paired famously throughout history. Before the advent of coolers, high volumes of sugar were a necessary component if your berries and apples and stone fruits were to be preserved and stored past harvest season: In *American Cookery,* published in 1796, Amelia Simmons advised using two pounds of sugar to preserve two quarts of strawberries. Granted, a considerable amount of sugar is required to exert the osmotic pressure needed to pull up the water from the fruit and keep the jar's contents germ-free. But I'd like to think that maybe, just maybe, food makers through the years have enjoyed sugar for its extra punch as much as its preservative qualities.

THE FARM MIGHT seem to be the only place to find honest flavor, with no embellishment. Plucked straight from the plant, the fruit is by nature sweet and delicious, but that notion of authenticity turns out to be a myth too. Humans have been trying to have it their way with nature for a very long time. Somewhere between 8000 B.C. and 4000 B.C., some very taste-obsessed Pacific Islanders decided that the sugarcane growing in their backyard wasn't as sweet as they liked it, and so they began cultivating a better variety. Our current species, *Saccharum officinarum,* is a sweeter version of earlier sugarcanes—including *Saccharum robustum* from Indonesia and *Saccharum sinese* from China. It seems that we've been hunting for the perfect sweet as long as we've consumed them.

Is it so surprising, then, that over the decades we have developed as wide a selection of real strawberries as of strawberry ice cream? Real flavors, in fact, aren't any more consistent than fantasy ones.

The changes are subtle, but we can be sure that the strawberry flavors captured on a farm decades ago, and brought to Sobel at FONA for evaluation, are quite different from those sent to him in a vial today. To find out why, I seek out Kirk Larson, at the University of California South Coast Research and Extension Center. Every spring, you will see him working his way up and down his rows of strawberry plants, each a potential new breed that in a few years may be in a grocery store near you. When I meet him, it is a typical May morning in Irvine, which means the sun is shining and the skies are blue. "Springtime is like heaven on earth in Southern California," says Larson, a horticulturalist by trade, who, in a checkered shirt, looks like a guy who just enjoys being outside. "It's the most unique climate in the world."

Brilliant springs, mild summers, and easygoing winters mean that California can harvest more than 1.6 billion pounds of strawberries each year, more than any other state. (Florida, where the climate is a bit too humid for the temperamental strawberry plant, is a distant second.) Eighty-seven percent of the strawberries consumed in this country are from the Golden State, so what happens to the strawberries here affects the taste of strawberry sundaes, jams, pancakes, and assorted parfaits and cookies all over the country. Larson's department is among the most prolific breeders in the industry, having produced the Albion, the Camino Real, and other hardy, commercially successful varieties in recent years.

Strawberries have been cultivated since the Middle Ages, but they were small and seedy. Like most fruit before modern times, they were also a lot more sour. It wasn't until a Virginia strain was crossed with a European one (by accident) that farmers ended up with something larger and sweeter. Since then, breeders have been trying to do even better. Spurred on by competition from packaged snacks and bolstered by technological advances in recent years, they have.

The average American consumes 99.6 pounds of fresh fruit a year, but this barely works out to two servings a day, less than half the minimum recommendation. Keith Kato, general manager at Dulcinea, a boutique grower of fruits and vegetables, believes fruit has fallen out of favor as a sweet snack because it's not produced and marketed with the customer in mind. "When we buy a box of cookies, we expect it to be up to a certain standard. If it's stale, we get upset. We might even return it," he says. "But with fruit, we react differently. If it's spoiled or sour, we throw it away and think, 'Oh crap, I got a bad batch.'" In other words, buying fruit is a risky proposition. It's no wonder that consumers might prefer to reach for strawberry cookies instead of strawberries. Kato believes that they would eat more fresh fruit if it were less of a guessing game. That's why some players in the $31.5 billion industry are beginning to run their companies like a snack-food brand in order to compete in the food business. They're attracting investors to fund efforts to make fruits tastier and easier to eat, and they're applying for patents and trademarks for their findings. Tastier seems to mean sweeter: a Fuji apple dipped in grape flavoring, known as the Grapple, has been wildly popular, as has Dulcinea's crisper, sweeter melon known as the Sweet'n Crisp Asian-Style Cantaloupe—sort of an apple-textured melon. But for now the challenges of creating the perfect strawberry are still formidable.

Kirk Larson is one of the patient ones. Every week during harvesttime, which in Orange County is between March and July, he works his way around the field, notebook in hand. He tracks every plant by its row and identification number, and if one catches his eye he will stop and assess its yield and its fruits' shape, color, firmness, and taste. The vinelike runners of the plant can't be too long, and the fruit can't be too small—both are obstacles to picking crops quickly and efficiently. Larson has to think pragmatically before a flavor fantasy can be realized.

He records his observations in his notebook, along with the date, and then he'll check that same plant a week later to see how it's doing. Many candidates might impress one week, displaying the right color, shape, and taste, but then will disappoint the next. Sweetness, in and of itself, is not enough. The look of the fruit must also say "ripe strawberry" because colors are important taste enhancers: a strawberry that's too white on the inside won't "taste" luscious enough; one that's too green on the outside won't "taste" ripe enough. Today Larson dismisses one that turned out not sufficiently red inside and another that has developed a nipple-like tip (both potentially unappetizing). We live in a hypervisual society, after all, where we depend on our sense of sight to guide us, even when it comes to issues of taste. In a report in the *Journal of Consumer Research,* subjects were presented with two different sets of glasses filled with orange juice: in set A, the juices were exactly the same but one was dyed a different color from the other; in set B, one juice was actually more highly sweetened than the other but had the same color. The subjects consistently said that the juices in set A tasted more different from each other than those in set B.

As Larson and I taste dozens of different strawberries, each a little tarter or sweeter or juicier than the last, I begin to wonder whether we can quite know what a strawberry really tastes like; we live in a world where fantasy and reality live so intimately with each other that they seem one and the same. I am reminded of a study out of the U.S. Army Soldier Systems Center, in which researchers told employees they were testing some new strawberry yogurts and made up a story about why they had to eat in the dark. The yogurt was actually chocolate, but that didn't seem to matter. Nineteen out of thirty-two subjects said that the yogurt had "good strawberry taste."

The point of the study was to suggest that we taste what we're told we're tasting, but I also wonder if we taste what we do because the definitions of particular flavors are so loose, especially compared to those of sound or sight. For instance, as the Flavor 101 class at FONA International explains, there are fifteen adjectives that can be used, alone or in combination, to describe different strawberry products. Professional flavorists might describe Smucker's strawberry jam as "jammy," "ripe," "cooked," and "caramellic." The strawberry Nesquik syrup, on the other hand, is "caramellic," "candy," "cotton candy," "creamy/milky," and "sweet." The typical eater may not consciously register the flavors as vastly different, but she's acclimated to register both tastes as strawberry. So even if we might think that the differences within a single flavor category (such as strawberry) are akin to the contrast between red and red-orange, in fact it's far more varied, like the difference between red and orange, or red and pale pink.

We are very exacting, however, when it comes to the *color* of flavors within specific food groups. Orange juice mustn't be the least bit brown, lest it's considered rancid. Apple cider and apple juice, on the other hand, *can* look brown. Apple soda is rarely, if ever, Red-Delicious-red or Golden-Delicious-yellow or, many other shades that apples might actually be; instead it's often—what else?—green, even though twenty years or so ago, green candies and sodas signaled the flavor of lime. In any case, strawberries must always be red.

Local varieties of strawberries bought at the farmers' market may taste sweeter than those from the grocery store, but Larson says it's not a fair comparison. When strawberries are picked at the peak of ripeness and consumed immediately, they will indeed be sweeter. The berries you get from supermarkets have the potential for sweetness too, but depending on the distance traveled, the timing may not be right. Strawberries don't continue to sweeten after they're picked, so distributors must compromise between flavor and longevity and pick early, or else supermarkets will have shipments of spoiled fruit on their hands. West Coasters are blessed: their strawberries are plentiful and the season stretches for many months. There's no need for the fruit to endure a five-day truck ride, as is the case in the Northeast, and so they arrive red and lush and at their prime.

Larson argues that, contrary to popular belief, size doesn't affect the taste either. The longer the fruit is left on the plant, the greater the amount of fructose in each and every cell, so it's the strawberry's age rather than its size that's relevant. To prove his point he gives me two: one small and one large, and they do in fact taste roughly the same: juicy, fresh, and sweet.

Strawberries taste better if you treat them well, he says. Wash only as many as you will eat at one time, keep the rest dry in the fridge so they stay fresher longer, and wait a few minutes before you eat them; they're more aromatic when you let them warm to room temperature. Sweetness requires patience.

Horticulturalists and geneticists have been actively cross-breeding strawberries for more than four decades, producing over 500 existing varieties. What's fun, he says, about these strawberries is that they are octoploids—they have eight sets of chromosomes, whereas we, as diploids, have two. The number of possible gene combinations is mind-boggling, but then again, the variations in people's preferences can be mind-boggling as well. Between 1982 and 2001, 463 varieties were developed from 11,000 breeding programs across the country—and possibly more, if you count the boutique backyard growers.

Americans like their strawberries a decent size, a bit firm, sweet, but with a trace of acidity, says Doug Shaw, who runs a breeding program in Watsonville, California. The French tend to like theirs smaller, softer, and with a floral note. Northern Europeans prefer theirs a touch lighter in taste. The Japanese like theirs softer in texture and very sweet, even if they prefer their pastries less sweet. These are just generalizations, of course, Shaw says; when you look at individual preferences the variations multiply, and the room for innovation is limitless.

The varieties that no longer exist? Breeders don't seem to miss them at all. Shaw keeps a library of runners from historical strawberry varieties as far back as seventy years ago (strawberries are propagated by their green, leafy runners, not seeds). Recently he grew some cultivars from the 1950s and '60s. There were some nicely flavored varieties, he says, but for the most part, they didn't have the aroma that strawberries have today, and they were very seedy. "It was surprising," says Shaw, when I asked him about them. "The idea that older cultivars had better flavor is pure mythology." Passers-by spotting those vintage strawberries in the field thought that they were wild, but in fact they were sold in supermarkets back then. (No wonder flavorists were creating strawberry flavors with cotton candy notes at the time.) Considering the taste and texture profiles we have now, says Larson, who tasted some of these cultivars, "we can never go back."

Fruit has pushed the parameters of our daily routine just as the beauty and fashion industry has. Naturally white teeth might no longer look white, thanks to the ubiquity of teeth whiteners; a size-8 woman might no longer look thin if we spend too much time watching the runways; and a naturally sweet strawberry doesn't taste like strawberry anymore either. As our fantasies shift, so do our realities.

AND WHAT of Marie Wright's new and improved oatmeal-flavored cookie? Out of the batch we taste together that day, Wright decides she likes the second variation, a nuttier version than the usual oatmeal cookie. (I prefer the second to the last, which turns out to have stronger notes of caramel.) And so she works with it some more, and in the end submits a cookie that has strong spice and raisin notes, with a creamy note in the background. That seems to her the perfect definition of a Heightened Oatmeal Experience, where the flavors of the healthy components ring out strong, even if their overall effect is the flavor of a comforting homemade treat that came right out of your mother's kitchen. Her client, she later happily reports, is pleased. If all goes well, it will soon land on supermarket shelves nationwide, just a few yards away from Larson's handiwork and hundreds of other strawberry concoctions created to fit your every fantasy.

Chapter Four

Always Room for Dessert

THE WAITRESS HAD A CONCERNED LOOK ON HER face when I, having already made a good dent in my burger, ordered a "Big Apple" pie and proceeded to devour it. "Are you okay?" she asked, seeming a little unnerved. But most certainly I was. Why would I not be? The filling felt soothingly warm, the crust thick, and the ice cream wonderfully cool. It was delicious. But for some reason, when a woman manages to eat an entire dessert, it's surprising, and maybe a little uncouth. Perhaps the proper thing to do would have been to share it or perhaps I was supposed to stop halfway. The truth is, I have never understood why that should be the usual protocol for desserts, especially since it's often perfectly fine or even expected for one person to order her own main course, be it chicken parmesan or a bacon burger, and finish it, if she so chooses. For whatever reason, there is a double standard when it comes to the last course. We flirt with the idea of desserts, saying how much we adore them when the menu is passed around, but when it comes time to commit, many of us retreat and wait until some-

one else makes the first move before we all (unfailingly) pick up
our forks and join in.

I say it's the fault of diet doctors, who have demonized desserts
all over the morning talk shows and newspapers, so that dessert-
phobia has become habit except on special occasions. A bestselling
diet-book author I interviewed recently called dessert one of the
two most dangerous things about eating out (the first being the
dinner rolls). I can't blame him, especially if weight-watching is in
order. Desserts are so tempting that they make us throw all logic
out the window. We can't help but eat dessert even when we're not
hungry and even when we know better.

The word "tempting" always comes to mind, but in actuality,
that's a bit of an understatement. The bread eating is understand-
able, since dinner hasn't arrived and we're hungry. But this cannot
explain dessert. With dessert, we feel compelled to consume it;
never mind that we said we were full three minutes ago.

Where does the power of dessert come from? The answer lies
not only in its tastes and textures, although certainly physiological
factors go a long way to explain that proverbial "dessert stomach"
people claim to have in reserve; it also lies in the more mystical
elements—the heart that's put into creating a dessert from scratch,
for instance, and the conviviality that comes with enjoying it. You
can't just fold up your napkin and walk away from that. In a small
way, our notions of the perfect dessert are windows into our soul.
It taps in to the natural tendencies and secret desires we all share,
and cajoles us into putting them in plain view for all to see. That,
to me, is the *real* reason why we think desserts are dangerous. We
like being in control, but they won't let us.

TO UNDERSTAND the remarkable hold dessert has over us, it's
worth taking a closer look at the digestive system, a system

consisting of deceptively simple tubular structures but governed by a marvelous web of feedback mechanisms. Once you chew your food, it moves from your mouth through the esophagus and into your stomach in a matter of seconds, and there it stays for about twenty minutes, stimulating the receptors around it and causing the stomach to expand, before your brain realizes you're full. The food sits for an hour or so longer, being washed in digestive juices, and then it progresses into the small intestine. The volume of an average person's stomach is about one liter; for binge eaters it's about two liters, though voracious eating can push past that capacity, since pressure, particularly from liquids, can help move the digested food to the intestines, thereby creating more room in the stomach more quickly. Under normal circumstances, however, hormones released in your gut and special taste sensors in your digestive tract will tell you to stop eating.

In any case, by the time your cake or pie or ice cream arrives, chances are that the latter part of the previous course is still in your stomach. You're absolutely "full," but by dint of some terrific force, you can't help but pick up your fork and sample whatever is offered. It seems that being full and feeling sated are separate matters. Somehow, by merely showing up, the dessert course has managed to outwit nature's own calorie-control scheme and charm its way into our meal.

Historically, doctors were convinced that it was the stomach alone that signaled satiety. At the turn of the last century, Walter B. Cannon, a noted physiologist, published several papers on the topic. For one experiment, he somehow convinced a fellow researcher to allow him to install a tube through his poor colleague's mouth and into the stomach. Suspecting that it was something the stomach did that would stir hunger, Cannon made note of the timing of his subject's perceived level of hunger with respect to the stomach contractions. Alas, despite the trouble both men endured to prove Cannon's point, the evidence remained mixed, and researchers have since discovered that matters are far more complicated than he thought. We now know that the brain and the endocrine system are important players too, a fact made apparent once our food proceeds to its next stage, moving from the stomach into the intestine, where it's dissolved with more digestive juices, not only from glands in the intestinal wall, but also from the pancreas and liver. Carbohydrates ultimately break down to glucose molecules; proteins, into amino acids; and fats, into fatty acids and cholesterol. Then, upon further processing, they get absorbed into the bloodstream, where they're carried into different cells of the body.

In the case of carbohydrates (a category that covers all sweets), the emergence of glucose molecules signals the pancreas to secrete insulin, which, in turn, sends the glucose molecules into the cells to be used as energy. What's not used right away is stored as fat. An increase of insulin in the bloodstream causes an increase of insulin in the central nervous system. This influx triggers an increase in another hormone: leptin. A rise in leptin, in turn, is sensed by the paraventricular nucleus, a group of large neurons in the hypothalamus, and it signals a decrease in a substance called neuropeptide Y. The upshot of all this activity is that our brain suddenly isn't interested in food so much anymore: *You've already gotten plenty of sugar in the system,* it tells us, *so stop eating.*

That's a simplified account of the story, of course. Many other hormones and neurotransmitters, working in concert, also affect the outcome. For instance, levels of ghrelin, produced in the stomach and upper intestine but sensed in the brain, rise in the absence of food and make us feel hungry. Levels of leptin increase with the accumulation of excess fat before we ultimately feel full. The lower the levels of neuropeptide Y, the fuller we feel.

Dopamine, acetylcholine, and serotonin also relay messages of hunger and satiety.

It's been said that our stomach, primed with nerve cells, is our second brain: stress on the mind sends butterflies fluttering in our belly; the anger that makes our head explode ties knots in our middle. When it comes to food, though, I can't help but think that our brain is our second stomach—telling it that it should eat or not eat, setting its own agenda as to when a meal is done.

The stomach may be sated when you've packed in enough food, but the brain is needier; it hungers for food that fulfills a *sensory*-specific satiety. In other words, it wants to be entertained with as many tastes, textures, colors, and temperatures as possible.

In the mid 1980s (at the height of my personal brownie sundae obsession), Barbara Rolls, at Pennsylvania State University, reported on the allure of variety in a meal in the journal *Appetite*. In her lab, with the intriguing name "Laboratory for the Study of Human Ingestive Behavior," she found that when two groups of people were offered a lunch with four identical courses of their favorite food, versus a lunch with four different courses, the group given the greater variety consumed 60 percent more calories.

A quest for variety is in our nature as living beings. Birds in the wild prefer worms, but after dining on worms for several days, they might try a cricket. When monkeys monitored with electrodes were repeatedly fed the same treat, the activity in the part of the brain concerned with eating waned, and so did their interest in food. But with the introduction of a new food—a peanut—those neurons perked back up and the monkeys began happily chomping away again.

This pursuit for variety may be a survival mechanism, and it kicks in most when when our options seem limited. Animals know this instinctually. When rats are exposed to their regular chow along with crackers, cookies, and chocolate, they eat more when each of these foods is provided in succession than when they are all available at the same time. We're the same way. In an experiment where people were offered different varieties of sandwiches in sequence, they consumed 15 percent more calories than those who were repeatedly offered the same one. A period of sameness seems to accentuate the allure of something different—just as a half hour with a savory dish would inspire a taste for sweet.

In food, as in life, variety is a spice; and over the course of a meal, dessert does just that—it gives us the change of pace that we're wired to crave. Our brain, burgeoning with receptors for different sensory pleasures, hungers to be stimulated by them. The more stimulated at one time, the merrier.

Sweets seem less likely to grow tiresome compared to savories. When a group of military personnel were fed the same forty-one food items over the course of five weeks, the savories bored them pretty quickly, while the sweet desserts and canned fruit remained desirable. In fact, scientists suspect that the taste of sweet slips past some of our body's usual satiety signals, outwitting them. And so we eat more and drink more sweetness even when we know we're full.

Desserts are the ultimate vehicle for sensory contrasts. Their acceptable parameters of temperature, texture, and taste are often more broadly defined than those of entrees, thereby permitting chefs to experiment with ingredients and provide exactly what our sensory neurons yearn for. For instance, Marcia Pelchat, an experimental psychologist at Monell, explains to me that she is a crème brûlée fanatic, while her husband prefers fruit crumble with ice cream. Each offers contrasting sensory experiences with every bite, a feature she calls "spatial contrasts." That is to say, there's a variation in textures and temperatures in a single mouthful. For instance, the crumble emanates warmth and has a roughness about it while the ice cream is cool and smooth. The crème brûlée (the top-selling dessert in upscale restaurants) boasts a crispy topping, still warm from having been fired to several hundred degrees, and at the same time, a smooth, thick, creamy custard, still cool from the fridge.

Certain dessert ingredients in and of themselves exhibit *dynamic* contrasts; they transform themselves within seconds of reaching your mouth, offering new textures and shapes before they're swallowed. Ice cream is one example; chocolate is another. Chocolate starts out in the mouth as a solid; then, with a melting point just below human body temperature, it dissolves into liquid (proof of the cosmic greatness of chocolate!).

Desserts have a sense of urgency about them. When they present themselves to us, we're overwhelmed with the impatience of youth, no matter how old we are, and we suddenly decide that we need to eat them right here, right now. We know that if we wait until we're hungry again, an hour later, we will risk missing something: the taste will fade, the dynamic contrasts that Pelchat refers to will vanish, and we'll never experience that dessert in quite the same way.

Consider a brownie sundae: it arrives in its prime, at a certain temperature, and it expires not too long after. The curvaceous scoop of ice cream eventually turns into a puddle; the cake, all warm and risen to its fullest potential, will cool and deflate; the nuts get soggy; and the chocolate sauce congeals. In his cookbook *Crave,* Ludo Lefebvre, then executive chef of Bastide in Los Angeles, wrote that there is something beautiful about creating a "gentle tug of war" between two distinct flavors, such as sweet and sour. The flavors sound like children in a playground, suggesting that the food is alive. And in a way, it is. Engineering the perfect dessert requires knowledge of the ingredients' biorhythms and a feel for good timing. For strawberry shortcake, the fruit, as we've seen, is best eaten soon after it's picked, before chemical reactions inside it change everything. For the biggest flavor, walnuts and pecans are best when baked for five minutes before being tossed onto a sundae. The window of opportunity for capturing those polarities in their most distinct, ideal state is small; but catch it, and the experience will be sublime.

IT IS HUMAN nature to be attracted to people and things that aren't exactly good for us, and dessert, as we've learned from a very early age, falls into that category. It's a contingency food, an indulgence, something we eat after we've finished our vegetables. In an effort to see if reverse contingency orders would get kids to eat better, Leann Birch, a psychologist at Pennsylvania State University, suggested to a group of preschoolers that if they ate their cookies, they could have their vegetables. The kids burst out laughing—that just made no sense! The sweets-as-treats association has been locked securely in the deepest reaches of our brain. As we get older, we come to believe that the diet doctor is right: desserts *are* dangerous, and if we don't want to overindulge, then we'd be wise to skip them entirely.

Dessert, it seems, has long been the food we want to eat—if only because it's natural to want something we think we shouldn't. For instance, when medical experts during Renaissance times warned that certain fruit taken as the last course was bad for the system, gastronomes enjoyed finishing the meal with it. These days, it's the stuff loaded with fat and sugar that's to be avoided, and by designating it off-limits, health gurus only exacerbate the temptation. When Manhattan restaurant consultant Arlene Spiegel added descriptors such as "sinful" and "decadent" to the names of certain desserts on a menu, sales tripled in one night.

Chris Gatto, executive chef at the restaurant chain Uno

Chicago Grill, knows how to play to our gluttonous tendencies, even if the chain's publicist takes care to let me know that there are many healthy options on the menu. For instance, his Deep Dish Sundae is, as he puts it, "a dessert gone crazy." An oversized chocolate chip cookie topped with vanilla ice cream and chocolate sauce, the sundae sprang into existence when someone had a wild and, yes, crazy thought: Hey, wouldn't it be cool to bake a giant cookie in one of these deep-dish pizza pans? It worked. It's adventurous yet safe—X-treme milk and cookies, if you will. He sells about 13,000 orders a week, and I wouldn't have expected any less: it's a dessert that let's you show your naughty side without anyone getting hurt.

Confronted with change, risk, and indulgence, our brain percolates with anticipation. Maybe it's our gustatory response to a frenetic, noisy, special-effects world. We want to taste and feel more on our palate, just as we want to see and hear more on the silver screen. We get bored quickly and constantly search for sensory stimulation and experiences that offer small, safe adventures. At the movies, we get our fix with action films, which spring into life with bright lights and loud noises; at the dinner table, we discover it in the perfect dessert.

DESSERTS HAVE always seemed to emphasize the humanity of the meal. Animals may seek variety by instinct, as we've just seen, but they don't really zero in on dessert. Dessert suggests that a proper meal has been served at a proper table, and that people have been enjoying each other's company and want to linger awhile.

Even before desserts were officially known as desserts and served exclusively at the end of the meal, sweet treats were about human relationships. The Ancient Greeks referred to the sweets eaten after a savory banquet (but before the symposium, the late-night drink fest) as *tragemata*. This literally meant "what one chews alongside wine," which, apparently, included nuts, honey, dried fruit, and an early form of cake, essentially a porridge baked dry by the sun. The revelers would lie back and drink and pick at the sweets casually—the food, a social vehicle to enjoying each other's company, unencumbered by the formality of the main course.

Japanese tea ceremonies in the fifteenth century featured the steamy brew along with light treats such as sweet bean pastes, biscuits and sponge cakes (you'd finish the sweet first, then turn to the tea; to do both would taint the purity of each taste). The ritual was a custom specifically meant to be enjoyed with others, not alone. As Donald Keene wrote in *Yoshimasa and the Silver Pavilion*, "Outside the room, where friends drank tea . . . there might be battle cries and the desolation of a city ravaged by warfare and neglect, but inside, there was the warmth of human companionship."

In the late Middle Ages, Europeans also retired from the banquet table for sweets when the gathering was small. Pretty dishes of sugar-coated nuts and fruits would be passed around and enjoyed with drinks at leisure. In some sense, we do the same today among friends and family. We finish the main course, then take our small plates and coffee cups to the living room where we have our cakes and pies and share a box of chocolates. Dessert served this way takes our guests away from the specter of dirty dishes and encourages them to relax and stay awhile. It serves a social purpose.

When and how sweets became a course in itself at the end of the meal is difficult to pin down. As Sidney Mintz reminds us, "There is nothing natural or inevitable about eating sweet food at every meal or about expecting a sweet course." Through much of the Renaissance, sugar was so expensive that it was used sparingly—as a spice for savories. A full-fledged sweet course wasn't typical in Western Europe until perhaps the eighteenth century or later, when sugar became more affordable.

Until then, sweets appeared intermittently throughout only the most lavish of meals. At Henry IV's coronation, sweets could be found in the third course, but not in the last. For his three-course thirty-eight-dish wedding banquet in 1403, sculptural "subtleties" marked the end of each course, and other sweets—cream of almonds, syrupy pears—were served at the beginning of the third. A glimmer of dessert appeared in fifteenth-century France, when two noblemen hosted a feast for the king, and sweets dominated the last three of seven courses.

It was probably the French who introduced the idea of desserts as we know it. The word *dessert* is in fact derived from the word *desservir,* to clear the table. Until the latter half of the 1800s, banquets were prepared *à la française*, that is to say, each course consisted of many dishes served together, abundant and artfully displayed, and the guests helped themselves at the table. The sweets first made their appearance as accompaniments, particularly in the second course, when the pièce de résistance (an enormous roast, for instance) was brought out with a flourish and embellished with sweetened ice, fruits, cream, or jellies.

The term *desserte* cropped up in the French vernacular in the seventeenth century, and it referred to the sweets that would be enjoyed—after the dishes from the previous courses were spirited away—on a newly reset table, or a second table altogether.

There would lie a bounty of sugar sculptures, cakes, confections, crêpes, and honeyed and sugared fruits, as well as meat pâtés and, as is also the case with today's dessert menus, cheese.

By this time chocolate also entered the fold. While dessert is nearly synonymous with chocolate to me, it took some time before it morphed from a sacred Meso-American drink to the sweet treats we indulge in today. The murky mix at first baffled and even repulsed the sixteenth-century explorers who met the Native Americans for the first time ("a drink for pigs," one Milanese traveler scoffed). But as the Spanish and Portuguese settled on the land and adopted local food customs, chocolate gained a European following, and the first official cargo of chocolate was shipped back home in 1585.

From Spain and Portugal, chocolate traveled to Italy, France, and other points north and west. In the seventeenth century, when the Italians invented the modern-day version of ice cream, they also tinkered with chocolate, trying it in all sorts of dishes. Needless to say, chocolate cakes, puddings, and sorbets caught on; chocolate pasta and liver fell out of favor. To celebrate the birthday of Elisabetta Cristina, the wife of Holy Roman Emperor Charles VI Hapsburg, the Austrian ambassador threw a bash on a summer evening in 1714, and he spared no expense for the dessert table. Iced fruits were placed amid chocolate foam, chocolate sorbets, biscuits, and ice cream.

The French created an impressive repertoire of pastries and confections in various shapes and textures including dragées, mousses, and marzipan. Their aristocrats embraced it in good times and bad. In a letter the Marquis de Sade wrote to his wife from his prison cell on May 9, 1779, the notorious sweet-lover pleaded with his wife for frosted chocolate cake—but not just any chocolate cake. "I want it to be . . . black inside from chocolate as the devil's ass is black from smoke," he said. "And the icing is to be the same."

Not to be outdone, the Germans created the thick and heavy Black Forest cake. A world away from the dainty concoctions from neighboring Austria, the cake celebrated the area's love for chocolate and its famed cherries and cherry brandy—both of which conveniently hid mishaps brought on by unreliable ovens. German immigrants to America introduced some of our favorite, generously sized treats, including jelly doughnuts and hearty plum tarts.

From Europe, chocolate desserts emerged in the Philippines, a Spanish colony, but after that the globe-trotting stalled somewhat. Middle Easterners, who went wild over honey and sugar in their confection making, didn't embrace chocolate to the same extent; and Asians and Africans, who preferred naturally sweet fruit over sugary treats at the end of the meal, didn't share the Europeans' chocolate zeal, either. Sophie and Michael Coe pondered this conundrum in their book *The True History of Chocolate,* and reported that cultural conservatism may be an explanation—after all, why would the Chinese want to replace, say, red bean treats with chocolate any more than we'd want to toss out our chocolate for red bean? Besides, while chocolate, in its original drinkable form, offered a new energizing beverage option to the Europeans, the rest of the world already had favorite caffeinated liquids: Middle Easterners were passionate about their coffee, and Asians were religious about their tea. There was no niche to fill, and perhaps that is why the dessert menus of these countries look so different to this day.

In any case, from chocolate cream cakes to perfectly poached pears, dessert emerged in full bloom in the nineteenth century in the Western world and its colonies. Serving dishes in sequence, as opposed to presenting them all at once, gradually became the norm. In this way of eating (known as service *à la russe*), a large banquet would feature a seemingly endless flow of distinct courses from the kitchen. And the dessert, meticulously crafted and gorgeously plated, earned its place as the grand finale of the meal.

Ordinary folk eventually gained greater access to desserts too. Before then, the poor often did without, either because the ingredients were too expensive, or because desserts were an exhausting affair. In 1747, when baking powder wasn't yet available, Hannah Glasse instructed the home cook to beat the batter *for an hour* "with your hand, or a great wooden spoon" just to make a pound cake. Fortunately, as we saw earlier, the cost of sugar and chocolate fell just as strides were made in the tools and ingredients used to bake with them. As the nineteenth century progressed, even those of more modest means also could mark the end of the meal with sweets.

This is important because by claiming exclusive rights to the last course, dessert acquired distinct powers. As the closing act, it has the special responsibility of prolonging a meal and the conviviality surrounding it. Ordering dessert is saying, "That was fun; let's not stop now." It goes hand in hand with the old-fashioned concepts of lingering awhile, savoring the atmosphere, enjoying the company and the moment. It is the opposite of a quick bite, eating on the run, or just dropping by. During the Middle Ages, sweet interludes were often accompanied by jugglers, acrobats, and musicians. That may sound a little excessive, but we have our own forms of entertainment today: our company, intoxicated by the effects of dessert wines and cake, might settle in for a DVD, parlor games, or more conversation.

Desserts also remind us that we're connected because, after all, when someone invites us to a dinner party, we might bring cake or a pie but not asparagus or pork loin. Unlike a burger or a filet of fish, dessert often exists in a form that must be shared: a cake is sliced, a batch of cookies is divvied up among guests, pudding or ice cream is dished out from a bigger bowl. When we eat this way, we must be considerate of others and take just the right amount so as not to insult the chef while leaving enough for everyone else. Like a bottle of wine, dessert gives everyone at the table a shared experience. We can't help but talk about it and compare notes. By offering dessert, we bring everyone together.

That is not to say, however, that desserts have no ego. After all, dessert, particularly of the plated kind, began as a privilege of the nobility and the rich and as such they have a curious way of simultaneously honoring both guest and host. The glorious sugar "subtleties" served at royal banquets were emblazoned with the signature arms of visitors to celebrate them; at the same time, the sheer abundance of sugar used also displayed the banquet giver's generosity and status in a public way.

Antonin Carême, the legendary French chef, knew the importance of fawning a little when it came to presenting desserts. In 1829, James and Betty de Rothschild, said to be the richest couple in France, enlisted him for duty. For a dinner honoring a famous writer, a Lady Morgan, he took the time to write out her name meticulously on one of the columns of an ornate Grecian temple constructed from pulled sugar. In doing so, he made the guest look good, he made his employers look good, but perhaps above all, he made himself look good. It's attention to details like these, after all, that earned him his celebrity-chef status.

Sugar is no longer a symbol of prosperity, of course, but desserts still often are. Roland Mesnier, who served as pastry chef at the White House for twenty-five years, tells me how much thought and work went into making the desserts for state dinners—often veritable feats of blown-sugar architecture, adorned with chocolates, meringues, and marzipan. For a delegation from India he created a large lotus blossom, made with edible pink-colored chocolate petals, mango sorbet, chocolate nougat, lychee, and toasted pecans. In paying tribute to their national flower, the dessert complimented the guests, but the evident degree of skill and knowledge necessary to have pulled it off also flattered the chef.

The same holds true for the rest of us, though on a more modest scale. As we saw earlier, a cake emblazoned with the birthday girl's name honors her, but depending on how beautifully it's decorated or where it was bought, it's also a showcase for the cake giver's talents or good taste. Desserts, it seems, let even the shyest person show off, in the quietest of ways.

AGE-OLD CUSTOMS concerning sweets hint that dessert isn't simply about food. It's about following shared rituals and traditions that we can't help but come back to time and again—the wedding cakes, the birthday cakes, the strawberry rhubarb pie at the church picnic, and the funnel cake at the county fair. We all have a bit of nostalgia in us, and desserts today play to that.

Words can enhance the effect. Brian Wansink, a professor of marketing, now at the Food and Brand Lab at Cornell, once did some creative writing with the menu at the café on the University of Illinois campus. For six weeks, the café alternated between offering zucchini cookies or "Grandma's zucchini cookies." At the end of the experiment, he found that sales increased by 27 percent on the days that "Grandma" baked—and customers who tried them actually rated the taste higher than customers who tried them on non-descriptor days.

Our olfactory system is closer to our brain's mood and memory center than any other sensory organ. When we see or hear something, those nerve impulses must travel from the eyes or ears, through the cortex, where thought processing occurs, before it registers deeper into the emotional parts of the brain. Scent bypasses this rational filter. When we sense the aroma of cake, the impulses travel straight through. And because smell and taste are inextricably linked, a whiff of pie will bring us a rush of memories just as the taste of it will.

This happened to my friend Mana, who has a penchant for beignets. Not just any beignet, but the kind that are hot and fresh, just like the ones her mother would serve when they had company, back in their old home in Congo. Mana moved to Chicago when she was a girl, but she recalls suddenly being whisked away to Africa when she set foot in the Café Du Monde in New Orleans and breathed in the scent of fresh pastries. This tastes just like *akate,* she said to herself when she bit into the restaurant's signature beignet. No one is more pleased than she, now that beignets have found their way onto many an American menu.

Scientists are only beginning to understand how we remember tastes and smells, and theories abound. It could be that our neural connections proliferate or that we become more efficient at firing the messages across the cell. It's possible that a memory may even change the structure of a cell membrane. Whatever the case may be, we tag each smell memory with a word, such as "lemon" or "chocolate," and when we encounter an aroma from the past, the label calls up the template of that earlier experience—and so we remember.

This presumably was on Kurt Hankins's mind when he created his crispy bread pudding à la mode for Applebee's. Besides promising plenty of spatial and dynamic sensory contrasts (the chilly ice cream and the warm pudding, the crispy outside and the smooth inside), the senior vice president of menu development knew he was providing a heaping portion of nostalgia as well. As we saw in an earlier chapter, cakes were meant for special company since the Victorian age, while puddings and pies were shared by family. It's been that way for so long, it's hard not to make the connection between humble sweet and home. "We used to eat it all the time," he said, as he explained his big idea to his team. "But the best was the crunchy part up top." Everyone agreed, yes, that crispy top part, you could never get enough of that. The trick, then, was how to re-create it so you get more of that crunch. They settled on cutting the bread pudding into twelve cubes (more surface to crunch) and frying them (more crunch to each surface). The result was a hotter super-crunchy outside and a cooler velvety inside.

Eventually the concept was tested with hundreds of surveys— from visitors to the Applebee's website to focus-group members and customers at select restaurants. "Want more ice cream with that?" Hankins's team asked. "What kind of sauce do you like?" "Does the name sit well with you?" People answered, and they were specific. They wanted more ice cream. They liked the caramel topping. Some thought it was more like French toast, but for most, the notion of bread pudding came through. Almost twelve months went by before the item finally debuted. "It's updated retro," said Hankins. "People loved it." It reminded them of home and transported them back to childhood, or at least to an idealized version of it.

Perhaps this points to why retro desserts have made such a strong comeback in the realm of family kick-back-and-relax dining, though honestly they were never gone. Even as purists like Alice Waters embrace the flavor of a simple ripe fruit, and experimental chefs concoct sweets with foam, gelées, and xanthan gum, there will always be someone eager to order the layer cake or the ice cream sundae. They're reliable standbys, even if pastry chefs might get tired of making them. We flock to them in the same way we enjoy viewing Hollywood classics again and again.

The same goes for the desserts at home. As Peter Dea, manager of food development at Mattson, put it, the idea of a goat cheese ice cream is fantastic, but do I really want it in my refrigerator? If you're going to buy a carton that you can turn to after a hard day's work, it'll probably be something with the flavor of what's familiar, like vanilla or chocolate. The allure of the familiar inspires even the most formal chefs to loosen their ties, so to speak, in order to win over their audience. French-native Michel Richard, at Washington, D.C.'s Citronelle, created Le Kit Cat, a dessert that plays on his favorite American chocolate wafer bar. Joël Robuchon, a culinary icon in Paris, with restaurant outposts all over the world, recognizes the draw of childhood sweets for Americans too; he uses Oreo cookie crumbs to top Le Chocolat sensation, a pudding-like concoction. Maybe because it recalls the taste of so many celebratory firsts, from the first birthday cake to the ice-cream cone on that first trip to the beach, the perfect dessert speaks to the wide-eyed child in all of us.

WHEN ANTONIN CARÊME started in 1816 as the personal chef to the prince regent in England, the portly royal was both pleased and reluctant. Pleased, because Carême was a star—the man who popularized the soufflé, no less—and he had this culinary genius at his disposal. Reluctant, and maybe even scared, because Carême, being the star, was sure to deliver on the prince's expectation for the most extraordinary of meals and he didn't trust himself to keep his royal appetite under control. "You will make me die of indigestion," he supposedly said to the chef, but that didn't deter Carême at all. "Your Highness," he said, "my concern is to tempt your appetite. Yours is to curb it."

That was as difficult to do back then as it is today. Whether it's a Red Velvet cake from a corner bakeshop or a confection from a star chef, the perfect dessert actively engages us and reveals a little too much. It brings to light that while we may pride ourselves on being self-sufficient, we prefer not to be alone. It exposes that we can act pretty childlike under certain circumstances, and it shows that we're saps for the good old days. Desserts speak to human nature, and we can't help but give in and have a taste.

Chapter Five

Sweet Tooths Anonymous

MELISSA SMITH KNEW SHE NEEDED HELP WHEN SHE ate, by her estimation, at least twenty Christmas cookies in one sitting. I was incredulous. I love sweets too, but twenty? Yes, definitely twenty, she said, but maybe even as many as forty. She had lost count. Someone had decided to bake all the cookies in his grandmother's cookbook and bring them into a meeting to celebrate the season, so she went around the room, taking one of each kind, then she went around the room again and took more. She felt terrible, but sweets were her weakness. If it wasn't cookies or candy, it was graham crackers and extra-sugary cereal, "soft porn" she called it, anything sweet and crunchy. "I'd eat half a box at a time," she confessed. Once, she ate an entire cake.

Smith (which isn't her real name) is someone you might say has a problem. Exactly what kind of problem is up for debate. Some might say she has atrocious eating habits; others might call her a glutton. But in her heart of hearts, Smith is convinced that she is a recovering sugar addict. A former alcoholic, she believes that in going sober she simply traded one addiction for another.

That meeting where she let loose on the Christmas cookies happened to be an Alcoholics Anonymous gathering. The meeting that finally pulled her out of her sweets dilemma was Overeaters Anonymous, which has members taking part in 6,500 groups around the world.

When I learned that sweets were suspect, I was both astounded and relieved. Astounded because I didn't want to believe that cookies could be broached in the same conversation as alcohol, cigarettes, or crack. Relieved because, frankly, I've had my own suspicions, and this validated my weakest moments. Addiction seems an apt explanation, but it's not exactly perfect. As much as we want to blame our brain chemistry, a cookie is just not the same as a cigarette, is it? There are certainly similarities—the cravings and the comfort, for instance, and the possibility of reckless consumption. But at other times a cookie is simply a delicious treat whose taste we savor and then we move on with our lives. How do sweets make that switch from friend to enemy in what seems like an instant?

IT WAS only a matter of time, I suppose, before someone claimed sugar addiction. We are an addiction-loving society; how can we not be, when there is so much to be addicted to? We're addicted to drugs and alcohol, of course, but we're also addicted to shopping, gambling, TV, and the Internet. We're addicted to oil. We're addicted to certain brands of jeans, smoothies, and mascara. On an Internet search, I found references to addictions to eBay, cats, crocheting, the BlackBerry, and Matthew Broderick.

We are a society that uses the term *addicted* very loosely, and it's difficult to know, unless you pry, who has crossed the line. Smith seems to have done so, but there are countless others who hover somewhere between normal and out of control. Chat rooms are full of people pleading, with multiple exclamation points, for help. "I need some support!!" types a member in one chat room. "I am sooo addicted to sweets. I get cravings all the time, and they are hard to resist," says another in a different online support group. One woman confesses that she wishes she could replace her meals with Oreos.

But does the sweet obsession of these chat-room users fit the definition of addiction? The National Institute on Drug Abuse (NIDA) defines it as a "chronic, relapsing brain disease that is characterized by compulsive drug-seeking and use, despite harmful consequences." That sounds about right. NIDA's brochure continues to explain that a drug is addictive if it is taken to "feel good" or "feel better." That seems to apply too. Smith herself confesses that anger or stress could send her down a slippery slope. It was partly the taste, she said, and partly the fact that cookies were a reward when she was a girl, the treat that often stood in for a hug or words of reassurance. The *Diagnostic and Statistical Manual of Mental Disorders,* Fourth Edition (the official manual of recognized mental disorders, otherwise known as DSM-IV, published by the American Psychiatric Association), also adds that "substance abuse and dependence" includes "continuation of use despite related problems . . . and withdrawal symptoms." Those sound appropriate as well. The DSM-IV states finally that addiction triggers a tolerance for the drug in question (that is to say, more of it needs to be consumed to achieve the same feel-good effect); there's no proof that this happens with sweets, but for me, more cake or cookies was never a bad idea.

Still, some aren't convinced that the taste of sweet is addictive per se. The chemistry of a brain on sweets is different from one on drugs. To appreciate the comparison, it's worth getting acquainted with two regions in the brain: the limbic system and the cerebral cortex.

The limbic system is the emotional brain. It allows us to feel sad or happy. It enables us to remember the experience and it lets us think, "This feels nice—let's do it again." The nucleus accumbens, one of many regions the limbic system is composed of, turns out be an important player when it comes to food. The nucleus accumbens mediates, with the help of the pituitary and other glands, feelings of pleasure and reward. Its trusty collaborator in this whole business is the hippocampus, which allows us to form new memories and remember these events for the long term. All together, the limbic system reminds us what we like or dislike, so that each time we're offered, say, a slice of Red Velvet cake, we don't need to ask ourselves, "Do I like this?" Instead, we know that we like it right away and we can order it again and again.

The cerebral cortex performs a variety of tasks, including controlling movement, processing sensory cues, solving problems, and making decisions. It's that part of the brain that enables us to sit straight at the table and mind our manners. It lets us assess the cake placed in front of us—how it looks, how it tastes, and such— and allows us to figure out whether we might want a second slice and how big that slice should be.

Billions of neurons communicate with one another in order for us to process a thought, feel a sensation, or take action. A message is carried by neurotransmitters, chemicals that are passed from one neuron to the next through electrical impulses. Two important neurotransmitters in the area of addiction are dopamine and acetylcholine. Dopamine is released in the context of sensory pleasure and translates that feeling into action. The memory and learning part of our brain records that feeling and reminds us about it so we're encouraged to do whatever we did before in order to experience that feeling again.

A team headed by Bart Hoebel, professor of psychology at Princeton University, demonstrated the compelling effects of these chemicals by wiring rats up to electrodes so that they could release dopamine by pressing a lever. When the clever rodents caught on, they ended up pressing the lever 3,000 times in order to stimulate themselves and they didn't stop until they were utterly exhausted. When the electrodes were placed in a sex region of the brain in male rats, they copulated with the female rats next to them; when the electrodes were moved to an appetite region of the brain, they devoured whatever food surrounded them.

Acetylcholine, under normal circumstances, signals us to stop. It's a chemical responsible for putting a damper on things. It increases when an animal is placed in a stressful hopeless situation, say, in the midst of large predators, causing him to lose his will to escape; it subsides when he's given Prozac, renewing his efforts to survive. In essence, acetylcholine turns off whatever behavior dopamine turns on. As levels rise, our appetite for food and sex plummets. As levels fall, we resume the activities that keep our species alive.

This elegant feedback mechanism backfires in the case of addiction. The drug-addicted brain is awash in dopamine in response to the drug, and acetylcholine fails to come to the rescue in time. When the object of the addict's obsession has disappeared, the addict experiences withdrawal. At this point, dopamine release decreases and everything in life takes a backseat to getting her hands on those drugs. She sets herself up for a binge and for the cycle to repeat itself.

Making matters worse, illicit drugs can also interfere with normal brain processing. In the case of marijuana and heroin, their chemical structures pose as neurotransmitters and warp messages neurons are trying to get across. In the case of amphetamines and cocaine, drugs may wreak havoc on the quantity of neurotransmitter a neuron releases.

Compulsive sweet eating may drive us a little crazy, but experts aren't ready to call sugar addictive. In another Hoebel experiment, rats demonstrated spiked dopamine levels when given sugar-water with their rat chow after a twelve-hour sugar fast; their intake increased day after day and when food was taken away from them, their paws shook and they displayed signs of anxiety, like a drug addict undergoing withdrawal. The conditions in this case were manipulated very carefully to reflect an addictive environment. Under normal circumstances the reaction wouldn't be as extreme, though I wonder if the feast-or-famine conditions human yo-yo dieters put themselves through might mimic these conditions. Hoebel says his lab's findings suggest that three factors may explain such behavior. First is the sweetness of the pure sugar; second is the schedule of feast and famine that leads to drinking the sugar in binges; and third is genetics—that is to say, some animals and people are more prone to addiction than others. This group, he says, needs to be especially careful not to binge on addictive substances. "This goes for both legal and illegal drugs, and sugar too."

I notice that he strategically placed sugar in its own category, and to many experts, this makes sense—sweets and other types of food just don't increase dopamine to the same extent that drugs like cocaine do. How high the levels rise varies depending on the drug, but the amounts of dopamine produced could be twice to ten times the amount triggered by food—and the euphoric effects from drugs emerge more quickly and last longer, since the chemical impact is so much stronger. Gene-Jack Wang, chair of the medical department at Brookhaven National Laboratory, prefers to consider overeating a *behavioral* addiction, like gambling. The cost of this vice may be devastating to the addict, he says, but compared to drugs and alcohol, sugar doesn't invite quite the degree of danger that drugs do.

Chocolate cravings, long claimed to trigger compulsive consumption, can't stand up to scientific scrutiny, either. One study provided chocolate cravers, on the onset of craving, with different iterations of chocolate: a chocolate bar, the caloric equivalent in white chocolate (containing none of the chemical components of cocoa), the pharmacological equivalent of chocolate in cocoa capsules (so you get the active ingredients in chocolate without the experience of eating a bar), placebo capsules, nothing at all, or white chocolate plus cocoa capsules (so you get the chocolate ingredients with the pleasure of eating a bar, though not at the same time). The researchers then asked their subjects to rate their craving levels upon consuming what was given to them. The result? Only the chocolate bar relieved cravings, and the white chocolate bar in both instances relieved cravings partially. The cocoa capsules were no better than the placebo or an absence of treatment. Chocolate cravings, it seems, weren't the result of a chemical dependency but a craving for the sweet experience itself.

WE'VE BEEN suspicious of sweets about as long as the masses have enjoyed them. A natural sense of unease overtakes us when numbers swell. In thirteenth-century China, when streets teemed with vendors hawking candied fruits and preserves, the sweet averse got a little nervous. One doctor at the time suspected that sweets not only rotted teeth but produced worms.

Centuries later, in the United States, sweet avoiders had more reasons to be frightened. The efficient new machines of the Industrail Revolution churned out more sweets more quickly, and railroads, mostly built in the 1800s, succeeded in delivering goods far and wide. Battalions of pastry makers, candy men, and cookie manufacturers arose in cities where there used to be none.

In the mid-nineteenth century, Sylvester Graham, an outspoken vegetarian and diet guru (and, ironically, the inspiration behind the modern-day crackers that partly drove Melissa to Overeater's Anonymous), preached against baked goods of various sorts. "The stern truth is," he wrote in *Lectures on the Science of Human Life*, "every

departure from the simple form of bread . . . [is] more or less detrimental to the physiological interests of man; and all those mixtures
and compounds of flour and butter or lard, and the sugar or molasses or honey, and eggs and spices, etc., comprehended by the
terms 'pastry,' 'cakes,' 'confectionery,' etc., are among the most pernicious articles of human ailment in civilized life."

In 1866, the prevalence of pies sent one critic ranting and rav-
ing, not entirely in jest. "We cry for pie when we are infants. Pie in
countless varieties waits upon us through life. Pie kills us finally.
We have apple pie, peach pie, rhubarb pie, cherry pie, pumpkin
pie, plum pie, custard pie, oyster pie, lemon pie, and hosts of other
pies," wrote C. W. Gesner in *Harper's New Monthly Magazine* in 1866.
"We enjoy less than any other people. We have no time for even
our pleasures. Pie is at the bottom of all this nervous unrest. How
can a person with a pound of green apples and fat dough in his
stomach feel at ease? It is too much to expect of him." Needless to
say, his sharp words didn't change matters.

Packaged sweets caused the most unease. In 1847, druggist
Oliver Chase invented the first candy machine, which essentially
worked like a printing press that cut lozenges. It unleashed large-
scale production of penny candies and inspired candy shops to
spring up across the land. In 1848, William Young invented a
spinoff of an early hand-cranked ice-cream freezer that removed
the need for muscle power, thus allowing for the mass production
of ice cream. Closed iron stoves, introduced in 1850, produced
baked goods more reliably than the old-fashioned wood-burning
fireplaces and brick ovens; efficient chemical leaveners, invented
around the same time, were a boon for cakes. (Never mind that
these leaveners lent a metallic taste to the batter—bakers now
simply could mask it with sugar, a commodity whose price was fast
plummeting.) In 1877, the first mechanically refrigerated rail car
began chugging fruits (not to mention meat and dairy) up, down,

and across the country, thus enabling consumers to enjoy nature's sweets—and make pies with them if they so chose—no matter what the local climate and harvest season. In 1879, Rodolphe Lindt (of Lindt chocolates) invented the conching machine, which ground the chocolate liquor, milk, and sugar into a velvety smooth, pliable texture that was much tastier than the grittier primitive chocolate bar. And in 1898, the National Biscuit Company (which eventually became Nabisco) introduced Uneeda biscuits, forerunner to Oreos, animal crackers, and other supermarket cookies we've grown to love. These were eventually packed using a new-fangled technique called the "In-er-seal"—which ensured freshness and allowed the manufacturer to box its product and appeal directly to the consumer (as opposed to shipping its goods in barrels and tins to a retailer to be repackaged for sale). Needless to say, branding efforts—the better to entice consumers with—soon followed. Yes, all these new innovations transformed the United States into a modern industrialized nation, but they also turned our land into a sweet-lover's paradise.

Worrisome types were appalled at the seemingly endless influx of sweets streaming down the assembly line and into a store near them. Critics feared that children's zeal for candy would trigger a host of unwholesome behaviors. After all, some of them were already playing betting games in order to afford a trip to the store; and cigar-shaped treats and the taste of sweet itself were thought to be natural precursors to tobacco and alcohol (some of the latter of which were made from copious amounts of sugar). At the same time, women's love for chocolate bonbons raised more than a few eyebrows. Alarmists wrote columns about how women were putting away pounds of chocolates and ruining their skin and figures in the process. As Wendy A. Woloson put it in her history of nineteenth-century American confectioneries, *Refined Tastes,* "Although confectioners encouraged them to buy sweets, and people eventually came to laud women as 'sweet,' it was simultaneously feared that once un-shackled, women's gustatory appetites, like their sexual appetites, might spin out of control and be the ruin of their households and, eventually, of the entire country."

Indeed, self-control was a preoccupation with Americans at the time, as Woloson explained to me later. "They wanted to deny having base appetites for food, sex, and vices. Since sugar was a rel-atively new commodity, it was a lightning rod for many prevailing cultural anxieties." More than a century later, sweets have found still more new ways to infiltrate our lives, and perhaps, like our an-cestors, we feel a little overwhelmed by the sheer abundance of them. The other day, I had countless opportunities to buy sweets without venturing more than a few blocks from my apartment. There were candy bars and cookies and other jumbo-sized snacks at the supermarket and drugstore, of course. But as the day pro-gressed, I could also have purchased some at the sandwich shop, the bookstore, a dress boutique, Best Buy, Blockbuster, the news-stand, and Staples (Staples!). And I don't even get out much.

Those who *do* will have even more chances to be tempted. Offices, hospitals, airports, and schools house not only vending machines (which sold $22.54 billion worth of goods in 2006) but also fast-food outlets. Meantime, the places that sell food are get-ting bigger. The average area of selling space in a supermarket in 2006 was 32, 396 square feet, compared to the average size in 1995 at 28,077 square feet. There are 945,000 restaurants in the United States, with a projected $558 billion in sales in 2008. In 1970, U.S. restaurants earned $42.8 billion, adjusted to today's dollars. The cravings triggered by the sights, sounds, and smells of sweets everywhere may convince sweet-lovers that they're addicted, even when technically they're not. We are bombarded with oppor-tunities to buy sweets all the time, and sales figures suggest that we don't resist. The supply just may have created the demand.

It's that ubiquity—and our loss of control in the face of it—that can turn something seemingly friendly into something feared. If we happen to feel hungry or unsatisfied (and who on a diet doesn't?), then hints of food can set off cravings and rob us of our control. Our brain, in other words, is very open to suggestion. When Gene-Jack Wang asked subjects to fast for most of the day, he saw increased glucose metabolism with increased hunger in the area of the brain that gets excited when addicts crave drugs. That area—a part of the limbic system called the orbitofrontal cortex—became even more activated when Wang dangled the subjects' favorite food in front of them without offering anything more than a crumb. (Fortunately, to make up for this torture, Wang treated the subjects to a free meal after the study.)

The *idea* of food, and not just the food itself, can also set off cravings. Marcia Pelchat, the physiological psychologist at Monell, put subjects on a strict fortified vanilla milkshake diet, the amounts carefully calibrated to equal the appropriate daily amount of calories and nutrients. As Wang did, she also asked her subjects about their favorite foods. She then flashed food-related words on a screen and took MRI scans of the subjects' brains as they watched. When words depicting their favorite foods (some of which were sweets, some not) appeared, she, too, saw activation in the very parts of the brain that become excited when an addict craves drugs. Pelchat's findings make me wonder, if plain words can do the trick, then advertisements and commercials certainly might too, turning foods that we love into those that we love too much.

I say "love too much" and not "hate" because the relationship doesn't exactly turn into that. Typically, when we see foods (or people, for that matter) as our friend, we like them and want to be with them; in this case, the emphasis on liking and wanting is the same. But when that switch occurs—when we begin to see those foods not as friends but as our downfall—we're still strangely attracted to them. The difference in the dynamic is that the emphasis falls more on the "wanting" aspect than the "liking." We forget to enjoy the food and we feel so bad about consuming it that we no longer like it at all even though we still want it.

Kent Berridge, a professor of psychology at the University of Michigan, has been studying the biochemical underpinnings of these feelings. With the help of brain imaging techniques, he hit on something he calls "hedonic hotspots." These hotspots exist as special neural circuits and are activated when we sense something potentially pleasurable, such as sex, food, shopping, drinking, and so on. When activated, hotspots give the thing we just sensed something Berridge calls a "pleasure gloss." It's because of these pleasure glosses that we like what we like.

A separate set of circuits governs our feelings of wanting. So far, Berridge has found both types in the limbic system, but he suspects they may reside in other brain regions as well. Wanting and liking seem as if they should work in tandem, but that is not always the case. When Berridge's team chemically stimulated the hedonic hotspots in rats with drugs related to heroin or marijuana, the "liking" reactions occurred; when he did so outside these hotspots, the "wanting" circuits lit up while the "liking" reactions remained constant or even decreased. This seems to reflect what happens with drugs like amphetamines: they stimulate the wanting aspects of the brain, but not so much the liking.

Berridge also tried injecting the hotspots with dopamine—that neurotransmitter that rises when we want to eat, mate, shop, or participate in any of life's pleasures. Curiously, it did not stimulate the "liking" circuits at all, just the "wanting" ones. And so while the rats worked hard for the sugar-water, they didn't demonstrate their liking for it by licking their lips or paws when they finally got it. Conversely, when Berridge performed the same experiment but with the dopamine receptors destroyed or blocked, the rats *didn't* try very hard to get their paws on the sweet beverage, though when they were offered it, they made a show of their liking for it. Dopamine, it turns out, isn't so much about pleasure as it is about possession. When our brain shifts to be all about the pursuit, that's when our favorite sweet transforms from innocent treat to something we don't quite trust.

Laura Milton, another recovered sweet addict, can attest to this. She would never order dessert when she ate with other people, but when alone, she would more than make up for it. Milton (a pseudonym) would pick up five doughnuts and eat them all in the car. When she was younger, she'd hoard packages of brownie mix and then eat the batter when her family wasn't home, afraid that the aroma of baked chocolate would alert everyone to her problem. Eating it provided comfort, but she had long lost the enjoyment of it.

CAN SO-CALLED sweet addicts say they love sweets more than the rest of us when for them the "getting" is more important than the enjoying? When sweets are recklessly devoured in record time, hoarded rather than shared, and (in the case of Milton) hidden lovelessly between mattresses, sweets become a tool for feeling better and are no longer an object of affection and a source of joy. If the taste has all but become meaningless, what can explain the allure that still remains?

It turns out, even if sweets don't send dopamine levels through the roof the way drugs do, they possess mind-altering powers of their own. Carbohydrates, a category that includes both sweet and salty snacks, boost our levels of serotonin, a neurotransmitter that bestows upon us a sense of well-being. This may explain why we reach for cookies and chips when our supply of serotonin is low— that is to say, when we're exhausted, depressed, or premenstrual.

Fat seems to complicate the relationship. One study out of Florida State University suggests women fall harder for sweets than men. When scientists prevented male and female rats from exercising and added condensed milk (a sweet and fatty treat) to their usual diets, both genders seemed to enjoy it—but the females ended up taking in 35 percent more calories than usual, while the males consumed only 15 percent more. When exercise was then allowed, the females cut down their caloric intake by only 20 percent, while males returned to normal. Humans don't necessarily do what rats do, of course, but the study does suggest that perhaps women's hormonal makeup, and specifically a form of estrogen called estradiol, has something to do with their increased snack size. Sweets may not be considered drugs, then, but we can't help but self-medicate with them nevertheless.

In some children, sugar might even ease pain. Julie Mennella and her team at Monell Chemical Senses Center measured the sweetness preference of 198 subjects ages five through ten, and then asked them to hold their hand in a basin of cold (50 degree F) water for as long as possible—once with a 24 percent sucrose solution in their mouth, and once with just water. It turns out, normal-weight children who enjoyed sweeter tastes were able to endure the chill with the sugar solution than without; but for normal-weight children who liked *less-sweet* tastes, the sucrose produced no effect. The results were strikingly different in overweight children. For these kids, the sugar-water was no better than the plain water at making the icy sting more bearable, even in the high-sweet-loving group. Incidentally, when the children's mothers underwent the same experiment, the sugar didn't appear to kill pain for any of them. More research is needed to explain the outcomes, but endocrine conditions and other differences may affect sweet preferences, and those preferences may in turn trigger different physiological responses.

Most of us are better acquainted with sweetness as an emotional stress soother, and there, too, researchers are exploring the science behind the personal anecdotes. A University of Cincinnati team recently reported that sugar has a scientifically measurable calming effect. Rats put under stressful conditions, both physiological (a rotating platform) and psychological (a well-ventilated but cramped space), displayed lower levels of stress hormones when fed sugar-water instead of plain water. Whether it's the sugar itself or the liking of it that lowers the stress responses remains to be seen, but I myself would pick a hot-out-of-the-oven yellow layer cake over a hot-stone massage any day.

THERE HAVE BEEN times when I thought for sure I was a sweet addict, but speaking with people who've devoured whole cakes in one sitting put me in my place. Meeting Brian Wansink did too. He is not an addict, nor does he experiment on them. Rather, he is the director of the Cornell University Food and Brand Lab and author of *Mindless Eating: Why We Eat More Than We Think*. His subjects are everyday people who eat more than they should, and his findings prevent them from crossing that fine line between love and a quasi-addiction.

Wansink does his work surreptitiously. So when he invites you into his kitchen, you had better watch what you eat. He may seem cordial, offering you a scoop of ice cream, and he may even show you a wonderful variety of flavors, but in fact he is watching you. He will keep tabs on how much you take; he will note whether you reached for the big cup or the little cup; he will watch whether you come back for seconds. And he will weigh—yes, weigh—your leftovers to find out exactly how much you've eaten.

Wansink observes how we eat in our natural habitats, much as a zoologist might study how orangutans feed in the jungle. Wherever people consume food, that is his laboratory, which is to say that the kitchen, the TV room, the car—the world—is his bailiwick. He has a lab on campus, specially designed to look like a home in the twenty-first century. Equipped with sleek kitchen appliances, a flat-screen TV, and dining tables and chairs, the lab transforms from a kitchen into a living room in a matter of seconds.

Not surprisingly, then, when Wansink invites me over to his lab one summer and offers me something to drink, I am very suspicious. He has a whole refrigerator of soda, but I decline. It is 9 A.M. and he is drinking Diet Coke. I think it is a trick, but it turns out he does in fact start out each day with a few cans of the stuff. "It's a great way to get that spurt of energy in the morning," he says.

Wansink is, in fact, a bit high-strung, but you have to be to dream up all the food projects he's published. His posters, often with amusing cartoons or pick-up photos (evidence of his previous career in marketing), actually attract a crowd at scientific conferences.

Wansink believes there are two kinds of people: those who eat according to internal cues and those who eat according to external ones. Most Americans, by dint of our culture, are external eaters. Others, such as the French, are internal eaters. The French will take a bite of a chocolate bar, say, and enjoy it, and then stop when they are no longer hungry. But Americans, he says, are different. "I'm full" doesn't so much mark the end of the meal as "I'm done" does. In other words, we assess our plates rather than our appetites. This is exacerbated by the tremendous proliferation of food establishments in recent decades. Not only can they stimulate cravings, as we saw earlier, they also tend to serve us big bowls and plates filled with food. As external eaters, we take it all in, because, simply, it is there.

To prove that point, a few years ago Wansink threw an ice-cream social for eighty-five of his closest colleagues, each pedigreed in the field of nutrition. He arranged it so that everyone was randomly given either a 17-ounce bowl or one that was twice that size. They were also handed a 2-ounce scoop or a 3-ounce scoop and told to help themselves while he watched. After they'd had their fill, the guests were distracted with a survey while the bowls were secretly weighed. It turned out that all but three guests finished their ice cream. Among those with the small scoop, those who received a larger bowl consumed 31 percent more ice cream than those who received a smaller bowl. Surprisingly, in perusing the comments in the surveys (which asked guests to guesstimate, among other things, how many scoops they had and how full their bowl was), the small-bowl users were likelier than the big-bowl users to think that they served themselves (and ate) more than they actually had. Most astonishing, those given the large scoop *and* the large bowl ate 56.8 percent more ice cream than those using a small scoop and small bowl.

In a set of similar experiments, Wansink found that teens at weight-loss camps served themselves 77 percent more juice in short, wide glasses than in tall, narrow glasses; and that bartenders poured 28 percent more liquor into tumblers than into taller highball glasses. Even when people were informed of this "vertical bias," the tendency didn't change, we're more addicted to filling our containers than to what's in the containers themselves. And since sweets are so easy on the palate (unlike, say, a bowl of chili), we're constantly vulnerable to eating enormous amounts.

Access is another accomplice to overeating. Wansink and his team gave bowls filled with thirty chocolate Kisses to employee volunteers on campus at the University of Illinois. Some of these bowls were clear; others were not. Some were placed on the desk within arm's reach; others required the participant to walk two meters to reach them. At the end of each day, Wansink took note of how many were eaten, and then replenished the supply to thirty again.

It didn't surprise me that the least visible and least accessible bowls were also the least visited: on average only 2.9 Kisses were taken from them each day. What did surprise me, however, was how vastly that number differed with the other scenarios. The volunteers consumed an average of 2.5 more candies each day when the bowls were clear but far away; 1.5 more when they were opaque but close; and 4.7 more when they were clear and close. It seems that we are victims of our own circumstances: we eat not because we're hungry, but because our choice of houseware items or an architect's layout dictates it. Over the course of eight days, as Wansink notes in *Mindless Eating,* the extra candies from the clear bowl nearby add up to 6,200 more calories, or two or three pounds gained in a year.

DRUG ADDICTS will scour the ends of the earth, selling what they own, disappearing from their jobs, desperately looking for another hit. But sweet addicts? The majority of us, it seems, can hardly be bothered to get up from our chair. Apparently we're not sweet addicts at all. We just eat as if we were—compulsively, unappreciatively—because it's easier to eat sweets than to avoid them.

Perhaps the trick is to focus on the "liking" of sweets and not the "wanting." Gail Civille, the director at Sensory Spectrum, says the more she has learned about sweets, the choosier she has become. Her career has actually made her lose weight, despite all the gum and snacks she must sample. Indeed, some of the most knowledgeable people I know working with sweets are also the most disciplined eaters. When pastry chef Wayne Harley Brachman examines a fruit Napoleon, he cuts it surgically, takes a bite, and spends time with it, noting the interplay of sweet and tart. When Wansink is served a plate of cookies—thick, chewy, and the size of my palm—he cuts them in quarters, decides which flavors he wants to try, and, miraculously to me, eats only a quarter of what he has chosen.

With knowledge, it seems, comes the ability to zero in on what we really like, respect it, and erase the clutter that surrounds it. It is harder than it sounds, of course. I remember sitting at my desk one day with two jumbo-sized soft cookies like the ones Wansink cut into quarters during my visit. I felt compelled to eat both, and I proceeded to do so, taking bite after bite, even as the flavors began to feel stifling and the textures hurt my tongue. As I lost control, I also lost my joy in eating them. One moment I was excited for a taste; the next, I was sick with regret. But I suppose that's expected with all pursuits that turn reckless, whether it's food or love or sex or money. Happiness, after all, is getting what we like when we didn't want it, or need it, that badly in the first place; the challenge is achieving that equilibrium.

Chapter Six

Does Sweet Make You Fat?

Esther Cook's kitchen is hard to miss. It's in a purple bungalow on the campus of Martin Luther King Jr. Middle School in Berkeley, California, and it's surrounded by an organic garden that spans an acre. Trips to that garden and the cooking classes Cook teaches are part of the Edible Schoolyard program founded by Alice Waters, the mother of greenmarket eating and chef-owner of Chez Panisse restaurant, a few blocks away.

The program sprang into existence in 1997, just as medical experts were voicing their concern about our expanding girth. Waters was determined to improve matters. It has been her hope that by letting children get their hands dirty in the soil planting seeds, cook, gather at the table, and eat their own produce, they will taste more thoughtfully, enjoy a healthier relationship with food, and restore all that is right with the world. It is *my* hope that by watching how the lessons are taught, I can rekindle my easy relationship with sweets, the one I had (the one we all had) during childhood, when foods of all sorts were enjoyed for what they were, without the worry of getting fat.

Back then, eating sweets used to be a series of small celebrations—from cracking open a fresh tub of ice cream to watching the chocolate chip–laden dough rise in the oven. These days, I still break for a snack and I still order dessert, but the experience is now tainted with worry, my mind addled with questions and on-the-spot risk assessments: *Should I have another cookie, or should I not? Should I walk away now, or should I indulge and then deny myself dessert tomorrow?* Such questions, spoken aloud or not, have become an inevitable prelude to any eating occasion. After all, as the headlines remind us, we're either fat or fear becoming fat, and sweets are often blamed for the problem. As a result, my own enthusiasm for sweets has cooled; blind devotion has given way to distrust.

What happened? It turns out our sweets have changed, and so has the broader context of our food consumption—from what we eat to how we eat it. In taking another look at the latter half of the twentieth century through the lens of food, I realized that the cultural shifts of the time had a great impact on how our bodies now look. Some of these shifts involve sweets, but some do not. While virtuous eaters might disagree, I believe sweets have been a scapegoat in our battle against obesity. Rather than being the sole cause of our weight gain, they're simply supporting characters in our fat-inducing, fast-paced lives.

THE MORNING I meet Cook (that is how she spells it, "believe it or not," she says), she is busily arranging in a massive blue colander the most orange-colored cut of pumpkin I've ever seen. There is also some lush rainbow chard and a giant stalk of celery, as well as leeks, beans, and beets, which (as she will later tell the kids) can taste wonderfully sweet. Cook used to be a chef and volunteered as a kitchen helper at the Edible Schoolyard. Eventually she came to enjoy working with the kids so much that she signed on full-time.

"We're making harvest soup today," she says cheerfully. I look on the blackboard, and indeed the words are scrawled in colored chalk, "Today's Special" style. A long list of vegetables follows, many sounding only vaguely familiar. My heart sinks a little, being a reluctant eater of greens; I force them on myself for health reasons, but prefer the more obvious sweet taste of fruit. Still, I can't help but be impressed with the gleaming bounty placed at the head of each table; it is fit for giants. "I've never seen vegetables so big and colorful," I tell her.

"They were just harvested in the garden by the last class," Cook says.

I look at this small blond woman with the calm demeanor and the large bowl of vegetables, and wonder if she can do it today—if she can really get a bunch of strong-minded preteens to appreciate what she has to offer. It's hard enough getting one screaming six-year-old to eat his vegetables, never mind twenty-four shouting, laughing, gum-smacking older kids and pots of soup filled with the healthy stuff. It's tough to stop and appreciate the sweetness of beets when there is ice cream and cookies to be had. If Cook's nicely set tables and friendly conversation can get them to listen, then surely we adults could sit down and focus for a few minutes and savor our food too, whatever it may be.

"Not everyone will like everything," she admits. "Kids are enamored of junk, so I just try to broaden their palate. I don't try to change their mind. If they don't like it, I ask them why. Just saying it's 'nasty' is not enough. They learn to pay attention to their food and communicate what they taste."

According to Cook, taking extra time to communicate is important, and yet we rarely allow for it at home. We don't live in a pull-up-a-chair-and-relax-awhile kind of world anymore. We think we're busy, so we eat and drink fast; we don't pay attention to the taste. We do a tally of the calories, but then we turn our attention elsewhere, to our computers, BlackBerries, or television. Despite our fat-fearing attitudes we end up eating too much anyway.

Cook also believes that our relationship with food has changed because the way we eat has changed. My visit with her made me realize that I eat in a distracted way, at my desk and on the run. How can we bring that focus back? I wonder. Marveling at how simple and elegant a centerpiece a few vegetables can make in a bowl, I eagerly wait for Cook's lesson.

ROBERT LUSTIG, a pediatric endocrinologist at the University of California at San Francisco, works across the Bay Bridge from Cook's kitchen and is director of the WATCH (Weight Assessment for Teen and Child Health) program for obese children. While he believes that the efforts of the Edible Schoolyard can't hurt, he's also convinced that the primary reason our bodies have changed is because our food has changed. And so, just as Cook is introducing good foods to kids at school, Lustig is helping parents to do the same at home.

If you ask him what's been put into our food to make us fat, he isn't likely to give you a quick answer. He'll have you at his office for a good hour or so, even though he's very, very busy. It's a complicated story, and it takes time to explain it, and so he will, because he is incensed over the whole matter.

Where to begin? "In the vernacular of the Clinton War Room, it's the insulin, stupid," Lustig says. As we discovered with Gene-Jack Wang at Brookhaven, insulin is the hormone in our body that regulates hunger and satiety through an elegant feedback mechanism. When you mess with insulin, you mess with that system.

"Our whole lifestyle is an insulin nightmare," says Lustig. He lists many reasons for the nightmare, including genetics and epigenetics (changes in cell function without change in DNA), stress, and an environment that discourages movement and calorie-burning. But what he seems to deplore most is the so-called insulinogenic food environment, a land filled with ingredients that wreck our body's chemical balance, making us fat.

To appreciate Lustig's point, it's worth remembering what happens when we eat foods containing carbohydrates (a category of foods that includes sugar). As they get broken down into glucose molecules and enter the bloodstream, the pancreas produces insulin. (Eating a lot of sugar at once triggers insulin to rush onto the scene, mop up those glucose molecules quickly, then vanish. A sugar rush, followed by a crash, is the result of this abrupt disappearing act.) As insulin in the bloodstream rises, so do the levels in the central nervous system, which in turn triggers additional changes in the brain, including a rise in leptin and a fall in neuropeptide Y. As a result, we feel full.

To keep this feedback mechanism working, a balanced diet—one that's low in fat, high in fiber, and not too high in fructose—helps. When this balance isn't maintained, it places undue stress on the system and wreaks havoc on our insulin function: As we keep flooding our bloodstream with glucose, insulin levels keep rising, and excess glucose molecules are transported into fat cells. What's more, dietary saturated fat, in high quantities, is linked to insulin resistance, though doctors aren't yet sure exactly why. Fiber promotes the metabolism of fat, so a fiber-poor diet promotes fat buildup, which in turn exacerbates insulin resistance. Fructose also makes matters worse because, in high levels, it compromises the liver's ability to respond to insulin. All in all, without insulin doing its job, glucose accumulates, the appetite feedback mechanism breaks down, we get sick, and chances are, we grow fat. And the fatter we are, the harder it is for our bodies to produce enough insulin, though scientists aren't sure why that's the case either. It's a vicious circle: obesity is linked to insulin problems and insulin problems promote obesity.

As Lustig sees it, our current foodscape has been hit by an insulin apocalypse. Food has gotten fattier, lower in fiber, and higher in fructose—precisely what we don't want. Many of these foods, while they look the same as they did at their introduction, no longer contain exactly the same ingredients found in their original forms. And it's these newfangled product iterations that put stress on our bodies. In the 1980s, new forms and levels of fat and fructose entered our diet, and (until recently, with the current awareness of its health benefits) fiber was taken out. The net effect of these three changes not only shrank the nutritional value of our diet but also magnified the negative impact of our occasional sweet binges. To understand what he means, it's worth a quick overview of how these food industry changes came about and how they affected our health.

First, let's consider fat. In the seventies, America experienced an influx of palm oil from Malaysia. The oil, extracted from the palm fruit, turned out to be an able stand-in for fat solids such as butter, lard, and partially hydrogenated soybean oil. It imparts a nice taste and texture to cookies and pies, not to mention French fries and fried chicken; and why wouldn't it? It contains 50 percent saturated fat, which is a little more than even lard. At a third of the price of soybean oil, the leading oil used in the United States, it worked itself easily and generously into plenty of processed sweets and eventually took the number-two spot on the market. Saturated fat worries in the late eighties triggered a temporary decline in palm oil usage. But with the current demonization of trans fats, palm oil has been enjoying a resurgence, finding its way into "healthful snacks" and quietly, unbeknownst to many consumers, raising the levels of bad cholesterol, just as trans fats do.

Now consider the disappearance of fiber. Fiber doesn't work with our on-the-run, convenience-driven society. This became obvious with the invention of the microwave oven. Introduced in 1967, this boxy gadget freed home cooks from countless hours of steaming, baking, and grilling. It originally cost $500, but by 1976, as the price dropped, it soon outnumbered dishwashers in American kitchens, reaching nearly 60 percent of, or about 52 million, U.S. households. Today 90 million homes own a microwave oven. This is important because as more Americans eat on the run—and have the technology to do so—they have discovered that fiber doesn't freeze and defrost well. Chicken, beef, spaghetti, and other conveniently made foods do; but whole-grain rice and other fresh foods, such as salads, don't. You can defrost frozen vegetables in the microwave, but they won't emerge as tasty as just-bought produce, and meats and starches that do heat well in the microwave are far more tantalizing anyway. Manufacturers obliged with truckloads of highly processed fiber-free foods—not simply because consumers liked them but also because they pack well and keep easily in inventory. The impact on our diets has been tremendous, says Lustig. "Medical anthropologists have gone spelunking in caves," he tells me, "and they've found people who've been dead for fifty thousand years. They'd take a DNA footprint of the bacteria in their stool, and determined that we used to eat 200 to 300 grams of fiber a day. We now eat less than 10."

Finally, there's the rising consumption of fructose, which proliferated after high-fructose corn syrup, developed in Japan in 1971, flooded the market in the early '80s. It won over consumers because it was found palatable in portable foods. It pleased manufacturers because it preserves well, resists freezer burn, and gives baked goods a golden brown color. Plus, it was cheap. By switching from a half-sugar, half-HFCS soft drink to a 100 percent HFCS version, beverage companies cut sweetener costs by 20 percent.

For Coca-Cola, which made the shift first, that meant a $70-million-a-year lead over Pepsi. Even today, as ethanol drives up the cost of corn syrup, it remains cheaper than sugar.

But there may be a downside to this sucrose substitute. When you're taking in high-fructose corn syrup, you're also taking in more fructose. HFCS tastes similar to sugar, but it has a higher fructose-to-glucose ratio than regular table sugar (55:45 instead of 50:50). Some nutrition experts say this isn't a dramatic difference, but Lustig believes it adds up, especially considering that the average American drank 828 eight-ounce servings of carbonated soft drinks in 2005 (with each serving containing more than 6 teaspoons of sweetener) and eats plenty of sweetener-laden foods we don't consider sweet, such as white bread, ketchup, and canned soup.

So what does the emergence of fast, processed savory foods have to do with sweets? Everything—because once upon a time, our diet was diverse. There were foods with fiber and foods low in fat and low in sugar. We had good foods three times a day, as meals, and we had indulgent foods—our high-fat, high-sugar sweets—in small portions once or twice a day, as dessert or a snack. But with the proliferation of all sorts of foods loaded with saturated fat and sweeteners and low in fiber, suddenly almost everything eaten over the course of the day transformed into an indulgent food, and sneaking in a cookie or candy bar at some point in the afternoon only magnified those extra calories we've already accumulated from our meals. Worse, with cheaper ingredients came bigger portion sizes, so in the end, even simple snacks became considerable calorie-laden treats.

When almost everything we eat is unhealthy, the impact of the occasional sweet treat is no longer counterbalanced by three healthy square meals. In other words, we lose that safety net of nutritious meals, which satisfy our hunger and save us from foraging for less-healthy fare. Without those square meals, everything we eat ends up falling into the "potentially fattening" category. Therefore Cook's classroom efforts are the perfect complement to Lustig's food theories: she teaches kids about the good options to balance out the bad, so that sweets and fats become the occasional treat they're meant to be and not the entire diet. And with an emphasis not just on the meal, but on the serving and eating of it, she hopes her lessons inspire them to create their own nutritious-food safety nets long after graduation day.

AT PRECISELY 11:30 A.M., the doors to Esther Cook's kitchen fling open and twenty-one seventh-graders burst into the room, their sneakers, damp from the puddles outside, squeaking on the blue linoleum floor. They are noisy and spirited, but not unruly. Without any prodding, they expeditiously drop off their backpacks and jackets in the back of the room, tie on their blue aprons, and pull up stools around the middle table, awaiting the day's instructions.

There are no groans or protests with the announcement of today's vegetable-laden dish. I wonder if it's because they know, subconsciously, that this late-morning session isn't so much about a recipe for making soup as for living a decent life. She tells one boy to throw out his gum. ("I hate gum," she had told me earlier. "It's all this mindless chewing. I don't let it in my class.") She reminds another to wash his hands after sneezing. And then she declares that something wonderful happened the night before. "Does anyone know what it was?" she asks. And to my surprise a few hands shoot up. "It rained," someone says.

Yes, it rained, and because of the rain, the plants are able to use the water from the sky, along with carbon dioxide from the air, and sunlight, to make sugar, thereby growing large and bright and delicious. Cook introduces each ingredient to her class, showing them how a snap pea makes a snapping noise when you break it, and how the bright purple liquid from beets makes a great stock. She holds up the big, flamboyant leaves of rainbow chard, and explains how it should be torn into smaller pieces. "It only makes sense, right?" she says. "Otherwise it won't fit on a spoon."

It occurs to me that her lessons are like the home-economic classes taught in schools back in the seventies and eighties. But packaged and updated for the twenty-first century as enlightened eating programs, these rather retro classes in cookery suddenly seem to be exactly what's needed to slow us down in these modern times.

Cook goes on to explain how to cut up the vegetables and how long they should be heated on the stove. The knives, neatly stored with other cooking gear in the center of each table, are not a child-safe version. They're professional-grade and sharp, and they need careful handling. The children, it turns out, are up for the challenge and no one gets hurt. Not just mere kitchen tools, the knives demonstrate to them that they are trusted.

When people talk about the Edible Schoolyard program, the discussion often turns to the garden, where the children grow and harvest vegetables and fruit, and where they learn what goes into a good meal. But in speaking to Cook, it becomes clear to me that the fresh produce is merely a platform for what's *really* being learned. By eating what they grow, the kids spend time at the table with an adult. She imparts to them her wisdom; she gives them her trust, and they give her theirs.

The class is divided into three smaller groups, each with its own table and stove. Today the fastest group is in the middle. Two boys are already stirring their bounty in a big pot, while the other groups are still chopping. When the soup looks done, Cook solicits their opinions. "Is it ready?" she asks the taller boy. He takes a sip and nods yes. She then asks his friend, and he, too, agrees. Only then do they pour the soup into a serving dish, and the little pre-lunch supper begins.

Meanwhile, some have begun setting the table; one begins grinding some peppercorns for the class. When they finally sit down and eat, they also talk. Sometimes they talk about the food in front of them and sometimes not. Cook remembers once asking her class about their favorite meal, and one boy raised his hand to say, for him, it was the night of the MTV Video Music Awards. His mother had bought dinner on the way home from work. It turned out that each member of the family had taken their own share and eaten it alone in their rooms. "I couldn't believe it," Cook says. "There's this gap in kids' lives. They come home and they put their dinner in the microwave. But some of the things they like doing are the homey things. They like hanging out with grown-ups. They need someone to say no, you can't eat potato chips for breakfast, it's not good for you."

Cook's kitchen classroom suggests that the way we live our lives today further exacerbates our current fat-promoting lifestyle. When I say our fat-promoting lifestyle, I mean our self-proclaimed busy lifestyle, which took off thirty to forty years ago with the rise of dual-income families, the proliferation of media outlets, and round-the-clock global businesses, all of which served to pull people's attention away from the family dinner table and into their own disconnected worlds.

We may feel that we're busier, but somehow we managed to eke out six more hours a day of TV-watching between 1965 and 1995. Meantime, most meals in America are eaten in fifteen minutes or less. If we're having lunch at a fast-food restaurant, it takes only eleven minutes. One out of five meals are purchased in a car. Sixty-two percent of people surveyed say they are sometimes or often too busy to sit down and eat. And yet, according to a 2007 Census report, we spent 3,583 hours engaging in some form of media in 2005, up 6 percent from 2000. The numbers for television-watching may have gone down from 793 hours in 2000 to 679 in 2005, but time on the Internet has shot up. This all makes me wonder: Just how busy am I really? Why don't I take ten minutes out of my evening to cut my cupcake in quarters and enjoy it, as opposed to eating it mindlessly while I'm on the computer, realizing queasily and too late that I ate more than I wanted?

Perhaps it's not that we're too busy, but that we're too distracted, at least when it comes to making food a priority. Eating has often become an undervalued act that we do along with something else, like surfing the Internet or tuning in to the stock reports on TV; we hardly consider it multitasking anymore. Appealing to that "busy busy busy" mind-set, food makers have come up with products like Go-Gurt, single-serving "breakfast cookies," pre-cream-cheesed bagels, and pre-peanut-butter-and-jellied sandwiches. As a result, home food has become fast food. With no effort required to make it, we no longer respect it with a place at the dinner table.

That wouldn't have been acceptable when I was growing up. Back then there were no computers, just the newspapers and books that my mother would tell us to put away when it was time to eat. The kitchen was the command center of the home, and my mother, the captain. The kitchen table, a hardworking piece of furniture that pulled apart to fit an extra leaf when we had company, was where we gathered three times a day, and where my mother dictated the rules. She wielded such authority that I never knew there was any other way and she provided the safety net: Milk was the proper mealtime beverage. Main dishes were a combination of protein and vegetable (chicken with green beans was a favorite, as were eggs with tomatoes). We never ate past full, so there was literally always room for dessert, which we always had.

At the time, "soccer mom" was not in our vocabulary, and neither was MySpace, playdate, or MTV. My mother did a heroic job shuttling us between tennis classes and piano lessons and birthday parties, but more often than not, we all managed to come home, set the table, and have dinner.

As I got older, however, a meal was no longer the center of attention but was pushed off to the side, next to the keyboard, or precariously balanced on the arm of the couch. That realization reminded me, guiltily, about author and classics scholar Margaret Visser and her thoughts on the virtues of a meal: when people gather around the table to eat, she says, the tenets of our culture are cemented; there are table manners to observe and patterns of communication to follow. In eating with other people, we are conscious of how we eat and how we enjoy the food. Conversely, solitary eating in front of the TV or the computer erodes the social restraints. Where and with whom we eat affects our choices, our intake levels, and whether we feel satisfied or want more.

This face time affects not only the eater but also the cook—a point made by Will Goldfarb, a New York City pastry chef and former owner of Room4Dessert, during a panel discussion at the French Culinary Institute in New York. His experimental-dessert bar was a warmly lit sliver of a spot downtown, and unlike many chefs who leave customers in the hands of underlings, Goldfarb was there most nights himself with a few helpers, serving customers on stools just a couple of feet away. A relationship develops because of that proximity, he says. He wants to do well for those eating his food, and they want to do well for him—by tasting it carefully, appreciating it, and taking pleasure in knowing that he made this for them personally. It's this feeling of responsibility that gets lost a little when the maker of the food isn't present.

Adam Drewnowski, a psychologist at the University of Washington in Seattle whom we'll hear more from later, suggests that there are repercussions to eating alone. French food experts, he says, held a conference about this in December 2006 called *Le plaisir: ami ou ennemi de notre alimentation* ("Pleasure: Friend or Foe of Our Food"). Eating alone is a factor in poor nutrition, he says, but it also "makes for poor social skills, interactive skills, and family life." What's more, in missing out on the pleasures of social eating, people might compensate by choosing meals that offer more extreme sensory effects, such as those that are sweeter, fattier, and saltier and more obviously delicious than the subtler-tasting meals that sustained them in the past. As opposed to desserts and once-a-day snacks, we end up expecting all-out indulgence all the time.

Depending on what we're doing, eating alone can affect portion sizes as well. If we were truly focused on our food, then the supersized quantity in front of us might actually alarm us, and we'd be able to make a rational judgment about how much more we want. But while we're distracted—channel surfing or e-mailing or online shopping—the quantity of what we've eaten doesn't register.

HOW HELPFUL ARE programs like the Edible Schoolyard? Experts say they certainly can't hurt, and some, like Leann Birch, the psychologist at Penn State, wish that they'd start earlier, when our eating habits are beginning to form. After all, as children grow older and attend school, their peers eclipse their parents in influence. She tells me about one experiment where she asked children what kind of vegetables they liked and what kind they hated. Her research team then seated children strategically—for instance, placing a child who hated peas but liked carrots with a group of children who felt exactly the opposite. For lunch, the kids were asked to choose their own vegetables. After about a dozen sessions of watching his peers choose peas, the kid who hated peas ended up liking them. If schools could take advantage of positive peer pressure, she believes, these programs could be more effective. I like to think they'd help kids tap in to their inner healthy-food safety net.

As for current programs, we have no scientific proof yet that eating well at school means eating well outside of it, much less improving kids' general health. The Edible Schoolyard is only beginning to track their progress, and as of this writing, results are a year away. Cook already knows her reach is limited once her students walk out the classroom; she often spots students up the street leaving a deli with soda and chips. But, anecdotally at least, there are bright spots. Cook speaks of a student who refused to try anything at first, but by the end of the year, after much encouragement, became one of the most adventurous eaters in the class.

At the Ross School, in East Hampton, New York, a doubling of the consumption of fruits and vegetables in school—as compared to the national average and control groups—led 80 percent of students' households to improve their buying, cooking, and eating habits. In Kissimmee, Florida, the Healthy Options for Public Schoolchildren program, which replaced certain items on the menu with healthy ones, found no change in the number of overweight children enrolled after one year, but after two years there was reason for cautious optimism: the overweight rate declined in schools under the HOPS program. The change was slight but hopeful, with 23 of the 486 participating children moving from the "overweight" designation to "at risk" or "normal."

At the Children's Storefront school in Harlem, an instructor with the Harvest Time in Harlem program reports having a conversation about rutabaga with a child. "Ruta-what?" the student had asked. The instructor gave her the whole story on the turnip-like vegetable, which, if you taste it carefully, balances nuances of pepper with sweetness. The student went home and told her mother about it, who hadn't a clue what it was. The mother in turn asked *her* mother about it, and she—the girl's grandmother knew exactly what she was talking about. And on that evening, instead of burgers or pizza, the three ended up picking up some rutabaga from the grocery store, boiling it up, and making it part of a meal, three generations of women together. As Ann Cooper, former chef at the Ross School who now works with the Berkeley Public School System, says, "It's about changing our relationship with food."

Inspired, I decide to spend some time knowing my food too, even when eating alone. I'll take my meals at the table instead of the couch, find out what's inside them, appreciate the unadulterated tastes of fresh produce as I chew and swallow. This way, I'll notice how much I'm consuming and I'll know that my sweet snacks and desserts will be the only foods I eat that are rich with fat and sugar, as they should be.

BACK AT the Edible Schoolyard, the class has managed to cook up a dish of harvest soup from scratch and share it. There are mishaps, of course. Two boys argue over who gets to spend more time with the pestle, crushing the peppercorns. The sweeping isn't exactly perfect. Cook orders a student to leave the class for interrupting. But somehow between 11:00 and 12:40, it all gets done. After the meal, everyone pitches in to clean up. I notice no slackers. The swishing sound of the broom, the clatter of dishes, and the faint scent of sweet, salt, and bitter flavors feel like home, the way it was when I was younger—evidence, day in and day out, that people had made a meal here and sat down at the table to enjoy it.

Chapter Seven

Let Them Eat Cake

I T IS A CHILLY NOVEMBER DAY IN SEATTLE, THE AIR still damp from ten days of rain. Adam Drewnowski, sporting a close-cropped haircut and mustache, rummages through the refrigerator he shares with his colleagues in the nutritional sciences department at the University of Washington. "Where is it?" he asks out loud, still a little jet-lagged from his trip to Paris two days before. "Has anyone seen it? It was right there." *It* being his can of Slim-Fast, which had been sitting in the fridge for years.

"There's a can in the back," a voice calls out. And indeed there is, the unmistakable 11-ounce can with that emblematic image of the frothy, "satisfying" meal-replacement shake inside. But Drewnowski is not convinced. He looks closely at the small print. It's an impostor. Someone had unwittingly consumed his vintage can of Slim-Fast and left a modern-day one in its place. There was a difference, he explains. That can had been living proof that the older Slim-Fasts were loaded with sugar.

More specifically, they were loaded with 34 grams of sugar and

220 calories, as opposed to the 180 calories in today's version, with half the sugar content. (I did not ask him whether the offender would be okay, having consumed such an old can of Slim-Fast. Whether yes or no, the answer would have been worrisome.)

The way he knows about the ins and outs of a nutrition label on a meal replacement might suggest to the casual observer that Drewnowski is watching his weight. But he is not on a diet (nor does he need to be). Rather, as a professor of epidemiology with a special interest in obesity prevention, he is fascinated not just by the contents of the can, but also by its cost, its target consumer, and the class and income of the people who actually consume it. Just as Robert Lustig believes that our foodscape has transformed over time, Drewnowski notes that our foodscape changes over space too. By space he means towns and neighborhoods, both rich and poor.

When I initially discovered Drewnowski's work, I knew I had to meet him. If I were truly to understand the nature of our relationship with sweets, I had to delve into issues seldom brought up except in the closest of relationships: class and money. In doing so, I realized why those matters are so taboo. They dictate the extent of the power you possess, the struggles you have, and the compromises you make because of them.

DREWNOWSKI, LIKE ROBERT LUSTIG, is well aware that processed sugar can make people fat. But what he has also noticed is that some sugary foods, like Slim-Fast, which has 180 calories and nearly 4 tablespoons of sugar in an 11-ounce can, are positioned to make us slim, while others, such as a 12-ounce can of cola, at about a quarter of the price and with the equivalent of 3 tablespoons of sugar and 150 calories, are said to make us fat. Why should sugar be an accessory to slimming in one context but not the other? He says this dual image is rampant. He points to another:

"There was something in the *New York Times* about removing soda and candy and sweets and so on from low-income schools in Los Angeles," he says. Sometime earlier, there was an article about Dylan Lauren, Ralph Lauren's daughter, and her candy shop, which she had opened on the Upper East Side of Manhattan. As Drewnowski tells it, the shop was reported to be a haven where kids could go wild and get cookies and candy and sweets and lollipops and there was absolutely no mention of diabetes or heart disease or anything like that—it was all good. "It was an incredible example of classism because food for the poor was automatically suspect in making kids obese and diabetic. It was very interesting and it tells us more about our attitudes than about the food itself."

I remember both articles, and he was right. The first one essentially talked about how sugary sodas in those machines are making children in public schools fat—that is to say, children whose parents, for the most part, can't afford private schools. The second described the sweet shop as the "destination for A-list moms and their children." The parents are presumed to have money, given that they can treat their kids to pricey chocolates and gummies from a splashy shop across the street from Bloomingdale's. Why are sweets bad in one context and celebrated in another?

"It's classist," Drewnowski maintains. And so after publishing hundreds of papers on sugary and fatty foods, he has turned his attention to the people who eat them. Why do some people get fat on these foods while others don't? Why are poor women often heavy, while rich socialites remain skinny? How can it be that in New York, obesity rates more than triple and diabetes rates more than quadruple in the span of a few blocks, from the tony Upper East Side to poverty-stricken East Harlem? And how can we fix the problem?

🍒

I'VE WONDERED the same thing. It always struck me that there's something of a chameleon aspect to sugar and its less expensive counterpart, high-fructose corn syrup. They have managed to work themselves in some way into every cuisine known to man. Sugar's ability to sweeten without altering the food's overall experience is uncanny. Honey and syrup, for instance, leave their mark, thanks to the flavor-altering minerals, nutrients, and other contents in them. But like salt, pure sugar and HFCS are the clear lip glosses and tan slip dresses of the food world: they remain invisible as they accentuate.

What sugar is and what it means changes according to where we happen to find it. It's a wholesome ingredient blended into down-home confections or it's the non-nutritive additive dumped into junk food. It's the pure and natural sweetener in fruity retro-chic sodas, or it's the stuff of evil lurking in cereal, baby food, and juice. It's a woman's food, in chocolates and cupcakes. It's a man's food, the stuff of sodas, energy drinks, and nutrition bars.

It's troubling, these multiple lives. As an equal-opportunity lover of all things sweet, I'd like to think the best of them. I'd like to believe they do no harm when enjoyed in moderation and offer only the most excellent things in life—if not good health exactly, then certainly good spirits, good times, and a sense of freedom that takes us back to our youth. But in reality, the taste of sweet can have positive effects and negative effects depending on the kind we eat, how often we eat it, and what else we're eating with it. Those choices we make color other people's perception of our level of sophistication and our wealth, as we saw earlier. They highlight the disparities between the haves and the have-nots, and between the strivers and the lucky ones who are already where they want to be.

THE WALLS in Adam Drewnowski's office are lined with seemingly endless layers of shelves, and the shelves, save for a lone box of Fig Newtons (a low-fat variety used in a photo shoot), are lined with journals and binders and books in such a neat and orderly way that if he wanted to cite a particular footnote—say, one in *Sweetness and Power* by Sidney Mintz—he could pluck it from his collection in a split second.

I suppose one needs to be incredibly organized in order to manage the impressive pile of food receipts that Drewnowski has managed to collect. By "pile" I don't mean the wad stashed between dollar bills in one's wallet. I mean 160 receipts collected over the course of a month from subjects living in the roughest neighborhoods in Stockton, California, where 39 percent live in poverty, and those in the toniest parts of Seattle, where barely 19 percent are poor and 51 percent of adults over twenty-five hold a college degree. These receipts are important because unlike food diaries or memory recall—which are commonly employed in nutrition studies—receipts don't lie. By collecting lists of what, exactly, left the restaurant or supermarket in a subject's stomach or hands, and at what price, he has gathered unflinching snapshots of how people really eat and how much they can afford or are willing to pay.

More important, he says, visibly excited at the thought, we see correlations between money and food choice. He sketches a quick graph on a sheet of paper. By plotting against calories consumed over a family's total food bill, he can see points where the data seem to cluster for different classes of people, indicating social trends. He can also take a closer look at the anomalies, the points that drift off on their own, and use those as clues to zero in on possible solutions. For instance, what does someone on a maid's salary eat? What does someone with an attorney's income eat? How realistic is it financially for the former to eat like the latter? And what's the story behind the handful of subjects with low-paying jobs but high food bills? Drewnowski is determined to find out.

Drewnowski later shows me some sample receipts. One is from Whole Foods in Seattle, totaling $45, which includes a couple of sushi rolls, some fruit-flavored soda, a sourdough baguette, and a chicken tortilla. Others are from Stockton. A Food 4 Less receipt amounts to $15 less but includes much more food, including a couple of boxes of Kraft Macaroni & Cheese for 68 cents each and iceberg lettuce for 59 cents. The pricier items, including beef costing between $3.25 and $7.74, are bought to feed a family, unlike the sushi rolls. A food-stamp customer at Wal-Mart spent a total of $6.51, which include two bottles of soda and a bag of Reese's Miniatures; another at Raley's supermarket bought pizza. This is just a snapshot, of course, but it gives a vivid sense of how a dollar can be stretched to feed more food to more people.

Having gathered data from the U.S. Department of Agriculture over the years while also collaborating with French public health officials on their projects, Drewnowski already has an idea as to what to expect. The poor will spend less money than the rich on food, and most of that food will be sweeter, fattier, and less nutritious. The reason, Drewnowski says, is not ignorance or sloth, as many thin, well-to-do types secretly believe. The reason, he says, is the price of food. "Good" sweets cost more than "bad" sweets.

The more sweetener, fat, starch, and unpronounceable ingredients in a product, the cheaper it is, since the ingredients themselves are cheap and pre-processed food is stable and easy to pack and ship—unlike fresh produce or meats. The discrepancy is apparent to the casual observer at my local supermarket, just a few blocks away from an invisible fence dividing a "good" neighborhood from a "bad" one. If you want to buy breakfast for a family of four, you could get a box of no-sugar-added muesli, which costs

$5.89, and flavor it with fresh strawberries ($4.99 for a 16-ounce clamshell box) and honey ($5.49 for a German variety in a 17.5-ounce bottle). Or you can buy a 14.25-ounce box of Reese's cereal for $5, which comes pre-sweetened (with 12 grams of sugar) for a difference of 46 cents per serving, which adds up to $671.60 for a family of four each year. If pancakes are on the menu, you can pick up a 12.7-ounce jar of Shady Maple Farms organic maple syrup, which costs $13.99, or you can buy Aunt Jemima syrup, which cost $2.69 for 24 fluid ounces. The Aunt Jemima will taste pretty good, but you get more than you thought you paid for—which is to say, corn syrup, *high*-fructose corn syrup, water, cellulose gum, caramel color, salt, sodium benzoate, sorbic acid, and artificial and natural flavors. If you simply want a snack, you could go for something nutritionists are apt to suggest: apples (I found a pack of four Granny Smiths for $4.99) and a jar of supermarket peanut butter, $2.99. This will feed four children one afternoon snack, with some peanut butter left over. Or you can buy a bag of Chips Ahoy! (a personal childhood favorite and in fact the second-bestselling cookie in America after Oreos), which costs a mere $3.99 for about 42 cookies. This, in contrast, will feed those children for a few days (if you can limit them to the recommended serving size of three cookies) and is virtually nonperishable.

The government spends tens of billions of dollars a year on farm subsidies, which keep corn and wheat, the staples of processed foods, incredibly cheap. Produce isn't subsidized, and so the prices remain much higher. The yawning price gap becomes even more apparent when one analyzes food in terms of price per calorie, as Drewnowski did. He reports that a dollar buys you 1,200 calories in the form of a package of cookies, but only 250 calories in that of a bag of carrots. Moreover, the energy cost of soft drinks is a bargain at 875 calories per dollar, while that of orange juice made from concentrate is considerably pricier: you only get 170 calories per dollar. "The difference in energy costs between fats and sweets and lettuce or fresh fruit was at times equal to several thousand percent," he says.

One would think a matter of a few dimes or quarters or dollars shouldn't matter. But it does, especially in a culture where food is a commodity and not something to be relished like a work of art. There is no room for savoring the nuances of strawberry flavor, with all due respect to Marie Wright at International Flavors & Fragrances—not when you have only so many dollars to spend and so many mouths to feed. Other than decent taste, people want their food the same way they want the other items they find in the supermarket, such as lightbulbs and tub-and-tile cleaners: accessible and cheap. It just so happens, the sugar-and-fat combination fits all three criteria.

Of course, there are healthier choices, but those choices often require a reallotment of funds. The mother who decides to cook salmon makes a conscious decision to spend more money on dinner that day instead of spending it on something else, whether it's clothing or entertainment. Or she may serve each family member a smaller portion of food, but that's a decision people rarely make. As former hunters and gatherers, we are calorie-hoarding creatures by nature, lest some untold Stone Age disaster keep sustenance at bay. It's a hard habit to break, unless there is means or incentive to do so. When resources are low, pricier foods on the shopping list give way to cheaper, not fewer, foods, says Drewnowski; people don't compensate by eating less until funds are depleted to the lowest levels. As one survey from the Bureau of Labor Statistics found, if an upper-income or middle-income person happened upon a few more dollars per day, they might use it to buy more vegetables and fruit. But if a lower-income person is given more money, they end up using it on rent and other necessities.

What's more, the food they eat turns into habit; it becomes part of their personal culture. "We make this mistake and say to people, 'Stop what you've been eating, and have some couscous salad,'" Drewnowski says, referring to British celebrity chef Jamie Oliver's strategy for fighting rising obesity rates in kids. "Those children wanted meat pies and French fries, and he gave them couscous salad. In working-class England? Come on! People don't necessarily move into someone else's alien diet."

In 1945, a farming journal suggested a way to eat cheaply and healthfully: on the menu were such dubiously tasty items as wheat flour, dried navy beans, evaporated milk, cabbage, and spinach. In 1975, the U.S. Department of Agriculture suggested a Thrifty Food Plan. Whether it offered a better alternative was arguable. Most of the calories in that early version of the plan came from refined grains (such as potatoes), added sugar, and fat, says Drewnowski. Beans, again, were the main source of protein. The recommendations have improved over the years—more vegetables and fewer beans—but it's still a pretty utilitarian diet.

Perhaps George Orwell said it best when describing a miner's tiny budget and how he chooses to spend it: "The basis of their diet . . . is white bread and margarine, corned beef, sugared tea, and potatoes. . . . Would it not be better if they spent more money on wholesome things like oranges and wholemeal bread or if they even saved on fuel and ate their carrots raw? Yes, it would, but the point is that no ordinary human being is going to do such a thing. . . . When you are unemployed, which is to say when you're underfed, harassed, bored, and miserable, you don't want to eat dull wholesome food."

To a certain extent, there is some sense of satisfaction gained from serving something that at least tastes good. In the choice between a generously portioned delicious meal and a small bland one, the former is the more attractive choice, except for the strictest ascetics (and perhaps swimsuit models).

In 2005, the highest quintile (20 percent) of households—those with an annual mean earning of at least $147,737—spent 6.8

percent of their money on food. The poorest—with a mean annual income of $9,676—spent 31.5 percent of their income on food. If you're trying to make ends meet on a minimum wage, then a box of cereal that satisfies a family of four over the course of a week might make more sense than a small bag of granola and a crate of strawberries, which might be enough to go around for a couple of days, assuming they don't spoil.

The thought makes us question how much freedom we actually have when it comes to satisfying our yen for the taste of sweet. When times are tight, we combine resources, multitask, we make do. We'll forgo a carton of premium sorbet if a two-liter soda on sale scratches that itch for something sweet. No matter how difficult things might get, we make compromises in order to overcome them, but only within the parameters of our comfort level.

IRONICALLY, THE MONEYED classes seem to be experiencing a peasant-chic food moment. Whiteness in food used to be a symbol of refinement, and the more refined the better. Purveyors of sugar used to wrap bricks in blue paper so that the crystals looked whiter. Today, a coarse brown sugar, like the kind imported from the island nation of Mauritius on the coast of Africa, is the choice sweetener at establishments also selling organic foods to those who can afford them.

At the same time, "buying local and in-season" is also a catch-phrase of the moment. This is another nostalgic reversion to pre-industrial times, when there was no highway infrastructure or railroad, and sea-trading was treacherous. The more distant and off-season your food, the richer you were perceived to be. But as we saw earlier with sugar itself, when physical distance is no longer an obstacle, an intellectual distance is imposed, separating those in the know from the unconnected and uninformed. And so restaurants boast about their local purveyors on blackboards, where the day's specials used to be listed. Imported chocolates still have their cachet, but more impressive are bars with fair-trade practices. Eating produce in season and from the farmers' market has also become a necessary foodie ritual. All very healthy, but now, ironically, also elitist. How can a family of four enjoy peaches from the farmers' market when a bag of them equals a sizeable portion of a typical week's food budget? How can they buy high-fiber steel-cut oatmeal when the only supermarket in the neighborhood carries just the instant kind and they don't have a car to go elsewhere?

Some studies have found that the situation is worse than we think. Rebecca E. Lee, from the University of Houston, inspected the availability of fruits and vegetables in Kansas City neighborhoods and presented her findings at the Obesity Society's annual meeting in 2004. In low-income neighborhoods, residents had access to a liquor store and to at least one convenience store that sold prepackaged fast foods, but supermarkets and grocery stores were few and far between. Worse, those few stores carried a limited supply of fresh fruit and hardly any vegetables. The high-income neighborhoods offered a whole different world, where residents could choose from several accessible supermarkets and grocery stores with a wide range of higher-quality produce.

Along these shopping aisles there are processed sweets with untold man-manipulated ingredients, and there are hallowed sweets with ingredients born out of nature itself. The latter may be perfectly sweet and perfectly good for us, but how perfect can they be, really, if only a sliver of society can find them or pay for them? My thoughts turn to the Mara des Bois strawberry, grown meticulously in boutique farms here and in Europe, and delivered urgently to four-star restaurants across the country. Is it really that much better a sweet than the strawberries we saw in Irvine or the strawberry cookies that Wright might cook up? As sumptuous as it is, the Mara des Bois has a flaw: it reeks of arrogance.

EVER SINCE SUGAR prices plunged in the nineteenth century, the taste of sweet had been a reliable friend during hard times, its taste masking the bland and the borderline fresh and easing the physical and emotional hunger pains of poverty. As Americans moved westward and factory work dominated urban areas, sugar slipped gracefully into the rhythms of everyday life. A good dose of sugar in tea and coffee (both relatively new to the country, having just gained ground in the mid to late eighteenth century) gave employees a pick-me-up in the middle of a monotonous afternoon—a most welcome respite as lunch could no longer be eaten at home. Paired with bread, the beverage turned sparse meals into something substantial and made for a worthy consolation prize in the absence of beer.

As is the case with cheap processed baked goods today, sugar mixed with wheat proved a highly effective means for survival in the untamed lands of early America. For the pioneers, pies were a clever way to bolster the food supply: they made paltry portions of meat go around the table a few more times, and they extended by several days the useful life of ripe fruits (baked inside and as part of the crust).

Angie Mosier, the Southern Foodways historian, recalled a time when sugar, gently and slowly heated with butter until it transformed into caramel, was thought to make an excellent cake filling. Households that couldn't afford a good oven would bake a modest cake in an unreliable one or in a skillet. Whether they came out even and moist would be anyone's bet. A little caramel or preserved fruit between the layers perked up the flavor and improved the texture of even the driest cake, and no one would be the wiser.

Sidney Mintz describes Coca-Cola as the right drink at the right time for mill workers in factory villages down south. Introduced in 1886, it offered a moment's respite in the middle of the afternoon, just as tea had offered a quick break for the first generation of factory workers in the wake of the Industrial Revolution. Soda did double duty, offering calories and caffeine. "It became popular when rural people were learning to live by industrial rhythms," Mintz explained to me. "It gave them that extra spurt of energy." Meanwhile, the big bosses at the mill were happy to oblige. They didn't want people falling asleep on the assembly line, or hurting themselves, after all.

Soda and snacks do the same for the modern-day worker, though in most cases, the energy spurt is less about preventing a fall into the machinery and more about breaking up the monotony. Vending-machine sweets, accessible and easy to eat within the time allotted, offer a break in the day. They provide pleasure during that small window in which we're free, even if we can no longer actually control the sugar content in our soda, as the colonists could with their self-sweetened brewed tea.

There are better options, however, if you are higher up on the social ladder. There would be the option of spending the $3 or so on a small bowl of fresh-cut fruit salad instead of a Pop-Tart, or if you are a socialite, asking the housekeeper to make you one. Either way, you can control what you want to eat, how much, and when. This is precisely where sweets discriminate between rich and poor. As Drewnowski points out, eating fruit salad not only assumes you have the extra money to buy it. It also assumes you have a kitchen, a proper knife, a cutting board, a refrigerator that's plugged in, and an electric bill that's paid, all of which require some money. "But a Pop-Tart," says Drewnowski, "assumes nothing."

SOMETIMES THE DIFFERING reputations for bad sweets and
good sweets are logical. Despite Drewnowski's issue with Slim-
Fast's health halo, at least it has the vitamins and nutrients that
soft drinks don't and it's meant to replace a meal, not accompany
one. But how to explain the difference between the candy at
Dylan's Candy Bar and at the 7-Eleven? And why are dishes made
with xanthan gum written up as culinary wonders in *Gourmet* when
it's used by a celebrity chef, and yet the ingredient is denigrated
when found in a supermarket salad dressing?

The halo effect depends not on the ingredients themselves but
on the eater, or more specifically, on the degree of control the eater
has over his or her food. Before the 1800s, sugar itself separated
rich from poor; now it is your state of mind while enjoying the
sugar that separates the haves from the have-nots. For instance,
Drewnowski's absolute favorite dessert is a slice of coconut cream
pie—not just any coconut cream pie, but the signature dessert by
Seattle's resident celebrity chef Tom Douglas. ("You have to share
it," he warns. "There's a lot of sugar and cream in it, but it's delicious.") So he and his dinner companion savor the slice of pie,
which happens to cost $8 (or the price of about two bags of Chips
Ahoy! cookies). Nice sweets with a big price tag are meant to be
appreciated like that. You eat a little at a time. Sensory-specific
satiety, as we saw earlier, may compel you to eat more than you
need, but chances are, if you're making at least middle-class wages,
you're not wolfing it down to ease hunger. Nor are you eating
sweets all the time. Sometimes you might have fruit; sometimes you
might have a cappuccino. If you're making at least middle-class
wages, then you have the freedom and the money to decide how
much to eat and when to eat it. That's how even down-market
foods can sometimes be elite in the right context. Lollipops at
fashion shows and Coca-Cola-infused sauces in trendy restaurants
aren't demonized because the people who consume such items in

those contexts have the power to choose something else entirely if they feel like it.

Sweets that escape demonization are also difficult to access. Dylan's Candy Bar, Tom Douglas's restaurants, Vosges chocolates: they are not available at a supermarket near you but at very specific locations.

"Bad" sweets are ubiquitous as well as convenient to eat, and if your funds are limited and you have little control over your time or how far you can travel, then "bad" sweets are also irresistible. "Bad" sweets require little else but an appetite.

But that's not to say that choosing soda or candy over produce is a passive decision. Rather it's an active choice resulting from a quick assessment of payback. The payback from vending-machine treats is immediate and pleasurable. The act of procuring a snack, opening the package, and eating it is a break in time; the snack itself is also a break for the senses, an escape from the whir of machinery and the smell of ink, paper, and carpeting. The sound of a bubbly, icy cola fizzing and the way it tickles the tongue, the scent and soft texture of chocolate chip cookies—all are an alluring time-out in the sensory ennui of day-to-day life.

But the degree of this allure is relative. When we choose one thing over the other, it's because the net benefit of that one thing overrules that of all other options. As a result, the poor become more "myopic" in their decisions, explains Avner Offer, a professor of economic history at the University of Oxford in England. The choice between *a*, which is available immediately, and *b*, which is available sometime in the future, depends on a couple of factors. It depends on when, exactly, the payoff will occur, whether it will pay off for sure, and whether that payoff has any relevance to their lives in the first place.

The *a* is a Pop-Tart or cookies; the *b* is forgoing that snack and embracing good health, not to mention a trimmer figure. The idea that it was an either/or situation arose as early as Victorian times; even then, the harmful effects of sugar were seen through a classist lens. As Alice Ross, the food historian, has explained, sugar, incorporated into homemade sweets like layer cakes, was a mark of sophistication and skill. Consumers of penny candies, however, were considered uncivilized. Not coincidentally, these candies were marketed to children from poor families and, like today's packaged sweets, could be had cheaply and easily.

It started out as an inkling, sugary snacks as the culprit underlying fat. But beginning in the late 1960s, the health benefits of option *b,* although less immediate, became more publicized. Into the '70s, the link between too much sugary snacking and diabetes and heart disease solidified and drove home the idea that poor food choices and habits would make you not only fat, but also sick.

American medicine has traditionally targeted middle-class needs more than those of the poor, so it wasn't a surprise that it was the middle class who made changes accordingly, tossing out option *a* and picking option *b* when it came to food choices laid out before them. This was particularly the case for middle- and upper-class women, partly because their circumstances made calories easier to resist (more on this later), and partly because the repercussions made doing so worthwhile. If she bothered to preserve her health, then she'd be able to work, make money, and reap the benefits of that money; she'd be able to watch her children grow older and enjoy their children as well. These outcomes are more of a guarantee in comfortable households than troubled ones.

A svelte shape is still (despite decades of feminism and all that it has accomplished) a sign of femininity and, as unfair as it is, a tool for gaining status, whether it's a high-powered man or a high-powered job. A 2005 New York University study found that every 1 percent increase in a woman's weight resulted in a 0.6 percent decrease in family income and a 0.4 percent decrease in her occupational prestige thirteen to fifteen years later. Heavier women were also less likely to marry; and if they did marry, the heavier they were, the less prestigious their spouse's job and the smaller his earnings. (No such decreases were seen in the case of heavy-set men. Their role in a marriage is still primarily economic.) Dalton Conley, the sociology professor behind the study, controlled variables by, for instance, comparing sisters with the same background, but he concedes that we never know for sure if it's a cause-and-effect situation; it could be that women with good jobs also tend to marry more successful spouses and to be thin. Still, in light of the positive possibilities that thinness brings for women, forgoing sweets (option *b*, in this case) seems to be worth the sacrifice.

For those already with such a man or such a job, avoiding sweets may be even more crucial: a love for sweets may be hardwired, but so is the search for status, whether it is in the form of fame, fortune, or respect. For those who already have it, losing it can be devastating. "Richer people have more to lose," says Offer.

Respect comes from your earnings and education level, and also, at least in a heterosexual context, from your masculinity or femininity. Men and women in Middle America, for the most part, do what they can to look and act within the social constructs that define their gender. Now for women, this is where the taste of sweet and the pursuit of status converge. Jeffery Sobal, at Cornell, observes that people "do gender" with food: Certain foods, like meat and liquor, are masculine foods. Others, like cake and confections, are feminine foods. When he first told me this, I thought it was one of the most sexist things I've ever heard, but when he explained it further, he won me over.

When Sobal makes references to food, he doesn't just mean the eating of it, but how we act around it—how we "perform eating identities," as he puts it. For a man, it's not so much the eating of steak that defines his masculinity and power, but how much he's willing to spend on it. For a woman, it is not so much the cake that enhances her feminine status but her ability to resist it and the maintenance of her figure in spite of it. (In Victorian times, as we recall, it was her skill in crafting the cake—not her enthusiasm for eating it—that boosted her status and that of her husband.) Control, not consumption, is the currency for status.

The lower classes, when faced with the choice between a and b, tend to weigh things differently. As Harvey Levenstein reported in *Paradox of Plenty,* the average American ate less sugar in 1977 than he or she did in 1965, but when you consider only the less wealthy, you wouldn't see that decline. The poor rarely cared, he explained, especially poor women, and in particular poor minority women. When asked about their food choices, taste, money, and time factors were among their top considerations. Only 4.6 percent of the responses mentioned health, and nobody at all brought up the notion of eating less to look slim. It's no surprise that more recently, a survey from the consumer research firm Packaged Facts found that those making less than $10,000 were the highest purchasers of processed snack cakes while those making more than $250,000 bought the least.

It's easy to explain the discrepancy by reverting to the Victorian idea that the poor lack control and can't be trusted to make decisions. In fact, choosing high-fat, high-sugar food *is* a decision. It's a decision to take what is immediate and a sure thing, as opposed to something in the unpredictable future that may or may not happen, considering the circumstances. In other words, there's not only a yawning income gap but also a large expectations gap, a chasm in the size of our dreams. For the poor, the considerations at hand are more pressing: the monotony of an unstimulating day job or an exhausting second shift, children to feed and keep out of trouble, and constant concerns about money. Making sacrifices now to bank on the future benefits of expensive healthier foods doesn't seem worth it.

Of course there are always exceptions. "Class isn't destiny," says Offer. But more often than not the educational campaigns to curb sweets and other junk foods work best for people who already *have* some education. They make sense to those who are better off and can afford healthier snacks and who can anticipate continued security. For the poor, the chances of scoring big on the labor and marriage market are slim to begin with.

I broached the topic with a senior policy maker in Washington. He had just lost forty pounds, despite his affection for fresh-baked cookies, and he had come by my office to promote the new food pyramid, which advises rather vaguely to "choose a diet moderate in sugars." (It has since changed to a more customized, computerized pyramid. When I type in my stats, I'm told to limit my extra fats and sugars to 265 out of a 2,000-calorie diet.) I asked him, "What if people just can't afford healthy food?" His reply was that if they can afford fancy sneakers and electronic games, then they can afford healthy foods; they just decide not to.

His argument made some sense, but it frustrates Adam Drewnowski no end. The iPod, he insists, brings immediate reward, and it's a small one compared to what the children frolicking in Dylan's Candy Bar expect, from fancy birthday parties to tennis lessons to winter holidays somewhere warm. In the absence of those high-end treats, a cookie, a soda, a pair of nice sneakers— these are life's pleasures. "Affordable luxuries, you mean?" I ask. "No, not luxuries," he says. Life's pleasures is all.

WHEN PUNDITS DOLE out nutrition advice, they pay only lip service to the fact that people tend to treat food as something we juggle along with our current work and family responsibilities. We fit it in. According to Drewnowski, this is probably why current initiatives to curb the consumption of high-fat, high-sweet foods don't work. The solutions are not relevant to everyone, particularly those whose lives fall below the middle class. "You can't tell a working-class person, 'Get healthy by eating mangos and playing tennis,'" says Drewnowski. "It just doesn't make sense." To ask people simply to change their diet is to ask them to walk away from their own reality and adopt an alien lifestyle. It's almost like asking an inner-city family to do their part in saving the earth by ditching their old clunker and buying a hybrid car.

As absurd as that sounds, it's true that healthy-eating messages haven't done much better, having been directed firmly at the middle and upper classes. The latest color-coded version of the USDA's food pyramid and its interactive website assume access to a computer, along with the time and permission to use it for personal purposes. The pamphlets that promote exercise assume you have a safe neighborhood for walking or money for a gym membership. The helpful hints to eat fruits and vegetables, as Drewnowski has pointed out, assume the money to buy them and the kitchenware to prepare them.

The current initiatives to eat local organic foods, as well-meaning as they are, also sprang up from a middle-class place. It started when the campus activists from the 1960s, who rallied for an end to world hunger, grew up and, as Levenstein tells it, "turned inward." After earning enough money from decent-paying jobs, they came to espouse wellness and the virtues of fresh produce and local organics. They also took up jogging and walking.

In 1971, as cheap sweeteners and fats invaded grocery shelves, Alice Waters opened Chez Panisse and reinforced the idea of unadulterated food. More than twenty years later, she set up the Edible Schoolyard in an effort to reach out to children in the public school nearby, children whose families had never set foot in her restaurant and probably never will. Programs like this are good, says Drewnowski, but despite the tremendous efforts of people like Waters and Cook, there needs to be a broader structural shift to eliminate the classist divide we find in sweets. Even though the consumption of produce rose in 2000, Americans still eat only 1.4 servings of fruit a day, and half of the intake is accounted for by the three cheapest varieties available: oranges, apples, and bananas. It seems that the pioneering chefs and espousers of fresh, sweet produce have done more to change the eating habits of the rich than those of the poor; and the talk about wholesome foods is doing more to tantalize so-called refined palates than to help badly nourished people who actually could use some quality food.

THE TWENTY-FIRST-CENTURY foodscape is vast, but you would never know it if you lived in the inner-city. East Harlem, a neighborhood one express-train stop away from mine, for instance, is a different universe. A city-commissioned health survey found that fast-food spots and poorly stocked bodegas outnumber supermarkets; and those bodegas were only half as likely as those on the Upper East Side to sell low-fat milk and seven times less likely to offer leafy-green vegetables. Surrounded by "Everything $1" stores hawking cold cuts, soda, and lottery tickets is a tuition-free private school, retrofitted from four prewar apartment buildings. A makeshift farmers' market opened for business in front of the school for a day, an annual event run by volunteers from Slow Food NYC, a nonprofit hoping to preserve local food traditions, and as its website puts it, "counteract fast food and fast life." Not unlike Esther Cook at the Edible Schoolyard, the organizers of Slow Food's Harvest Time program hope to teach children that an array of healthy and fun food choices lie within their reach. Children who attend the school come mainly from Harlem and the South Bronx; some live in homeless shelters. What they have in common is parents who want a better chance for their kids and who had the incredible foresight to place their child's name on a list practically the day she was born. The waiting list is 1,200 names long.

Today the lesson was apples. The children chose from three different kinds, cut, peeled, and ready to eat. Farther down on the long folding table, apple cider and apple butter were served with saltines. Off to the side, the kids created apple prints. The teacher, a young fresh-faced woman with straight golden hair, admits her surprise at the children's enthusiasm. "When I was a child, I was disappointed when they brought out fruit instead of cake. But these kids get excited," she said.

It's hard not to be skeptical about these programs after speaking with Drewnowski. Even if the children become enchanted with, say, the Jonathan apple, or even with Kirk Larson's Albion strawberry, how will they obtain it on their own? I wonder, if the kids have enough fun with the fruit, will they plead with their parents to spend the time to seek it out? Will they impress their mothers with their knowledge and enthusiasm enough to persuade her to spend a little more money on their weekly grocery bill and bring home a bag of Gala apples?

In dismal circumstances, knowledge isn't power; money is. It takes creativity to bring in the funds necessary to put that knowledge into action. Sweet fruit, after all, lends itself to imagination, as is the case here. The apples are colorful, possess an array of textures, and can be cut up to make kebobs, dried to make a packable snack, and even carved to make stamps with food coloring. They may not be more fun than an iPod or expensive sneakers (their sense of immediate pleasure not quite as enticing, as Drewnowski likes to point out), but it's a step in the right direction. In some ways, the perfect sweet depends on your state of mind, and fruits could use some more marketing of this sort. After all, the National Cancer Institute allots $1 million a year on their campaign to get people to eat more produce; the soft drink industry spends $600 million.

A thin girl with dark eyes and a neat ponytail said cookies are her favorite snack, though she quite liked the apple butter. It tastes like cinnamon, she explained, eating it happily with her crackers. "It's like applesauce," said another. After the fifth-graders left, the second-graders streamed in. They tried everything. And when the teachers called for them, some lingered a little longer; some who had extra money purchased an apple or two and put them in their pockets. Others picked up a few extra crackers with apple butter, wrapped carefully in napkins. For them, these were the perfect sweets, if only for the afternoon.

Chapter Eight

Guilty Pleasures

A FEW YEARS AGO, A TEAM OF DETERMINED PSY-chologists and their students hunted down hundreds of unsuspecting travelers going about their business in air-ports and railroad stations in four different countries on three continents. A few phone calls to residents in the local area wouldn't have sufficed for this project; their task required a much broader, intercontinental James Bond approach. They wanted to shed light on an international mystery, the mystery behind why we Americans have such a hard time taking real pleasure in our food, compared to people in other countries. And so they set forth in Belgium, France, Japan, and their home base, Philadelphia in the United States, to confront potential, subjects with a two-page survey, quizzing them about their health concerns and their tendencies to diet.

The most interesting aspect of the exercise, at least to me, was the word-association portion of the survey, and the sweet-related words in particular. The Belgians and Japanese offered varying responses, but the contrast between the French and the Americans was stark. When asked which word "belongs best" with ice cream, the French generally chose the word "delicious," while the Americans countered with "fattening." For "chocolate cake," the French women responded overwhelmingly with "celebration," while the American women checked off "guilt." For "heavy cream," the French replied "whipped," while the Americans said "unhealthy."

The difference between French and American attitudes immediately brings to mind the French Paradox, the curious reality that the French are blessed with lower heart disease rates than Americans despite an affection for rich foods. While Americans clearly have a robust appetite (as evidenced by our famously large portions and growing obesity rates), we don't seem to like food nearly as much as the French, or at least we don't like it *enough* to squelch our paranoia about its ill effects or to articulate our affections for it to the same extent.

Paul Rozin, a professor of psychology at the University of Pennsylvania and the lead author behind the study, believes that this may help explain why we eat so much. Extra calories may be the immediate cause for excess weight, but perhaps it's in fact guilt and fear that pave the way for our unhealthy relationships with food—guilt that we've eaten something "bad," fear that we'll get fat. As we've explored earlier, our nation's culinary tradition is young and amorphous; our choices in food are more a mark of distinction (or disgrace) than a source of national pride. That said, in a melting-pot nation with arguably no national cuisine—and therefore no signature flavor—guilt and fear have emerged as the standout ingredients, leaving us with adjectives of quantity (big, excessive, hearty) instead of quality (spicy, garlicky, creamy) to describe our food.

Rozin explores our love-hate relationship with sweets (and food in general) from an attitude standpoint as opposed to a calorie one. His findings make me wonder whether the secret to savoring

sweets is like the secret to enjoying that other biological drive necessary for our species' survival, sex: physiological factors matter, of
course, but what ultimately defines the experience is all in the
mind.

Perhaps it was fate that Rozin came to study food, culture, and
guilt. He had the sort of mother who made him clean his plate because children halfway around the globe were starving. I'm not
sure why cleaning off my plate would help, he says, settling into a
big chair in his cozy parlor of an office, but then again, that was
how children were disciplined at the dinner table back in the days
before portion control and organic baby yogurt.

As nutritionists, chemists, and obesity doctors search for that
miracle food that might explain why certain nationalities tend to
be slim, Rozin zeroes in on the mind-set that separates us from
them. To him, it's not just about red wine or dark chocolate or wild
salmon or olive oil. It may not even be the amount of good fat or
bad fat that makes the difference. It's the emotional circumstances
under which we eat, and how and what we end up eating because
of them.

Rozin's study broaches the question, What is food anyway?
Depending on how we answer it, we feel either blessed or dis-
tressed when we eat. For many cultures, food is a sensual experience, an expression of love, a work of art, a means for celebration,
tradition, ritual, and memory. When I met Adam Drewnowski, he
had just returned from a conference in France sponsored by the
French Nutrition Institute, a government agency equivalent to our
health department; the invited speakers were not only medical experts, but also philosophers, psychoanalysts, and historians, and
the topic of discussion was the future of eating.

You wouldn't likely find such a government-funded dietary-
health gathering in Washington, Drewnowski said during my visit.
Indeed, in the United States, food tends to be about calories, fat,

sugar, antioxidants, omega-three fatty acids, cholesterol, salt—the result of one big natural or man-made chemical reaction. We filter out the heart and soul of a food, leaving behind a list of ingredients that can be dispensed easily into "good" and "bad" categories.

"There is a sense among many Americans that food is as much a poison as it is a nutrient," observes Rozin and his coauthors, "and that eating is almost as dangerous as not eating." Unlike the vast majority of nutrition papers that focus on the obesity epidemic, this one takes a good look at what Rozin calls an "epidemic [of] food worrying."

Sweets, needless to say, tend to fall into the "poison" category. The exceptions, of course, are fruits, but even *they* are not necessarily consumed simply for pleasure. Blueberries, pomegranates, and açai have made inroads because they've been marketed not so much as delicious foods but as super-foods; dieters might not be able to describe the taste very well, but they can certainly tell you about their antioxidant levels. The California Strawberry Commission, touting a fruit that is rich in antioxidants as well as vitamin C and fiber, is busily conducting research on its medical benefits. After all, the health pages in newspapers and magazines have become a good food marketing spot. Since news of blueberries' antioxidant effects on heart disease and cancer hit the headlines a few years ago, sales have soared. Americans brought home 105 million pounds of fresh blueberries in 2002; that number rose to almost 500 million pounds three years later.

In any case, the "bad" sweets are parsed down further to bad ingredients—ice cream dissected into sugar and cream; store-bought cookies reduced to sugar, butter, and high-fructose corn syrup—so much so that the nostalgic image of them runs the risk of being forgotten or remembered only in TV commercials for frozen cookie dough. In our concern about being healthy and slim, we sometimes toss the joy out along with the wrapper. Girl

Scout Cookies, making an appearance but once a year, have come under scrutiny. A tradition that started in 1917 with home-baked cookies sold door-to-door for 25 cents, the cookies have been denigrated for their sugar, fat, and calorie contents, even though trans fats no longer show up on the nutrition label. In a column in the *New York Times* not too long ago, one nutritionist and former Girl Scout leader went so far as calling those beloved Do-Si-Dos part of our "toxic food chain."

Our language exacerbates the insanity. As we busy ourselves putting foods into categories, our wordsmiths get pretty creative about what those categories might be. We're especially good at emphasizing the negatives, having come up with terms like "empty calories" sometime in the sixties, and "junk food" in 1973 thanks to a *Washington Post* letter to the editor bemoaning vending machines in schools. In other languages, there are terms for snacks but they're unlikely to pass judgment on the food itself. Food is simply food, an entity to be enjoyed and one that's neither junky nor empty nor worth counting calories about.

When Gary Hirshberg, CEO of Stonyfield Farm yogurt, began thinking about launching his product in France, he was pleased to discover how receptive the French were to fat. "Sometimes in the States, I just want to say to people, 'Just let me add a little more fat and it will taste much better,'" he says, "but the Americans won't have it. In France, taste is important; they're not afraid of fat."

Only 4 percent of the French eat less fat than the amount recommended by the American food pyramid (i.e., less than 10 percent of total caloric intake), and yet 71 percent of French males and 73 percent of French females describe themselves as healthy eaters while only 33 percent of American males and 23 percent of American females do. In fact, only about 42 percent of the French population is overweight or obese, compared to about 66 percent in the United States. Cardiovascular disease is much less prevalent among the French than among Americans. Of course there could be plenty of reasons for this: good genes perhaps, or less stress. But I'd like to think that maybe, too, there is some magic in positive thinking.

IF AMERICAN FOOD is considered a mix of vitamins, minerals, sugar, and calories, what, then, is the flavor of America? That was the question posed to the Baskin-Robbins product development team as they prepared to create two new ice-cream varieties to celebrate the company's sixty-first summer. I had visited their Boston headquarters a few months before meeting Paul Rozin. Had I met him first, I would have fully fathomed the enormity of the challenge before them.

The company, the world's largest ice-cream conglomerate, with scoop shops as far-flung as Russia, China, and Kuwait, invents new flavors every season, but this time they aspired to more. "There's been so much conflict and unrest in the news. We seemed to be looking for comfort," says David Nagel, director of Brand Excitement, the company's marketing and communications task force. "You've also got the Fourth of July, the season's biggest holiday." So it just felt right, he says, to explore the concept of Americana, and "bring ice cream back home" so to speak. In doing so, he hoped to accomplish something that Baskin-Robbins and other makers of sweets strive for with every product launched: to create our next favorite flavor.

But how to describe America's sweet tooth? We certainly enjoy our chocolate brownies, chocolate chip cookies, and yellow layer cakes, but none of these say "America" necessarily—at least not in the way crème brûlée speaks of France, flan of Spain, green-tea mochi of Japan. When potential customers view ice cream as a scientific concoction of good and bad substances, how do you design a flavor that resonates national pride?

The culinary aspect of such conundrums is tackled by Stan Frankenthaler, who won wide acclaim for his creative fusion cuisine at Boston's Salamander restaurant before taking the reins as head chef at Dunkin' Brands, Baskin-Robbins's corporate parent. Here he's still very much involved in the business of fusion, though his thoughts now lean toward cookie-dough nuggets and other ice cream "inclusions" as opposed to sesame-ginger dressings.

The October before the July launch, Frankenthaler, Nagel, and their marketing and food science cohorts sat around the brand's big black chef's table and free-associated with the word "American." Abstract concepts and packaged goods were mentioned as often as food. There was talk of sweet potato pie and apple pie and root beer floats, but "red Corvette," "red-white-and-blue," and "baseball" were also thrown into the ring. By the end of the afternoon the free-for-all was whittled down to a workable list.

It makes sense, perhaps, that the cars and colors made the cut as often as the edible things. The United States was built on ideas and ambitions, its food borrowed and adapted from the Native Americans and the newcomers who made their homes here. Foods that say "American" do so not because of their taste but because of their stories. The concept of apple pie conjures the image of a mother in an apron pulling out the sweet, golden pastry from a hot oven. The notion of root beer float takes us back to the soda fountain and Saturday nights gone by. For Nagel and his team, patriotism, with a generous helping of nostalgia, is as good an ingredient as any.

SWEETNESS HAS long had an uneasy footing in the United States, and almost since the beginning, there was plenty to feel guilty about. Before sugar became public health enemy number one, it was the stuff of questionable ethical origins.

As we saw earlier, the British defeated the Spanish and the

Dutch in the race to rule the sugar trade. They succeeded in part because they most effectively exploited the use of slaves. Between 1500 and 1800, the British shipped 11 million Africans to the New World. In dominating the slave trade, they overtook the sugar trade as well. They kept most of what they reaped for themselves, causing sugar prices to rise for everyone else, including their subjects who lived so close to the very land that produced the crop. Exorbitant prices limited sugar to the tables of the wealthiest until the nineteenth century. In colonial Pennsylvania, raw sugar sold, wholesale, for as high as 58 shillings per 112 pounds, while the same amount of flour never cost more than 21 shillings.

In the 1790s, amid anti-slavery protests, the anti-saccharites formed their own society and organized boycotts of sugar throughout Europe. One such abolitionist was George Fox, who was morbidly specific on the toll sugar took on human life: Giving up five pounds of sugar and five pounds of rum each week for twenty-one months, he said, would "prevent the murder or slavery of one fellow-creature."

The warnings were ineffective for the most part. Between 1701 and 1810, British consumption of sugar skyrocketed 400 percent; about a century later, the sugar rush seized Middle America. "Free" sugar (that said to be made without slave labor and presaging our current interest in blood-free diamonds and fair-trade coffee) didn't catch on, though the slave trade ended in the British-ruled sugar kingdom by 1838 anyway, primarily because machines proved more productive.

IF A CONCERN for general human moral values didn't sway consumers away from sugar, the Protestant ethic at least roused some guilt, even if it didn't necessarily persuade all good Christians to drink their tea plain. Explains Rozin, there was a Protestant notion that food was not supposed to be pleasurable. "Eating was a personal responsibility. You are responsible for your weight. You're in charge. What happens to you is because of what you do. There was a lot of body guilt."

In the Garden of Eden, the Tree of Knowledge taught Adam and Eve that bad things can come out of taking a taste of a fruit that's a "delight to the eye." I've always thought the fruit in question to be an apple, but in reality the Bible doesn't specify what it was, though, like the most indulgent of desserts, it left them guilty and ashamed of their bodies. My assumption left an indelible link between sweetness and forbidden behavior.

I have trust issues when it comes to delicious food; the more indulgent it seems, the more suspicious I think I should be. Even as fruit earned its good-for-you-darling status, thanks to its high fiber and vitamin content, the principles that underscored the fall-out in Eden that day live on in Middle America, where how and what we eat is a measure of not just our sophistication and income, as we have seen, but also our virtue.

A few possible theories might explain our heightened culture of "lifestyle correctness," to borrow a term from Howard M. Leichter, the chair of the political science department at Linfield College. He believes that food morality might be a result of our early American "frontier" spirit and the value we've placed historically on "rugged individualism." Out in the unpredictable wild, colonists had to rely on themselves in order to stay healthy and survive. In the Northeast, the early Puritan settlers, who moved to New England to escape the excess in the Old World, lived frugally and ate their food plainly in order for it to last through the long frigid winters. The Quakers, dedicated to a simple life, thought it better to avoid the fancy stuff too, eating their food boiled, rather than embellished with the sauces you might find in southern European Catholic countries. The simpler the meal, the less likely they'd be tempted to enjoy their food too much, the better their health, and the more pious they were in the eyes of God.

Self-reliance and self-improvement were important tenets back then. And they still are in America today, in the form of diet dictums. The irony now is that forgoing pleasurable foods seems more pious in the *absence* of religion. Leichter suspects that weakening church and family ties might motivate the diet and fitness obsessed. Without the support and love of a parish, we're afraid to be caught sick without any help. I'd like to think, however, that we're a little more independent than that. Without strength from God or a social network, we supply our own strength, a physical one that is nourished by low-sugar snacks and high-priced gyms instead of charitable donations and prayer. When we neglect this temple that is our body, we feel guilty, and that guilt is tapped in to by the marketing strategies of the diet and fitness industry, modern-day crusaders who feed off our desire to do penance.

The notions of restraint and personal responsibility made it easy for the teachings of some very odd characters to catch on in the nineteenth century, during what has been called "the Golden Age of food faddism." The time was right. The rise of city living took people away from nature and the physical work of farm life, and instead thrust them in the middle of mechanized labor, urban squalor, and, as we saw earlier, a proliferation of packaged goods, including packaged sweets. People got sick. Someone had to come in and save them—or inspire them to save themselves, as the case happened to be.

At that time, Christians also happened to be in the midst of creating a new type of Church. In place of the wrathful God of the Calvinists emerged a benevolent God. While disease was no longer the mark of a sinner, the church still didn't cut us a break when it came to our food. Disease and ill health turned into something that a good Christian should avoid or overcome to achieve salvation. After all, notes James C. Whorton in *Crusaders for Fitness,* "The body housed the soul, and, as the most marvelously intricate construction in all of nature, provided the most dramatic evidence of divine wisdom. In this light, it was easy to regard physiological knowledge and hygienic living as Christian duties." Nature, then, is good because it's what God intended. Excessive consumption changes nature by making us fat, and, so the thinking goes, whatever *tempts* us into this excessive consumption—the irresistible tastes of sweet and alcohol, for instance—is bad. To save our souls, and to escape the mess that is the secular world, we have to save ourselves.

In the 1830s, Sylvester Graham personified the muddling of food and religion, espousing healthy living as the key to holy living. An ordained Presbyterian minister, he preached cleanliness and vegetarian eating (including the consumption of a specially ground wheat flour that became known as Graham flour, the main ingredient of Graham crackers). He also preached abstinence from just about anything vaguely exciting, including alcohol, unmarried intercourse, condiments, and—as we saw earlier—pies.

A couple of decades later, Mary Mann (the wife of Horace Mann) warned against wedding cake, which she declared "indigestible" and inappropriate for a Christian table. In her book, *Christianity in the Kitchen: A Physiological Cook Book,* she asked her dear readers to control their animal appetites lest they risk "premature decay, and untimely death"; it offered recipes too.

Horace Fletcher, another health crusader who rose to fame in the latter part of the nineteenth century and beginning of the twentieth, was a retired businessman with no medical training, but his saliva-centered theory somehow caught on with the public. Fletcher preached the importance of masticating your food completely. The technique, he said, allowed food to be digested thoroughly (thanks, in theory, to a "filter function" in the back of the mouth), prevented overeating, and promoted well-being. If you chewed and chewed until the taste disappeared, the food would be ground to such a slimy state that it would slide down the throat almost by itself. As he saw it, taste was nature's safeguard against the unvirtuous behavior of eating too much too fast.

In 1876, John Harvey Kellogg, a Seventh-day Adventist, took the helm as head physician at a Battle Creek, Michigan, sanitorium where the meals were vegetarian and breakfast consisted of grains he called "corn flakes." The product, along with that of imitators, such as Charles W. Post's Grape-Nuts, touted hygienic packaging, convenience, and promises of health.

Today, few corn-flake eaters are aware of their breakfast's Seventh-Day Adventist roots, though they have an inkling that it's a pretty healthy choice. The explanations behind these food faddists' teachings may have been long forgotten, but an abbreviated version of the ideas stuck in the minds of Americans (chew well, eat light, no pie, no cake) and directed their eating habits for generations to come, whether or not they made sense anymore.

Never mind that the simplified directives can seem silly out of context. These rules-to-eat-by handily primed Americans for the guilt trips that emerged in the next century. World hunger and, again, secular unrest caused church-going folk to look inward— and to reconsider the doughnuts and cupcakes and punch at their fund-raising suppers. (Spicy foods were a no-no too, but they already distrusted that stuff anyway.) Pure, plain food was the holier way to go, and regardless of your religion, plates were to be cleaned, lest (as Rozin's mother might point out) some poor child in Africa go to bed hungry. There was a fine line between feasting and gluttony.

Some doctors adopted an almost an evangelical mission to

spread the word. John Yudkin was one of them. In his 1972 book, *Pure, White and Deadly,* he warned: "Avoid sugar, I say, and you are less likely to become fat, run into nutritional deficiency, have a heart attack, get diabetes or dental decay or a duodenal ulcer, and perhaps you also reduce your chances of getting gout, dermatitits and some forms of cancer, and in general increase your lifespan." Yudkin had been a self-described sugar addict, devouring "pounds of milk chocolate and liquorice of all sorts and cakes each week." But when he swore off sugar, he became convinced that it was the source of his medical woes. He exaggerated and employed fear tactics: The reason why sugar needs to be washed and filtered during the refining process, he said, is because in its natural state, it's dirty. "It contains particles of sand and earth," he said, getting the attention of the hygiene-loving middle class. There might even be "mould, bacteria, and sugar lice."

The new warnings awakened the Puritan tendencies in middle-class Americans. Unlike, say, the French, who've long appreciated fine foods, or the Japanese, who have always taken pleasure in the beauty of a meticulously prepared dish, Americans held food in no such high regard. If health gurus were telling them that certain foods were bad, or that they should eat less, then they would surely believe it, even if they didn't do anything more to adjust their behavior than to feel guilty about it.

&

IF WE AMERICANS practiced what has been preached, then perhaps we wouldn't feel so guilty. We would eat less, feel healthier, and live our lives without dietary regret. But we don't, because as much as we embrace the idea of determining our own health destiny, we also love the notion of a bargain. In the land of plenty, boundless opportunities, and the American dream, bigness appeals more than exquisite taste or delicate artistry in food. We assume that it's human nature, but it's in fact Americana nature. Except for the major cities, where space is at a premium, Americans who can afford them often luxuriate in outsized SUVs and houses. Certain possessions—the ones that we take the most pride in, it seems—we simply like big.

But not everyone shares our fondness for bigness. When Godiva opened its first boutique in Japan, business became considerably brisker when it *decreased* the size of the chocolates. American heft didn't have the same allure in Tokyo, Sharon Rothstein, the vice president for global marketing and merchandising, later told me. Their Japanese clients, it seems, wanted a more delicate sweet treat. They wanted explanations with their box of chocolates, and they were more visual in their decision-making process. Godiva's giant strawberries were a hit for Valentine's Day in the United States, while elsewhere, small, precious strawberries appealed. Meanwhile, high-sugar desserts are absent from Tokyo's Dean & DeLuca stores, and bagels there are half the size of those found in the stores' hometown, New York, and almost twice the price. As Rothstein put it, "Americans tend to appreciate things larger."

But is it things in general, or only certain items, such as food, our frontiers, cars and highways—the things that define us? When Paul Rozin and his team surveyed items in French and American supermarkets, they found that in 14 out of 17 instances, packaged foods came in larger sizes this side of the Atlantic. A Nestlé Crunch bar was 1.41 times larger, a bottle of Coke was more than 1.5 times larger, and a microwave cheeseburger was almost 2.5 times larger. (Interestingly, French and American cats share the same size box of cat food and the French have larger washcloths, napkins, and toilet-paper squares than Americans.)

Rozin found a discrepancy in restaurants too, even within the same chain. A McDonald's grilled chicken sandwich weighs 175 grams in Philadelphia and 155 in Paris; a medium bag of fries is 135 grams in Philadelphia and 90 grams in Paris. At Häagen-Dazs the items sampled averaged 1.42 times larger in American stores, and at local Chinese restaurants in the United States the items were on average 1.72 times larger than those in Paris.

In recent years, food marketers, beleaguered by bad press stirred up in the wake of the obesity crisis, have started to downsize, but big and proud portions are hardly a remnant of the past. Sure, in the past few years we've seen the introduction of Kraft's 100-calorie-snack cookie pouches and Dannon's smaller yogurt packs, and the demise of the super-sized meal option in many establishments, but we've also seen the rise of the king-sized candy bar, the Thickburger from Hardee's, and dessert-only restaurants serving multiple courses of sweets. At McDonald's, one order of apple pie is two pouches. And as we might recall, at Uno Chicago Grill, the bestselling dessert is still the monster-sized cookie baked in a deep-dish pizza pan and topped with ice cream. The Japanese may talk about "the shape of the taste"—the delicate way the food is carved or trimmed, the meticulousness of the plating—but we Americans seem to be more impressed by its size.

It is no wonder, then, that even as the Baskin-Robbins team was uncertain as to what the final winning candidates would be, they knew one thing for sure: there has to be something big about it, and in the ice-cream industry, that often means big flavor made by big inclusions.

Ice cream isn't just a snack or a dessert in and of itself anymore; it is a vehicle for *other* snacks and dessert items, including chocolate chunks, chopped Oreos, Reese's peanut butter cups, and cake batter. It is the inclusions that often give today's new flavors their names, not the nature of the ice cream itself.

After whittling down their ideas to about a dozen workable concepts, the Baskin-Robbins team created a wish list of what each one should taste and feel like, and delivered it to the food lab, where basic flavors like vanilla, chocolate, and sweet cream are mixed with combinations of crunchy inclusions and sweet flavor "ribbons" (that thing that makes a fudge swirl a fudge swirl). There were many factors to consider, from how it would look next to other flavors in a 3-gallon drum to whether the concept would appeal. The only limiting factor on inclusions would be how big they can be before a scoop falls to pieces under the pressure.

EATING SWEETS can be quite stressful when experienced amid the dissonance between the two equally staunch beliefs, "think big" and "eat less." The French, I think, have it much easier. They have faith in fine things, whether it's a vintage coat you pass down across generations or a pastry sampled at Pierre Hermé, and that attitude is consistent. It's unlikely that they'd fall into food traps as much as I do, whether a bargain is offered or not. Scanning the menu or price list, I realize I'm constantly asking myself: Why *not* get the gargantuan size latte or a much, much deeper pouch of M&M's for a few dimes more?

The French, and other older cultures, seem to have an innate trust in their food and in their bodies' ability to handle it, while we Americans tend to micromanage our dealings. I calculate calories. I make excuses for finishing the plate when I don't have to ("It's a waste of food and money," I'll say, or "It's a nuisance to bring it home"). I calculate how much time I need on the treadmill to delete the damages of this afternoon's cupcake.

I can't remember when I last let my taste buds and appetite centers be. It is as if I were an overprotective parent. Food sociologist Claude Fischler, from his health post in France, coined a term for this neurotic thinking: *gastro-anomie*. It suggests a state of instability and recklessness in eating. But who can blame us?

Raised in a value system that contradicts itself, we're utterly confused. We either eat helter-skelter or we feel pressured to call in the experts, even though, as we've seen with the quacks at the turn of the nineteenth century, they can make matters worse. Hence, in recent years, those of us who can afford to be choosy have deprived ourselves of carbohydrates and sweets in the name of Atkins, Sugar Busters!, and the Zone. We've said no to ice cream and cheesecake for the sake of the likes of Ornish.

We eat with our heads and not with our hearts; we overanalyze; we second-guess ourselves: Is this good for me? Will this leave me hungrier later? Sometimes we work ourselves into such a state that we think we need direction from diet doctors and nutrition gurus and trainers. This only encourages them to give us more advice, which then leads us to second-guess ourselves anew.

Other cultures aren't so inclined to listen. The Japanese, who live longer than just about everyone else, have built a cuisine around carbohydrates. Northern Europeans, who certainly have no qualms about their beef specialties and cream sauces, live longer than those on the so-called Mediterranean Diet. For all the bells and whistles on our latest version of the food pyramid, the French have no dietary guidelines. There is no fitness industry in France comparable to what we have here. A few years ago, when I was talking to some French women who had just given birth, they were heading to a spa to be treated with seaweed wraps instead of some class with a name like "Abs and Thighs."

To cultures that enjoy their food, what's important is not what you eat but how you eat it, and perhaps in what quantity. While American habits, from snacking to eating fast food, are slowly chipping away at longtime eating traditions around the globe, certain customs still prevail. Peter N. Stearns, professor of history at George Mason University, suggests that in France the rhythms of eating and enjoying are inculcated in children's minds when very young. Rather than learning about good and bad nutrients, they learn about good and bad times to eat, and their parents are strict about it. The French believe that children need guidance when it comes to food, just as young American boys and girls would need guidance in playing a fair game of ball. Parents instruct children on the four distinct times to eat over the course of the day: breakfast, lunch, an afternoon snack, and dinner. Veering off this track would be unheard of, like leaving the office in the middle of the afternoon for a shower. This kind of "disciplined eating" crosses class lines, explains Stearns; fine food deserves savoring, and for those whose food is not so fine, watchful intake ensures sufficient shares for everyone.

In America, the consumption of snacks, particularly sweets, has been a freestyle affair, especially for children. Until the 1970s, doctors obsessed over finicky eaters and underfed children as opposed to overweight ones. And even as the medical community began changing its directive, parents didn't. Lollipops stood in as pacifiers, a convenient bribe to cut a tantrum short. A cookie was a reward for a coloring project well done.

An increasing number of school districts have banned this practice as well as celebrations involving cupcakes. Still, in 2005, the Texas legislature found it necessary to pass the Safe Cupcake Amendment in response to parents' outrage over the restrictions; and more recently, at least one school in Philadelphia has promoted the use of candy and other trinkets as a means for positive reinforcement. Sweets remain a conundrum to this day, especially when adults are impatient and children are fussy.

SWEETS WERE never a contingency food for me, and for that I feel blessed. I have only my adult self to blame for my calorie-counting habit. In my childhood home, ice cream was simply a reassuring

presence in the freezer, like ice cubes and leftovers, and that alone
has helped to make me less neurotic than others. My father would
create ice-cream sandwiches: scoops of coffee flavor between two
slices of Wonder bread. We would get chocolate-vanilla swirl at
the diner by the lake, or a scoop at the ice-cream shop by the
movie theater (I, the banana, and my mother, the strawberry). I
have nothing but fondness for these memories, but then things
changed. I happened to catch a comment from some expert on TV
who said that ice cream contains *sugar and fat, the worst possible combination you can possibly consume.*

Ice cream with large inclusions could just possibly be the perfect sweet (it's half a dozen desserts in one!), if it weren't for the
guilt factor. To override it, ice-cream makers know they have to
come up with something particularly nostalgic, delicious, and irresistible. After several months of tastings and testings, the Baskin-
Robbins team decided on two new "American" flavors: apple pie
(reminiscent of the irresistible mess you get when you scrunch
vanilla ice cream into a dish of it) and baseball (Cracker Jack–like
inclusions). The decision made perfect sense to me. Of all the
dessert staples sold in an American bakery, pie certainly stands out
(though I wonder if I would still have thought so if it weren't for
that famous Chevrolet jingle that ran in the mid-'70s: "Baseball,
hot dogs, apple pie and Chevrolet, they go together in the good ole
USA"). And surely the idea of mom in her apron baking pie in her
kitchen and dad taking the kids out for a game of ball captured the
idealized idyllic American life.

Once the team arrived at the decision, they tweaked the tastes
and appearances to perfection. They asked themselves, What do
Americans think is the perfect apple pie? And what does baseball
taste like? For the apple pie, the lab crew set out to grocery stores
in the local area (a logical move, since that's how so many people

get their pie: they buy it rather than baking it themselves). In general, that means apples sweetened with cinnamon, sugar, and perhaps apple juice, and a thick, satisfying crust.

The final flavor was a combination of a few brands, which the Baskin-Robbins team then matched with products from inclusion suppliers—companies who manufacture, say, chocolate chips or pretzels made specifically to incorporate into other snack foods such as ice cream. The apples here had to be Granny Smith and Golden Delicious, which stand up to freezing temperatures without getting mushy the way the Red Delicious might. The crust is specially treated with butter to prevent it from getting soggy when incorporated into pre-frozen ice cream.

The flavor pushed the limits to satisfy America's taste for "big." Each scoop is designed to pick up about fourteen half-inch pieces of crust, the maximum amount that allows the scoop to hold its shape without breaking apart. The crew was equally generous with the fruit "filling." Four scoops give you the equivalent of one apple—and every avid reader of health pages knows that apples are chock-full of nutrients (never mind that you're having ice cream with it).

Putting the baseball concept into practice would seem to be a bigger challenge, but not if you consider that most pastimes in America go with food. We have food to drive with (coffee with a sip lid), food to watch movies with (popcorn), food to run with (PowerBars), food to study with (pizza). With watching baseball, there were a few options: popcorn, peanuts, and Cracker Jack. Naturally they went with their own version of the third option, which is essentially the first two coated with caramel, and hence twice as delicious. With a coating of butter on the popcorn, the finished flavor featured a nice clean crunch too.

I taste one, and then the other, and through the wonders of food science each of the ingredients sings out clear and loud without getting soggy, stale, or lost in the ice cream. You get a lot in a mouthful, as was the intent. The big taste was worthy of a big American serving. And in trying them both, the notion of fattening *and* delicious crossed my mind.

Will Americans ever think, simply, *delicious*? Perhaps a broad downsizing in our foodscape may obliterate the *fattening* thoughts, but whether it will get rid of them completely is questionable. Except for an elite group, we've always loved our sweets large, and food makers have obliged by engineering food that indulged our appetites and addressed our various food issues: If fat is your enemy, then there's fat-free ice cream. If carbs are the culprit, there are low-carb cookies. Does sugar make you crazy? Then try pretend sugar. In a land of plenty and plenty of food technology, it's easy to have our cake and eat it too. But enjoying it guilt-free? That's another story.

Chapter Nine

A More Perfect Sweetener

I CAN'T REMEMBER WHEN, EXACTLY, I FELL FOR PRE-
tend sugar; there was no eureka moment. It wasn't as if I discovered it in a local diner one day and my coffee was changed
forever. All I know is that it happened sometime in the mid-
1980s, just as my metabolism began its downward slide and my
pants started to feel tight. As if appearing out of nowhere to my
personal rescue, Diet Coke and Diet Pepsi came through with
sugar-free soft drinks that tasted pretty close to the real thing. Curious, I did some research and learned about the marvels of aspartame, an artificial sweetener that came in blue packets and tasted
worlds better than the older pink-pouch saccharin.

Over the years, I expanded beyond diet soda and stocked my
kitchen with aspartame-enriched fruit yogurts, flavored instant
coffees, and cocoas. I hoarded those blue packets, keeping a stash
in my purse at all times for emergency use, pouring them into
bowls of cereal and mixing them, two at a time, into my daily
"venti" dose of caffeine, the Big Gulp of coffee. Do not get me
wrong. I still had doughnuts and muffins and brownies and cakes.

But when it came to everyday staples that happened to be sweet, that's where I sacrificed the real stuff for the fake. I saw nothing wrong with having Equal (the brand name of the tabletop variety of aspartame) and skim milk in my latte, even as I paired it with Red Velvet cake à la mode and other foods far more caloric than sugar itself, because every small bit counts. Apparently others embraced aspartame with as much enthusiasm, if not more. Shortly after its introduction, aspartame became the number-one-selling artificial sweetener in the country.

THE STORIES of artificial sweeteners are both old stories and new stories—old, because like sugar centuries ago, these sweeteners seemed to have appeared at the right place at the right time, only to be caught in a swirl of suspicion over their health effects; new, because the circumstances, of course, are drastically different, reflecting our wants and needs in a specific moment in history. In both stories, we end up pouring them on even as we suspect we might regret it, thinking in the back of our mind that one of these days we'll collectively realize *this jig is up*; eventually we're going to become fat or stupid or very, very sick. Still, 48 percent of all households have a stash of them somewhere in their cupboards. We fear these sweeteners to some extent, but we also fear the prospect of living without them.

It's this inherent imperfection in sweet things, and the fear and wanting, I think, that has kept sweet-minded food scientists busy. Despite the options we already have, we still crave a more perfect incarnation of sweetness, and it's precisely this unending pursuit of sweet perfection that has quietly pushed the boundaries of life as we live it.

TENS OF THOUSANDS of years ago, primitive men and women spent their days searching the forest and inspecting flowers, fruits, and nuts for something to eat. It wasn't always easy. There were 200,000 or so wild plants at the time, and only a few thousand were edible. Eventually the most resourceful of the bunch kept tabs on the good choices and planted them so that more would grow. Around 4000 B.C., the Sumerians cultivated the first fruit crops in the Fertile Crescent; these included figs, dates, and pomegranates. After much trial and error, they succeeded in adding more to their repertoire, including apples, pears, plums, and cherries. The more they had to pick from, the more secure their survival.

The labs are the Fertile Crescents of today. Scientists pore over new substances, purifying, mixing, and matching them in search of food that's better—whether better means tastier, healthier, longer-lasting, cheaper, or more filling. Sometimes they might stumble upon something new and tasty by accident, which has been the case with the major sweeteners currently in use. With the genetic coding for sweet receptors a mystery until a few years ago, scientists had to rely on luck and timing to track down the sweet substances, like primitive hunter-gatherers stumbling upon a new plant bearing fruit.

For instance, James Schlatter, a chemist at G. D. Searle, a pharmaceutical company, discovered aspartame in 1965 while hunting for treatments for gastric ulcers. He was in the midst of creating a tetrapeptide, a chemical compound consisting of four amino acids; to do so, he had to make a two-amino-acid chain first—something called aspartyl-phenylalanine methyl ester. In the course of the experiment, a dusting of the chemical landed on his hand. When he licked his finger later, reaching for a sheet of paper, he realized it tasted sweet. He told his boss, who apparently decided the public needed a new sweetener more than a new stomach medication.

Samples underwent further processes for refinements. Tests were conducted. Sixteen years passed before allegations questioning its safety were placated (more on that later) and the Food and Drug Administration finally approved it. Blue packets, emblazoned with the brand name Equal, quickly cropped up on tabletops everywhere. Over the next decade, aspartame, which is about 200 times sweeter than sugar, found its way into packaged food products under the name NutraSweet. These products took on a cute little logo resembling a red and white swirled lollipop. Like a seal of approval, it materialized on the labels of a range of sweet treats from soft drinks to yogurt, announcing to consumers that there's something worth trying inside. Before "Intel Inside" and "Gore-Tex Guaranteed to Keep You Dry," NutraSweet pioneered the practice of giving otherwise invisible products a way to declare their brand directly to the consumer.

NutraSweet wasn't the first faux sugar, and Diet Pepsi and Diet Coke weren't the first sugar-free sodas. The first diet bubbly, No-Cal, appeared in 1952 and—like the original Coca-Cola and sugar itself—was a well-intentioned product for the sick. Sweetened with cyclamate (which, too, was serendipitously discovered—by a grad student who put his cigarette down on his lab bench and then tasted sweet when he picked it up again), No-Cal was meant for diabetics and allowed them to enjoy a sparkling refreshment like everyone else. When it became obvious that otherwise healthy folks looking to shed a few extra pounds also wanted a no-calorie product, conventional soda companies threw their efforts behind more sugar-free sodas and eventually came up with Tab, Diet Rite, and Fresca.

By then, saccharin (another accidental discovery—by a visiting scientist at Johns Hopkins playing around with a colleague's coal-tar experiment) was a major sweetener, and the new products that contained it tasted as unnatural as the neon colors on their cans.

But no matter. Determined dieters managed to adapt to it and even prefer it. If you give yourself enough time with a food, and no other options in its stead, as in the case with the most conscientious of dieters, you will adapt. New neural connections form, telling you that this is what will quench your thirst, and eventually it begins to grow on you and you reach for it again and again.

In any case, the timing of aspartame's FDA approval couldn't have been better, though some might say suspicious. While aspartame was still in limbo, the feds pulled cyclamate from the market for being possibly carcinogenic, and slapped a warning label on saccharin after a long-running debate over the relevance of rat studies indicating incidents of bladder cancer. The public was in imminent danger of losing their no-calorie sweet kick. But as luck would have it, the newly elected president, Ronald Reagan, was a friend of Donald Rumsfeld, an executive at Searle at the time. Not long after Reagan moved into the Oval Office, Rumsfeld became his personal Middle East envoy—and, more important, aspartame finally got the green light, much to the delight and relief of sweet-loving dieters across the land. (Eventually both cyclamate and saccharin would be declared safe too.)

For those who never quite had the willpower to think pink, aspartame was a godsend. Suddenly millions of women, starved by their diets and exhausted by their careers, family responsibilities, and aerobics, could reach for a refreshingly sweet caffeinated drink along with everyone else. Aspartame was a modernized improvement on saccharin, just as sugar was a high-tech and more versatile alternative to honey. Aspartame-sweetened soda made a dieter's meal of bland steamed vegetables more enticing. Poured into yogurt, aspartame helped tide me over to dinner just as my stomach began to grumble mid-afternoon. I didn't realize it at the time, of course, but for me and millions of Americans, it did what sweetened tea did for the working-class families at the dawn of the Industrial

Revolution: it made a paltry meal satisfying. Like sugar, aspartame managed to make itself relevant to the social rhythms and taste expectations of the times.

WHEN ASPARTAME EMERGED it was as close to sugar as anything I'd ever seen, but how helpful is that if sugar itself is far from perfect? The early Americans enjoyed their sugar as we do: amid warnings. Critics had declared that sweets made people fat, crazy, and possibly vulnerable to alcohol addiction; anti-saccharites reminded consumers of the link between sugar and slavery. Today the public relations battle continues. The carb-counting culture of the Atkins trend may have finally dissipated, but low-fat and low-sugar diatribes, with names such as *Sugar Shock!* and *Sugar Busters!,* continue to elbow their way onto the crowded diet-book shelf. "Sugar seems to be blamed for everything," says Melanie Miller, vice president of public relations of the Sugar Association, "from obesity to teeth falling out to all kinds of bad things." Her organization is fed up. "We had just gotten to the point where our members just said, 'Enough is enough.' We're tired of everyone else defining our messages for us. We need to take that back and define our own messages."

And so her organization has petitioned the Federal Trade Commission about its issues with sugar impostors, namely Splenda and its "made from sugar" and zero-calorie claims (Splenda, in fact, has four calories, but because foods under five calories may legally refrain from reporting them, it's fair game). She's also in the midst of campaigns to promote the touchy-feely side of sugar. She screens a soft-focus TV spot for me on her computer; it features families baking and a gentle reminder that the genuine article is only fifteen calories a teaspoon.

But fifteen calories is not zero, or four for that matter. With the prevalence and serviceable taste of zero-calorie sweeteners today, we've become spoiled and expect to get a lot of sweetness without reducing portion sizes. Fifteen calories lie just beyond the boundaries of what we're willing to sacrifice. Still, where regular sugar lacks in the calorie-control department, it carries an advantage in the safety arena. We simply refuse to believe in foods that are too good to be true. If it tastes good, it must be fattening—or worse.

In the case of NutraSweet, "worse" runs the gamut, no matter how hard scientists at the company have tried to convince us of its safety. Methanol, one of the breakdown components of aspartame, along with aspartic acid and phenylalanine, is the component that gives some people pause, but in fact it's contained in other foods and is processed by the liver. A 12-ounce can of Diet Coke contains .024 grams of methanol, which is more than the potential amount in the same portion of apple juice (.020 grams) or grape juice (.045 grams). According to over 700 studies, aspartame is safe, except for a small group of people (1 in 15,000) with a hereditary disease called phenylketonuria, who lack an enzyme to metabolize phenylalanine. Newborns are regularly screened for it, and so those who must stay away from aspartame know who they are.

Still, every once in a while a new study comes along and my doubts resurface. In 2005, Morando Soffritti, the scientific director at the European Ramazzini Foundation for Oncology and Environmental Sciences in Bologna, published a study on aspartame's effect on rats over the course of a lifetime. He split 1,800 rats of both sexes into groups and fed them varying amounts of aspartame. Three years later—the time it took for the rats to die a natural death—he found that rats fed as little as 20 mg/kg of aspartame (the rat equivalent of five 20-ounce bottles of diet soda a day for a 150-pound human) were more susceptible to lymphomas, leukemias, and other cancers. The acceptable daily intake for humans in the United States is 50 mg/kg of aspartame per day, or 18 to 19 cans of diet soda for a 150-pound person.

Soffritti's work created a stir within the sweetener industry and the scientific community for its unconventional protocol: he observed the rats until they got old and died, as opposed to killing them off after two years, as is how these studies are traditionally done. This, critics say, can confuse the results, since advanced age makes both test and control groups vulnerable to disease. Moreover, they weren't happy that he didn't provide his 35,000 pathology slides to the agencies for review following publication of his article.

"Misleading" and "flawed" is how a member of Ajinomoto Corporate Services, a seller of aspartame, described it, calling the "slight" increase of cancers "incidental." Soffritti responded by saying that because Ajinomoto holds 45 percent of the market share for aspartame manufacturing worldwide, the argument was suspect, and besides, researchers funded by the sweetener industry have never been required to submit pathology slides either.

But before anyone could even seriously succeed in quitting aspartame, news came out that assuaged our fears. By the following spring, the European Food Safety Authority had issued an opinion that Soffritti's findings did not present enough evidence to persuade the agency to modify its current position on aspartame's safety. The FDA issued a similar statement almost a year later, in 2007, taking issue with his protocol and concluding that there was no reason to issue recommendations against consuming it. Never mind that between the time it said it would investigate and the time it reached its conclusions, its magazine, *FDA Consumer,* had already run a feature article on sugar substitutes: "No Calories... Sweet!" the headline declared.

More recently, Soffritti extended his research to the effects of aspartame on rats exposed during fetal development. He again reported increased incidence of cancer, including a marked rise in breast cancer in female rats. Again he carried out his experiment until the animals died naturally. "Cancer is a disease of the aging," says Soffritti, who is now about to explore the effects of sucralose on mice. "So what happens when you sacrifice the rat at two-thirds of the lifespan? You're not going to see what happens during the last third." He remains unruffled by the criticism, and points out that if experiments were cut short, we never would have demonstrated the carcinogenic risks of certain fuel additives (like MTBE) and pesticides (like xylene). Our conversation gave me pause, but it hasn't exactly scared me into depriving myself completely. With no official ban from the FDA, no outright disapproval from well-known medical groups in the United States, and no proven explanation yet as to why aspartame might cause cancer, I found it hard to motivate myself to quit, and so I continue to enjoy my aspartame-sweetened yogurt, if only once in a while.

IN THE MEANTIME, sucralose, the leading tabletop sweetener, has been experiencing its own drama. Like aspartame and saccharin before it, sucralose sprang into existence by chance after a chemist in London accidentally created a small explosion of compounds in his lab. He was in the midst of developing new, non-food products made from sugar, including an insecticide, as one rumor goes, and had been adding sulfuryl chloride, drop by drop, into sugar solution. His adviser told him to test it, but he misheard the instructions as "taste it." So he did. It was sweet, and he informed his supervisor of his discovery. Excited about the profit-making prospects, they perfected the formula, running through scores and scores of chlorinated permutations before they settled on the present formula, which is six hundred times sweeter than sugar. Yellow packets of sucralose, labeled "Splenda," began appearing on tabletops in April 1998. The FDA had initially approved its use in fifteen food and beverage categories (the largest initial approval given to any food additive); in August 1999, it expanded its permission for use as a general all-purpose sweetener.

But as is often the case with artificial sugar, some experts remain suspicious. Over the course of safety studies, rats ingesting sucralose had a mean body weight gain that was 13 to 26 percent less than that of the control group, even though the sucralose group took in only 5 to 10 percent less food. This drop in weight, to some, seemed excessive, though as the company points out, strong-flavored food can do this to rats. What's more, one of its breakdown products was found to be a weak mutagen in an Ames test, the biological assay used to assess the mutagenic and carcinogenic potential of chemical compounds. But other test results failed to prove any ill effects, and so the FDA ultimately concluded that sucralose, all in all, doesn't pose any danger in humans if they stick to the acceptable levels of daily intake—5 mg/kg per day, or six cans of diet soda for a 150-pound person.

WHAT IS IT about fake sugar that engenders distrust, elicits our worst fears, and prompts us to think we need to find something better? The most tragic adverse effect in fake fat seems to be a case of the runs. But with fake sugar, the purported potential disasters are no joke, as talk of brain tumors and cancer pervades the rumor mills. Perhaps the irony of our sweetest dream turning into our worst nightmare is just too delicious a story; we can't resist half-believing it.

"We all love conspiracy theories," says Ihab Bishay, the director of research and development at NutraSweet. But the fact is, he points out, more than 200 million people in over a hundred countries have been using aspartame for the past twenty years without incident. An amiable polymer scientist of Egyptian heritage who grew up in Canada, he never thought about diet soda until after his mid-thirties. ("In Egypt, diet products are primarily consumed by diabetics and not by the general population," he explains.) But now he's a convert, having seen the benefit of saving himself a few hundred calories every week, and he has no worries about his adopted habit. So why should I?

Nevertheless, a few months before the release of the Soffritti findings, a different rumor started circulating. This arrived in the form of an article by David Benton at the University of Wales, Swansea. In a survey study reported in *Nutrition Research Reviews,* he wondered whether artificial sweeteners ultimately caused users to take in more calories than they would have if they just consumed sugar; after all, dieters have had varying rates of weight-loss success with them. This was also a scenario too enticing to resist: a zero-calorie food that actually ends up making you fat! How funny is that? It's a notion I continue to read about every few years or so (as is the case with sugar scares and sweetener-cancer links), and I've never paid it much mind. After more than ten years of use, I never got fat. But then again, I never got any thinner either.

Benton's survey article cited past findings that suggest sugar substitutes may not be the free pass we thought they were. For instance, a French study suggested that artificial-sweetener users were heavier and had higher levels of triglycerides (a major form of fat) and poorer glucose tolerance than non-artificial-sweetener users. Critics, however, pointed out that causal connections are difficult to draw. Are people using artificial sweeteners because they were overweight to begin with, or did the artificial sweeteners make them fat?

Benton doesn't claim to know the answer, but he does point out that current studies are too short term. People using artificial sweeteners are obviously watching their weight, so they'll of course be counting their calories carefully. More interesting, he says, is the question of what will happen after many months or years, when most dieters begin slacking off. Rather than using artificial sweet-eners as a way to cut calories, do they eventually see them as a free pass to eat more food when willpower wanes? Do they uncon-sciously end up consuming more calories than they saved?

One study found that with normal-weight people, the use of sugar substitutes didn't help them curb calories at all; but with the obese, it was another story—presumably very determined to lose weight, they kept their calorie intake low. In another study, men consumed slightly fewer total calories with artificial sweeteners than with sugar, but women ate as much as they usually did, if not more. Both sexes ended up eating more protein; men also con-sumed more fat.

To underscore Benton's point, a separate 1988 *Physiology & Be-havior* article compared three high-intensity sweeteners (saccharin, aspartame, and acesulfame-K) with glucose and plain water. Sub-jects drank sugar or sugar-substitute solutions, and were asked to rate their level of hunger. Then they ate a carefully monitored meal. Those who drank saccharin and aspartame solutions before the meal had higher hunger ratings than the glucose subjects, and they also ate more at the meal that followed. The aspartame subjects were particularly ravenous. Glucose, in contrast, quelled hunger immediately and gave the subjects a full feeling for the next forty to fifty minutes, causing them to take in less of the meal later pre-sented to them. Real sugar, it seems, is likelier than fake sugar to keep you satisfied.

To understand why artificial sweeteners might not always be an effective diet aid, it's useful to remember that appetite is con-trolled by many feedback mechanisms. Earlier, Robert Lustig ex-plained how glucose in the bloodstream triggers an insulin response, which tells us we're full—and it's tempting to think that without real sugar, we don't set that natural appetite-control system in motion, so we keep eating. The reality is, however, that the insulin loop is just one of more than a dozen feedback mechanisms influencing our food consumption. It's hard to know exactly what's at work behind how much we eat.

For instance, Susie Swithers, a professor of psychology at Purdue University, has a slightly different take on the matter. She suspects that the taste and texture characteristics of food—including sweetness and viscosity—affect our appetites. It's as if the sweetness in a sugar cookie and the richness of a full-fat yogurt kick-start a mechanism that in turn monitors the calories consumed. When the sweetness or fat is an impostor, then perhaps that switch doesn't get turned on and our body loses track of how much it has eaten. Diet soda, of course, with no sugar and no fat but much sweetness, seems a particular danger. These are just theories for now, she says, and it's worth pointing out that dieters who are making a truly conscious effort might very well be able to override the deregulation effects—though, as for everyone else, we can't be too sure.

The bottom line is that results are too varied and there's no proof that artificial sweeteners will foil a diet. For every study that suggests the paradox, there's another that reports the effectiveness of the sweeteners as a tool for weight loss. One such paper, published in the British Nutrition Foundation's *Nutrition Bulletin* in 2006, reports that subjects consuming food and drink sweetened with aspartame instead of sugar lost about half a pound a week. Such conclusions are enticing but not completely sound. They often depend on memory recall of food intake (which is prone to error), and are funded at least in part by artificial-sweetener-industry sources. It's tricky to tell whether the subjects lost weight because of the fake sugars or because of plain old willpower. Another study, in the *Journal of Food Science*, found promising results too, but also conceded that artificial-sweetener users tended to be older, better educated, and wealthier—all factors that feed into our eating habits and affect our shape.

"The problem is the complexity of the mechanisms, both biological and psychological," says David Benton. "A study in a laboratory for half a day does not easily map onto life as we know it."

ADVANCEMENTS IN SCIENCE have grown by leaps and bounds since Victorian alarmists warned against candy-eating, but ironically we're more confused about the benefits and dangers of sweeteners—and our food in general—than ever. Internet postings and blogs are the modern-day flier, turning up the volume and reach of any rumor. Obscure studies can get forwarded many times over if they're interesting enough. If a lone complaint resonates, it's quickly joined by others who feel the same way, until suddenly, with the strike of many "send" buttons, one bad experience becomes amplified and somehow more real.

I often wonder if it's such an uphill battle for sugar substitutes because they are exactly that: substitutes. It's hard to convince people that a substitute is as stellar as the real thing. Even if it is—as in a substitute teacher at school or an understudy in a play—we can't help but feel a twinge of regret about not having the original. There is something fleeting about the idea of a "substitute." If it were good, it would be permanent and welcomed to stay.

The other commonly used term, "artificial sweetener," doesn't shine much of a positive light on the situation either. I think of artificial British accents, artificial nails, and polyester, all things that try to be what they're not and fail miserably. The genuine article stirs up feelings of fondness that its artificial counterpart never could. One researcher who spoke at a sweetener conference wondered out loud whether the label "artificial" actually psychologically makes people think there's a bad taste. The industry often prefers "high-intensity sweetener," but that seems to channel the notion of high-octane gasoline or X-treme sports and didn't seem right either.

There have been attempts to drop the descriptors and just call it sweetener, which seems to make sense. If it sweetens, then it's a sweetener; why segregate it? And yet it doesn't seem fair to put the stuff in the same category as honey, agave, or maple syrup, which exist on their own in nature. Artificial sweeteners take some man-power; we need to coax them into being.

Splenda seemed well aware of this gaping divide between natural and unnatural. Discovered just as the organic and natural food move-ment was gaining ground among mainstream shoppers, Splenda marketed its product to appeal to consumers who wanted something natural but didn't want the calories that came with it in its natural state. Sucralose's ability to withstand high heat and its claim that it is "made from sugar" seemed to offer a savvier alternative to cooks and picky eaters. Just as sea blockades during the Napoleonic wars helped to give rise to beet sugar, and penny pinching led to the popularity of the cheap and transportable high-fructose corn syrup, the turn to-ward natural and home-grown sent consumers looking for an alter-native. At the same time, carbohydrate-counting was just gaining ground, and that diet movement proved even more detrimental for the sweet industry than calorie-counting. It was perfect tim-ing for Splenda, observes Robin Steagall, a dietician and spokesper-son with the Calorie Control Council, an association representing the low-calorie and reduced-fat food and beverage industry. "Made from sugar so it tastes like sugar" became a mantra ingrained in everyone's mind, and soon its yellow tabletop packets surpassed all others, including sucrose. According to Datamonitor, a marketing research firm, sucralose was used in 1,436 new products all over the world in 2004. Just one year earlier, it was used in only 573. Today 3,500 products contain sucralose.

The truth is a little more complicated than the hype. The "made from sugar" part is especially vexing for the sugar industry as well as the makers of NutraSweet and Equal. Sucralose starts out as sugar, but it doesn't stay that way for long. Three hydroxyl groups are removed from a sugar molecule and then replaced with three chlorine molecules. So certainly you can think of it as sugar, but only as much as an heirloom engagement ring is still an heirloom when the diamonds are replaced with cubic zirconium.

The Sugar Association ultimately filed a lawsuit against McNeil Nutritionals, the maker of Splenda, for false advertising. Splenda countersued the association for orchestrating a smear campaign; as of this writing a trial is still pending. Merisant, which produces Equal, also became embroiled in a case against Johnson & Johnson, the parent company of McNeil, making similar complaints.

The legal skirmishes highlight the enormous selling power of the notion "natural." Splenda earned $212.3 million in U.S. sales in 2006, outpacing Equal by a long shot. The former leader—until Splenda came along—made only $48.7 million that same year. In the midst of "Sugargate," as the case between the makers of Equal and Splenda came to be known, the *Philadelphia Inquirer* conducted a reader poll and asked: Did you switch from Equal to Splenda? The answer surprised me: a whopping 59.5 percent said yes. (Just for the record: 10.1 percent said no; 9.4 percent use both; and believe it or not, only 20.9 percent didn't use either.) McNeil lawyers insisted that consumers embraced Splenda because it tasted better—and besides, it spent almost twice as much as Merisant in marketing its product. In truth, though, McNeil's own focus-group findings suggested that its fans mistakenly believed that the product was, in fact, a natural form of sugar.

Not too long ago, my own taste buds were confused at a lunch, for which Splenda officials gathered the best chefs in the country and transformed L'Ecole, the restaurant at the French Culinary Institute in New York, into a real-life Splendaville.

Splendaville (not a term I made up) is the sweet paradise depicted in its advertisements at the time, where everything has a bright golden glow about it. Everyone eats; no one picks at her food or pouts. No one is fat. There are smiles everywhere, and cakes and cookies and thick frosty shakes, and laughter.

"It's like going to Disney World for your taste buds," the then marketing manager of Splenda remarked to me over sweetened ribs. He was actually talking about the event at hand, not the commercials, but today they are really one and the same. What felt like a continuous parade of pastries surrounded us—all replicas of the chefs' signature creations, save for the sugar. Richard Leach, famous for his architectural desserts in the 1980s and at the time a chef at New York's Park Avenue Café, baked chocolate coconut macaroons; Rebecca Rather, from Rather Sweet Bakery in Fredericksburg, Texas, whipped up her signature Texas Big Hairs Lemon-Lime Tart. Gale Gand, of Tru in Chicago, prepared a blueberry peach cobbler. The guests stared dumbstruck at the gigantic plates placed before them, each holding a half-dozen different desserts, plus the communal dishes of brownies and more cakes wedged in between.

I wasn't shy about digging in, and I started with the lemon-lime tart, then the cobbler and the brownies. The woman next to me deemed the treats too sweet, though I disagreed. It was just a different kind of sweet. A real brownie made with sugar would have been a good couple of octaves deeper in flavor; it would have coated the tongue all over. This one gave an intense splash of sweet on the surface, but it's short-lived. Whoosh, and then it's gone. Not an unpleasant sensation, but not the same either.

As auspiciously as the afternoon started out, I left feeling more confused than satiated. Was I feeling a phantom sugar rush, or did

I simply eat too much? ("You probably just ate too much," Drewnowski said when I asked him later.) Did I not feel indulged because it wasn't as satisfying as the real thing, or because I simply *knew* it wasn't the real thing? I had a hard time teasing what I felt from what I thought.

The distinction doesn't seem to bother most sweetener users, at least from Merisant's standpoint. Its lawyers believed the company deserved $200 million to make up for the sales they lost, thanks to McNeil's alleged false advertising, and that's what they demanded last spring in that courtroom in Pennsylvania. After a month-long trial, the two sweeteners jointly settled for an undisclosed amount, just as the jury reached a verdict.

THE EXACT MECHANICS underlying sugar's distinctive sweet taste has, as of yet, been difficult to pin down. There are so many unique things to like about the taste of authentic sugar, many of which we take for granted and can't explain. There's the onset of sweetness, the way it feels on the tongue and as we move it around in our mouth, the way its taste is round and full and then disappears as cleanly as it emerged. We may not notice the details but they're there, day in and day out. We miss them only when they're gone.

When you eliminate sugar from a drink or pastry, you not only take away the sweetness, you also compromise the texture. "Once you remove more than 25 percent of the sugar in a soda, you begin to lose that mouthfeel," Ihab Bishay explains to me. "You can see there's a thinness to it. The people who are drinking regular cola are drinking it not just for the sweetness profile but also for the syrupy thickness. They want that."

The business of creating a sweetener isn't so much like mimicking a painting as replicating the pigments themselves—creating a cobalt blue that looks the same, but isn't. Sweetener molecules act differently in the presence of a sweet receptor. Some prefer to keep to themselves and to make contact with the receptor, briefly, halfheartedly, before they slip away. Others are clingy. They'll grab onto a receptor and refuse to let go, so that the molecules that emerge in the area soon after have nowhere to attach; that explains why subsequent bites of food have a weaker taste. In other cases, a sweetener might have molecules that wander onto bitter receptors, as is the case with saccharin. What some tasters end up with, then, is a bitter aftertaste.

In liquids, aspartame and acesulfame-K (or Ace-K, a sweetener found primarily in packaged goods) seem to have a synergistic affect—that is, putting the two together gives you a taste that's 30 percent sweeter than the sum of the two. Depending on the context, aspartame and saccharin may be synergistic in low concentrations but not high concentrations.

When sugar activates the taste buds, it's thought that it attaches to two receptors, T1R2 and T1R3. Attaching to these receptors is not as simple as fitting a square peg into a square hole. There are grooves and curves that must be matched. Sucralose, aspartame, and neotame (a recent entry from NutraSweet that handles high heat) all interact with T1R2, for instance, but they hang on for different lengths of time, affecting how long the taste of sweet lasts on your tongue. The taste of sweet that results may be close enough to sugar for some, but for others it's as unsatisfying as scratching an itch that's just out of reach.

Aspartame and Ace-K work in tandem to re-create that sugar taste we crave. The first sweetener is thought to alter the shape of the receptors to allow for a stronger binding of the second sweetener. At the same time, aspartame reduces any bitter or metallic aftertaste characteristic of Ace-K. Ace-K provides a quick upfront sweetness that's missing from aspartame, while also reducing aspartame's long sweetness duration. The pair is arguably the best sugar imitator we have now, says Bishay. Generally, the more sweeteners in a blend, the closer the profile might be to sugar.

PERFECTION REMAINS ELUSIVE, however. At the American Chemical Society's Sweetness and Sweeteners symposium in Atlanta in 2006, biotech firms joined traditional flavor and food companies in sharing their findings, signaling that the quest for the perfect sweet has become truly an interdisciplinary affair. Less than ten years ago, the gene coding for the sweet receptors was still a mystery, and so were the steps that occur between tasting sweetness and registering it in the brain. With its discovery, the journal *Cell* in 2001 celebrated, appropriately enough, with chocolate cake on the cover, and out of the floodgates burst a rush of genetically inclined new ideas. As a result, a number of scientists set up shop, searching not for the next miracle drug, but for a completely new way to create the taste of sweet.

They're a new breed of sweet pursuers, more apt to use terms like "G proteins" and "laser capture" than "strawberry" or "vanilla." They work for companies that don't hope to make their money by manufacturing the product, or even distributing it. Instead, they hope to create a blueprint for sweet-enhancing and sell that blueprint to food companies who will manufacture the product themselves and pay them royalties for the privilege. In other words, for the first time ever, it's not just sweetness itself that's a commodity, but the *idea* of it.

Many of the scientists come from a pharmaceutical background. Their search for the perfect sweet—an understanding of the essence of sweetness itself—is stripped down to a rather simple goal: to find compounds, made by man or Mother Nature, that will attach to one or more of the multiple pockets found on the sweet receptors. To understand the approach, it helps to know that one of the founders of Senomyx, a San Diego firm that presented at the sweets conference, was Charles Zuker, among the first researchers to discover the sweet receptor gene. After his moment in *Cell,* he founded the company and hired a team of researchers who eventually created artificial taste buds. With these superhuman taste buds, the firm hopes to find not only sweet enhancers but also salt enhancers and bitter blockers. (A savory enhancer is already in a partner product.) Think of them as invisible bass boosters and amplifiers, which don't produce music in and of themselves, but make the music better. Industry reporters meanwhile have opted for a more provocative way to tell the story: Senomyx, one newspaper headline said, was creating ingredients that "trick" the brain into tasting salty and sweet.

Words like that concern Mark Zoller, chief scientific officer of Senomyx. "I don't like the use of the word 'trick,'" he says. Understandably so—he has the delicate task of touting the cutting-edge nature of his work without making people's stomachs do cartwheels because of the *Star Trek* nature of it. After all, we are talking about food. Consumers are bringing his products into the comfort of their homes, not to mention into their mouths.

"All we're doing is making the receptor more efficient so that it's responding to a lower level of sugar and sending that signal to the brain. The brain is sensing as it normally would. It's not really a trick," he says.

However you choose to describe it, his methods are not exactly conventional, at least in the flavor industry. The sleek, post-space-age machinery makes the discovery of aspartame seem quaint. And unlike Marie Wright at International Flavors & Fragrances, who sees herself as a bit of an artist, creating people's flavor fantasies, Zoller considers his work a natural evolution of his job in pharmaceuticals. "What interested me is that we have this potential where you can lower the amount of sugar and fat in food and affect the health of a lot more people," he says. "From a scientific standpoint, it made sense to work on the prevention of disease and not just the treatment of it."

Senomyx and other firms like it hope to make the world a little sweeter with a little less sugar; and as food-technology think tanks, they have created a brand-new field. Discontent with what we had, we've inspired new companies to knock down the walls of conventional food making and find another way.

Creating food always involves some element of chance, whether it's a soufflé or a new ingredient. You start with some basic culinary rules, but the merits of the final products are often subjective. There's room for argument, a bit of improvisation, and joy in the occasional surprise. Senomyx, however, prefers to assume nothing and to leave nothing to chance. Components of fruits, vegetables, plants, or compounds engineered in the lab, whatever they might be, all get run through its equipment.

"We take a broad approach. We're not biased," Zoller explains. "Our receptor-based assays can go through hundreds of thousands of chemical systems, and what we're looking for is one component that binds to the receptors we're interested in." In the past couple of years, Senomyx has tested around 300,000 compounds in each of its taste-receptor systems. One out of 1,000 or even 10,000 might stick, and if it does, they'll take it to the next logical step: testing the compound with other taste receptors, such as bitter, to make certain the ingredient doesn't elicit tastes that we don't like.

As of this writing, progress in the sweet area remains to be seen. One promising enhancer, referred to as simply S5742, has so far demonstrated an ability to allow for the same level of sweetness with 40 percent less sugar. Because these taste enhancers and blockers will be present in such minuscule amounts, and because they're considered *flavor* ingredients, not food, they are not subject to the same lengthy FDA approval process as our current artificial sweeteners. Still, the road to market is a long one, because even if an ingredient passes the scrutiny of high-tech machines and regulatory authorities, it still has to stand up to trusty old machines in the kitchen and finicky home cooks. You've got to be able to chill it and bake it and toast it. You've got to be able to keep it on the shelf. At the end of the day, you've got to be able to put it in your mouth, enjoy it, and live to tell about it.

In the meantime, some food makers are going back to nature, but with more focus than our primitive ancestors. The food company Cargill has been working with farmers around the globe to find a better-tasting stevia-based sweetener. Stevia, an herb native to Paraguay, has long been sold in health food stores and heralded as a safe and natural supplement, but not as a food. There have been complaints about its aftertaste and questionable links to liver conditions and infertility. To eliminate these drawbacks, Cargill, in partnership with Coca-Cola, has sifted through two hundred or so varieties of stevia, and crossbred them for a more consistently sweet plant. They've tweaked it in the lab and cultivated it, thereby not only "optimizing" the plant, as Ann Clark Tucker, the director of public affairs, puts it, but also "squeezing more sweetness out of each acre." The search for sweet, it seems, has inspired us to push the boundaries of even nature itself.

ALL THIS TALK about fake sugar has made me wonder about the real thing. I've eaten it only in pastries and candy for so long that I've forgotten what it tastes like sprinkled straight from its white packet. And so one morning I indulge myself. I get some strawberries and sprinkle a little sugar over them. It's real sugar after all (and I rarely go through a whole packet of Equal), so I don't think I need more than that. And yet when I take a bite, I taste only the softest whisper of sweetness. I pour some more sugar over the berries and still find them sour. I empty the entire packet, and still the fruit tastes a bit too tart for me. It isn't until I nearly finish the second packet that the sweetness level is to my liking. Apparently my brain has rewired itself, expecting the fruit to taste a certain way and being disappointed when it doesn't. The line I've subconsciously drawn between "not sweet enough" and "sweet" has moved. Like the eighteenth-century Brits, I've been enjoying my new-fangled sweets a little too much to ever go back.

Chapter Ten

And Good *for* You

IN MY FAMILY, WE ALWAYS PLAYED BY OUR OWN RULES when it came to seasonings. The salt and pepper rarely left the cupboard, but sweeter stuff would make regular appearances next to the soy sauce on the dinner table. To add a sweet-and-sour kick to fried rice, my siblings and I would apply ketchup. My mother (as celebrated chefs now admit to doing) sometimes poured soft drinks into pots of savory stew, giving rise to the name of one of her best-loved specialties, 7UP chicken. My father sprinkled sugar on open-face toasted cheese sandwiches and stirred peanut butter into beef noodles, and I thought they were delicious, all.

This is probably why, until I left for college, it never occurred to me that the taste of sweet was such a terrible thing. It was always mixed with something good, and I never thought anything strange about it. Moreover, I prided myself in my openness to experimentation. I'd eat anything, especially if it was sweet.

I am therefore surprised and even disappointed in myself when, one morning, I bite into a piece of kale and feel a wave of disgust, precisely because it is sweet. I had expected something bitter. It tastes terrible, and I tell the person who served it to me.

Valerie Duffy doesn't take offense. You see, I am not at a restaurant, but near my childhood home at her nutrition lab at the University of Connecticut Allied Health Sciences Center. In conducting an experiment with kale as well as Brussels sprouts and asparagus, she makes no attempt to spruce up the presentation. Each bite-sized portion of the wilting pieces of blanched vegetables is served up plain in a clear plastic cup, like the one you'd find on top of a cough medicine bottle. But this is what she has to do in order to find out how super-tasters and non-tasters perceive their greens.

Duffy, who is both a registered dietitian and a sensory psychologist, is unlike any nutritionist I know. Being in the magazine industry, I usually meet nutritionists who are almost celebrities themselves by virtue of their association with real celebrities whom they've whittled into shape after a pregnancy or for a boxing movie. They make their reputation by giving their clients a list of don'ts, as in "Don't eat grapes at night," or "Don't have a cookie when you should have almonds." The program zeroes in on what's bad (sweets) and formulates lists of avoidance strategies (don't eat sweets).

Duffy approaches the situation from a rosier standpoint. Instead of pointing a finger at what overweight people are doing wrong, she asked what healthy people are doing *right* and why. She now hopes to use the answer to develop an eating strategy that we all can use. Duffy likes to say that she preaches nutrition from the "neck up," though I think it's a lot more profound than that. In exploring the "why's" of eating, she acknowledges that not all of us are working toward a nutritious diet from a level playing field. It's harder for some than others.

People eat certain foods because those foods taste good to them. This includes foods that are healthy for us, namely vegetables. But, as we've learned from Linda Bartoshuk, how good a food tastes is not a constant among all people. Some of us like the taste of vegetables; others don't, no matter how hard we try. But rather than having us fight our taste realities and change the individual, Duffy believes it makes more sense to change the food. What might do the trick, she says, is the taste of sweet.

Yes, believe it or not, the taste of sweet, the magic ingredient food manufacturers have been using for over a century to entice us into eating products that are bad, is now being used by a nutritionist to get us to eat things that are *good*. The weapon for turning profits is finally being tapped as a tool for health.

Will her plan work? And will sweetness do enough good to erase the guilt that has been associated with it for so long? If the answer is yes, then it's a testament to the fact that the taste of sweet can be anything you want it to be, if placed in the right context. My visit with Duffy convinced me that sweetness can be a deterrent, but it can also be an asset. It can be good or bad or something in between. Like anything else in life, it's what's you make of it.

TODAY DUFFY and her team have cooked kale, Brussels sprouts, and asparagus in various sugar and salt solutions: a modest start to a potentially groundbreaking way to get children and picky adults to eat their vegetables. I say "groundbreaking" because ever since Americans began packing on excess pounds, the verdict has been that people who are overweight have no one but themselves to blame. We might condemn food makers for warping portion sizes and putting too much sugar and fat in their products, but ultimately, the popular thinking goes, it's the unsuccessful dieters who often make the bad choices, who eat too much candy and greasy foods (or even upscale pastries) and imbibe too many cocktails, compared to their thinner counterparts, who eat copious amounts of greens and whole grains. Heavy adults, it's often presumed, are either too lazy or too reckless to care, or too stupid to know any better. As for children, the good ones supposedly listen to their parents and eat their vegetables; the naughty throw tantrums, cry for sweets and chicken fingers, and get chubby on them. It's the *person* who needs to change, the old diet dictums have declared. But Duffy is part of a new wave of food thinkers looking beyond willpower for answers to poor eating habits. Some, like Gene-Jack Wang, are peering into the brain; others, like Adam Drewnowski, are looking for economic explanations. As for Duffy, she's saying: Let's change the food.

To begin with, Duffy hopes to shed light on the assumption that vegetables taste the same to everyone. Up until now, the dieter who can clean her plate of broccoli is applauded for having more willpower than the dieter who can't. But what if they're not experiencing the same sensation? What if the broccoli is actually tasty to the first dieter, so it doesn't take much effort to incorporate it into her meals. And what if the bitterness of the broccoli seems so strong to the other dieter that the two bites he took were a feat of sheer willpower? If differences in our genes and our taste-bud count can cause disagreements over what's sweet enough and what's too sweet, then it makes sense that we'll also have quibbles at the other end of the taste spectrum: between what's sweet and what's not sweet at all. In other words, those who consume seemingly less-than-tasty food are in fact eating it not because they're more virtuous, but because it tastes pretty good to them anyway.

It turns out that vegetable-lovers detect a hint of sweet in their greens—not just in the obvious suspects, such as the fresh beets uprooted from the Edible Schoolyard, or corn, or red bell peppers, but also in more difficult-to-love varieties like asparagus, Brussels sprouts, and kale. In contrast, according to studies conducted by

Duffy (who did her postdoctoral sensory work with Bartoshuk and her colleagues), those who hate eating vegetables can't sense any sweetness at all. Apparently they are so sensitive to bitterness that it completely overwhelms the sweetness.

To understand how vegetable enthusiasts perceive the presence of sweetness in their salads, Duffy explored the nuances of bitterness. Humans have been found to possess a couple dozen bitter-receptor-taste genes. These genes code for an array of receptors with varying levels of sensitivity. If a particular ingredient activates the receptors in a way that produces a strong bitter taste, it will overpower what little sweetness that ingredient possesses. Appreciating that sweetness would be as difficult as hearing a whisper in a loud, crowded party. In the case of, say, saccharin, that little tinge of bitter is enough to eliminate the enjoyment of the sweetness. Imagine, then, what happens with vegetables, which are loaded with bitter health-promoting compounds such as phenols, flavonoids, isoflavones, and glucosinolates: for some, nature's own medicine can taste as bad as the kind you get at a drugstore. Duffy hopes to find out who these people are, what their genetic makeup is, and how they can be helped from a taste standpoint.

One bitter receptor gene is the hTAS2R38, which helps control our ability to taste PROP. Two forms of the gene are the PAV and the AVI forms. Some of us possess a pair of the same form; others have one of each. Scientists at Monell have found that those who have the PAV-PAV or PAV-AVI are more sensitive to bitter taste than those with the AVI-AVI pair. In contrast, those possessing two AVI forms were one hundred to one thousand times less sensitive to the bitter taste of PROP.

As we might recall, PROP tasters tend to be very picky eaters. In a study Adam Drewnowski conducted some years back, PROP tasters tend not to like grapefruit or green tea. They also tend to despise vegetables. With this in mind, Duffy takes some of the most bitter vegetables she can find in the grocer's freezer and sprays them with a non-nutritive sweetener diluted in water. She then feeds these differently seasoned vegetables to subjects tested for their taster status and finds out what they like best. In doing so, she hopes to establish some taste-preference parameters and to offer a customized approach to food preparation and meal planning. I cringe at the thought of sweetened vegetables. But as if reading my mind, Duffy reminds me that it really is "just a spritz." "We're not adding a lot," she assures me. The idea, she says, is not so much to sugar-coat vegetables as to balance out the bitter.

AS INNOVATIVE as Duffy's protocol might sound to us consumers, the notion of using sweetness for good harkens back to ancient times. Before sweetness was the obesity culprit it is today, it was a medical wonder with an expensive price tag. In Ancient Greece, sugar and honey were often prescribed to reinstate the balance of humors when it was lost. Galen recommended sugar for melancholy children—melancholia being thought to be related to an unsteady state in the liver. The concepts of humoral medicine eventually spread into other parts of Europe and reigned for centuries, and sugar continued to be a star. The name of the species cultivated to this day—*S. officinarum*—in fact means "of the apothecary shops," and the saying "like an apothecary without sugar" was a way to describe someone who lacked something important. Sugar was thought to help cool a fever, quiet a cough, soothe the stomach, and moisten chapped lips. It was considered good for the breast and the lungs. Blended with pearls and gold leaf and crushed into a powder, it was to be blown into an ailing eye to cure it. On the issue of whether sugar was allowed during Lent, Thomas Aquinas gave the "sugared spice," as he called it, his stamp of approval—after all, he said, people took it not for nourishment but to aid in digestion.

(Incidentally, some church leaders centuries later also awarded the same hallowed seal of approval to chocolate, albeit amid some controversy.)

Buddhism was born in the heart of the sugarcane fields in India, and the religion is rich with sugar references. Sugarcane juice is what Buddha supposedly reached for after his fast for enlightenment. Medical texts from India and China, written by monks as early as the fourth century, upheld sugar as a form of treatment. Besides stomach problems and itchiness, it was, at least at one point, thought to promote strength and produce sperm.

Sugar eventually fell out of favor among the health establishment because of concern over its fattening and tooth-decaying properties—but even so, it still came in handy to facilitate wellness. As we saw earlier, the taste of sweet was, and still is, mixed with bitter medicines, from lozenges to syrups, to make what's good for us go down "in a most delightful way," as the *Mary Poppins* song tells it. If vegetables taste as bad as medicine for some people and are just as good for them, why not mask the bitter? And why *not* look to the taste of sweet for help? The taste of sweet may have a disgraceful reputation these days, but even the bad can turn into good, given the right opportunity.

Jeffery Sobal, at Cornell University, explains that there have always been "diet darlings" and "diet demons." A food could be considered a darling one day and a demon the next, and attitudes could differ widely across the oceans and across time. Back in medieval days, some fruits were diet demons. Consumed raw (as opposed to baked, dried, or preserved in syrup) at the end of the meal, they were believed to send poisonous vapors to the brain. The solution, some European medical experts offered, was to cook the offending fruits with wine. Of course later in America, during Prohibition and for decades after, wine turned into a demonized food—only to become a darling again, thanks to the culinary habits and comparatively good cardiovascular health of the French and, more recently, research into its anti-cancer effects.

Chocolate, introduced to the Europeans in the sixteenth century, most probably by Mayan nobles visiting Spain, was originally consumed unsweetened and considered a health drink and a luxury, while vanilla was thought to be dangerous. Centuries later, with mass-production techniques, larger infusions of sugar, and cheap price points, chocolate was demoted to junk-food status and demonized. But after yet another couple of centuries, chocolate makers focused their efforts on scientific research, and in doing so they were eventually able to prove that the cocoa bean did indeed possess some of those good-for-you compounds; in fact, they eventually managed to turn their product (at least the dark forms of it) back into a darling. All things considered, sugar and sugar substitutes are long overdue for their "darling" moment.

Duffy is working toward that. Besides, customizing the sweetness of vegetables might do more than provide good nutrition; she's hoping it will also help prevent disease. Given that decreased vegetable consumption increases the risk of certain types of medical conditions, Duffy wonders if super-tasters (who can't stand vegetables) are more susceptible to certain types of cancers. Early research, which she conducted with Bartoshuk, suggests they are. In a sample of 251 men, her team found that those who tasted PROP as more bitter had a higher number of colon polyps, especially if they were older than sixty-six years of age. Indeed, subjects who gave PROP the bitterest ratings were also those who ate the smallest amount of vegetables, the fiber content of which helps to prevent colon cancer. Of course not all polyps turn into cancers (in fact, most don't), and it could very well be that PROP tasting simply makes people more susceptible to polyps and not to the cancer itself. More studies are needed, but the fact is that eating more vegetables can't hurt, and instead of being the problem, sweetness can be, at least in a small way, part of the solution.

DUFFY'S WORK broaches a seemingly contradictory issue: If non-tasters are presumably salad eaters, why—as Bartoshuk has informed us—do they also tend to be overweight? It turns out that while a lower taste-bud count sweetens the taste of vegetables, it also encourages greater intake of rich foods, such as those that are fried or laden with cream or fat. In one study, Duffy had seventy-five subjects sample heavy cream and eight high-fat foods, including extra-sharp and very low-sodium cheddar cheese, cream cheese, mayonnaise, milk chocolate, bittersweet chocolate, and regular and low-sodium potato chips. After each tasting, she asked them to rate the level of sweetness, saltiness, sourness, bitterness, creaminess/oiliness they detected, and their degree of liking/disliking. Her findings intrigued me. The more bitter the subjects rated PROP, the more creamy or oily they rated the fatty foods; the more creamy or oily they rated the fatty foods, the less they reported liking them and the less they consumed. It seems that we all want some texture to our food, but not so much that it's overwhelming. For tasters and super-tasters, the degree of texture in certain foods feels already too intense; for non-tasters, they've hardly reached the saturation point. Because the food doesn't feel as rich, they eat more in an effort to overcome a weaker taste experience.

Taste and texture play into our drinking habits as well. Non-tasters say they detect a trace of sweetness in scotch. They also report drinking more wine and beer than tasters do and enjoy it more too. Meanwhile, tasters and super-tasters undergo a completely different experience and tend to be the ones sipping on sparkling water or soda at a cocktail party. That's because alcoholic beverages not only taste bitter to them but also irritate the mouth. Taste buds come in contact with fibers from a nerve that mediates touch sensations, including oral burn. Given that super-tasters have more taste buds, they also have more of these fibers, which accentuate the discomfort of that tannic feeling from drinking red wine. Beer seems no more enticing. So unpleasant is the taste and texture experience that even among freshmen in college (arguably the most intoxication-prone population in America) super-tasters have been found to drink less beer than their non-taster counterparts.

BACK AT Duffy's lab, I am still working my way through twenty-four variations of flavored vegetables. How sweet is it? How bitter? Do you like it? All of these answers are inputted into her database, and slowly, with enough people, a profile of what super-tasters, tasters, and non-tasters like to eat across the sweetness spectrum will emerge.

By the end of my session, I feel pretty full even though I spit most of them out. (They weren't at all as tasty as the oatmeal cookies in Marie Wright's laboratory.) Duffy had used the same assessment scale as Bartoshuk, with zero being the equivalent of a dimly lit room and 100 being the brightest light I've ever seen. When asked about liking, I gave a score of zero to vegetables simply treated with water and higher points to the salted ones. I assigned negative ratings to those with sour notes and (despite my love for cookies and cakes) for those with a trace of sweetness too; vegetables, I thought, shouldn't taste like candy.

Sweetness can be helpful, but perhaps only with a little more creativity. As we saw earlier, much of tasting is learned, and being the conscientious healthy eater that I am, I've learned that vegetables are supposed to be bitter, even though my semi-super-taster taste buds don't like them. Perhaps sweetness in the form of vegetables produces too much dissonance to be considered the perfect sweet. After all, we have a history of eating our vegetables plain, especially here in the Northeast. While those in the South may have experimented with sauces, thanks to a mixed ethnic population, the Quakers, for instance, took theirs boiled with salt, pepper, and perhaps butter if available; canned yams were not for them. Simple eating was virtuous eating, says James McWilliams, author of *A Revolution in Eating,* and besides, taste was rarely an issue at the time. "When you're living on a settlement, you're much more concerned about the food supply."

It can take a while for an exotic food combination to break into the mainstream, though it may take less time today, now that technology has made us one big community and businesses have gone global. But still, sugar or sugar substitutes in place of salt on the dinner table doesn't seem exactly exotic. It just seems strange. Nevertheless we experience the sweet-vegetable flavor all the time, even though we may not always add the sugar ourselves. We caramelize our onions and carrots to make them sweeter, and some of us put marshmallows in our yams. Any able home cook knows that many recipes, even vegetarian ones, require a secret spoonful, if not more, of sugar. Never mind, either, that food manufacturers use it generously in their savory products. A can of bean-with-bacon soup, for instance, contains 2½ teaspoons.

We believe sugar pairs naturally with dairy (cheesecake, ice cream, chocolate milk) and protein (honeyed walnuts, glazed ham, sweet-and-sour chicken), but for most of us sweeteners with vegetables sounds unappetizing. It's as if we don't want to tamper with something that grows from the earth, at least not at the dinner table. For many Americans, vegetables with sugar is like "ketchup on ice cream. They don't want to think about it," says Paul Rozin, who besides studying the culture of food is also exploring the issue of disgust.

In coming all the way to Duffy's lab in rural Connecticut, expecting to find what might be the healthiest and perhaps the most perfect sweet, I stumbled on the one instance for me where sweetness isn't appealing at all.

MONTHS LATER, I check back with Duffy, who has since been conducting her experiment on children in the local Head Start program, with interesting results. When she brought out sweetened and unsweetened vegetables and asked them to choose, two-thirds of the children picked the vegetables with sweetener. "It was a slight misting," says Duffy—less than a teaspoon, but it made a difference.

She has braced herself for some controversy. Do we want our children to be consuming more sweetness? After all, sweeteners often insinuate themselves into the main course, especially if it's packaged; and kids certainly get enough of the stuff in their breakfast cereals and snacks. More sweetness, even a small amount, seems counter to the message to eat healthy. Then there's the fear that children's palates may never expand beyond sweet, and this may limit their food choices in the future.

Duffy is well aware of these problems, but she doesn't think our current strategies are working. "Children aren't eating their vegetables," she says. "They're limited to potatoes and tomatoes"—mostly in the form of French fries and ketchup. Depending on age, gender, and activity level, children should have at least one to three servings a day. What people of all ages should be eating are the serious varieties, such as Brussels sprouts, kale, and spinach. But it's not in our nature, as a French experiment at the Gaffarell Nursery of the Dijon Hospital illustrates. There, researchers asked two- to three-year-olds to choose among meats, fish, cheeses, breads, pastas, rice, fried potatoes, and vegetables. Not surprisingly they chose vegetables less often than meat. Children gravitate to what's caloric and what will quickly make them full, and greens don't tend to fall into that category lest it's spinach with cream sauce, which the subjects here quite liked. Without succulence or sweetness, most vegetables are difficult. You have to spend some time getting to know them before you learn to accept them.

If it's hard for the typical child, consider the child who has a taster parent and is a taster herself. If her parents don't eat vegetables, chances are she won't have the positive reinforcement and habit of eating hers, either. Besides, there are plenty of other foods to keep the child happy, and a happy, unfussy child is what parents want after a busy day, even if good nutrition goes by the wayside.

In this case, perhaps a spritz of sugar could come to the rescue, providing better-balanced meals with less drama. Eating vegetables in this way may be a good method for getting acquainted with the taste of bitterness. It may seem strange in the context of greens, but people have done this many times before. Some go through a period of drinking coffee with sugar and milk (and even whipped cream and flavored syrups) before we eventually transition to black. We grow up eating sweetened cereal before graduating to corn flakes. And some start with flavored yogurt before enjoying the unsweetened real thing. Of course, many don't make it to the next step. But in the case of vegetables, where any intake is helpful, who's to say picky eaters wouldn't be better off than before?

If we look at the foods that people enjoy—fat, salt, and sugar—sweeteners may provide the most efficient tool. Adding fat will not kill the bitter, nor will salt substitutes, at least very effectively. And while real salt does the deed, it's still generally bad for the cardiovascular system if you use too much of it, which people tend to do. Sugar substitutes (and if you don't mind the calories, sugar or honey) may be the best hope we've got.

Duffy has found that some vegetables don't need as much sugar to temper the bitter as others, though it will take more

research before she can give details. For now, it looks as if each vegetable possesses unique compounds that impart varying abilities to
suppress sweetness. Ironically, the efforts of some producers to
breed for more healthy nutrients may actually make them even less
tasty. But if Kirk Larson can produce a sweeter strawberry, then why
not a sweeter vegetable? In the past twenty-five years scientists have
made much progress in carrots—by taming the harsh notes and
fine-tuning the texture for greater succulence, they've allowed us to
enjoy a sweeter carrot now than a generation ago. "On a five-point
scale," says Philipp Simon, a USDA geneticist and horticulturalist,
"they're up to a whole point sweeter." Sales, too, have risen—by up to
15 percent.

Success remains to be seen with leafy greens. "Sometimes
spinach can taste sweet, other times grassy," says Teddy Morelock,
a professor of horticulture at the University of Arkansas. "But we
haven't hit on anything consistent to breed for yet." The sweetest
spinach he's ever tasted was still only half as sweet as a watermelon.

Meantime, in the course of her research, Duffy has also begun
to notice that people with different tasting abilities have different
sweetness threshholds. One particular concentration of sweetness
might change "dislike" to "like" for tasters but will tip the scale to
"too sweet" for super-tasters. Duffy compares it to wine tasting.
"You must choose the right balance that works for you," she says.

That balance skewed sweeter centuries ago. While the English, who
had influenced early American tastes enormously, may have eaten
their vegetables plain, this was not so on the Continent. There, the
nobility enhanced their savory dishes with sugar as soon as they got
their hands on the spice. Many were protein-based, though some
Italian dishes featured vegetables, including candied lettuce and
sliced turnips with sugar and Parmesan. Bartolomeo Scappi, the
great sixteenth-century Italian cookbook writer, mixed eggplant

with mint, parsley, garlic, pepper, cinnamon, and, among many more spices, sugar. Another Italian author, Cristoforo di Messisbugo, recommended baking a pie filled with sweetmeats, udders, or eyeballs from veal, then topping that off with a flourish of sugar, as well as raisins and chopped proscuitto. In the middle of the seventeenth century, there is a recipe from another Italian, Bartolomeo Stefani, who fries his brain fritters in butter and sprinkles them with sugar. I read about these recipes in disbelief, chronicled meticulously by food historian Ken Albala in *The Banquet,* and suddenly a mist of aspartame on asparagus doesn't seem so bad anymore.

Food anthropologists have observed that countries with meat-based cuisines, like the United States and Germany, typically season their food less enthusiastically than those with plant-based cuisines, like China and Mexico, who are often avid users of spices and sauces. Borrowing cooking customs from these vegetable-loving nations might change the way we eat for the better.

If anything, Valerie Duffy's research has persuaded me to think out of the box and improvise, even more than my family ever did. I might add more broccoli than usual to a sweet-and-sour chicken dish, dress Brussels sprouts with a little honey mustard, mix caramelized onions with kale. In the cookbook *Hot Sour Salty Sweet,* I find a recipe for a Thai dish in which green beans are tossed with cherry tomatoes, cabbage, and, among other seasonings, sugar "to taste." Another instructs the reader to steam cabbage, beans, and carrots with sweet squash or pumpkin. Thai cuisine features plenty of sweet but healthy recipes—the sweetness being a large reason it has become so popular in the States, says Paul Rozin. (The Thai Trade Commission counted approximately 3,000 restaurants in 2006, a 3 percent growth from the year before.)

Cooks farther west sweeten greens too, though the practice gets short shrift when compared with salting and buttering. In researching a story on maple syrup, I found recipes for pouring it on

Brussels sprouts. Chef Iacopo Falai, at his restaurant Falai, in New York, candies fennel and serves it with chocolate hazelnut cake. His *tuiles* are made with beet juice instead of red wine, and he serves arugula with crème brûlée. One doesn't have to go that far, but a little creative use of sweetness may not be such a bad idea. It opens the door to seeing sweetness in a new light and leaving social constructs behind.

IT'S FUNNY to think that as much as I love the taste of sweet, I've taken it for granted. I've wolfed it down without letting it sit on my tongue for a while and taking note of its nuances. I've overlooked it in places where it has existed, and I've missed opportunities for using it in places to help me out. I'm often doing or thinking about other things when I'm eating—whether it's surfing the Internet, reading, or writing. And sometimes I even say to myself, "I shouldn't be eating this," or "I wish I were eating something else."

There is a simple elegance in perfect things. I think of science experiments, geometric proofs, and poems. There's a marked effortlessness in the most arresting of them. They unspool naturally. Natural, of course, doesn't always mean safe and harmless, as the artificial-sweetener industry likes to remind us, but there are plenty of foods in nature that are superior to the man-made variety, and these foods tend to be sweet—the milk that an infant gets from her mother, the sap that resurfaces on a tree, without fail, year after year. It's irresistible, this natural desire for sweetness, as manufacturers also like to tell us. But perhaps this natural desire can be satisfied only by nature itself. It would be simplest, and most elegant, that way.

Still, I realize that perfection means different things for different people, and maybe aspartame or saccharin is the preferred sweet for some, whether it's because they actually enjoy the taste or they've grown accustomed to it. Whatever the case may be (choose the sugar-free blueberry muffin if you will), be sure to enjoy it; savor it for what it offers rather than fixating on what it doesn't. Fear and guilt will bring only doubts, disappointments, and a binge later on.

Aristotle's sensory hierarchy may seem archaic, but in some ways his basic assumptions survive; it's still on the bottom rung and we don't pay as much attention to the sense of taste as we do the other senses. But we should. After all, in our mouths our genetics and our environment intersect; our taste buds determine whether we should swallow, and whether we should become the foods placed before us. Our choice changes our body in some way, and over time, we live out the sum of all our decisions.

On the way back home from visiting Valerie Duffy, I take the same roads we'd driven a million times when I was a child. There are new take-out restaurants and grab-and-go spots. But there are also the old standbys—the produce stand, for instance, selling sweet corn, and luscious stone fruits, or whatever bounty of the season. We would take it all in, my family, sometimes browsing the farm goods with ice cream from the previous stop still in our hands. The perfect treat was anything and everything we wanted it to be because we let it, and life was all the sweeter for it. Chances are, my parents would be discussing what might be nice for dinner, and my siblings and I would agree or disagree, still licking our cones. "So much activity!" we thought, though it was the smallest of farmers' markets, on the side of a country road.

Notes

Introduction

3   *simple foods:*
Harold McGee, *Food and Cooking: The Science and Lore of the Kitchen* (New York: Scribner, 2004), 670–93.

4   *70 percent:*
For some basic information about sugar's production, check out the Sugar Knowledge International Limited (SKIL) website http://www.sucrose.com.

4   *two inches:*
John N. Warner, "Sugar Cane: An Indigenous Papuan Cultigen," *Ethnology* I, no. 4 (October 1962): 405–11.

4   *Historians suspect that:*
Sidney W. Mintz, *Sweetness and Power* (New York: Penguin Books, 1985), 17. Mintz's book and his conversations were of enormous help in compiling the historical and anthropological facts for this and the second chapter; they also inspired some of my thoughts presented in chapters 8 and 9. Also extremely enlightening was Noel Deerr's *The History of Sugar*, vol. I (London: Chapman and Hall, 1949–60).

5   *The Ramayana:*
Translated into English prose from the original Sanskrit of Vālmīki by Manmatha Nath Dutt, M.A. (Calcutta: Deva Press, 1891), 18.

5   *A southern Chinese poem:*
         Sucheta Mazumdar, *Sugar and Society in China: Peasants, Technology, and the World Market* (Cambridge, Mass.: Harvard University Asia Center, 1998), 17.

5   *Sailing along the Indus:*
         Mintz, *Sweetness and Power,* 19–20.

5   *a "concreted honey":*
         Ibid., 20.

7   *fruity martinis:*
         An interesting account of the sweetening of our cocktail hour appears in Noah Rothbaum's *The Business of Spirits: How Savvy Marketers, Innovative Distillers, and Entrepreneurs Changed How We Drink* (New York: Kaplan, 2007), 97–127.

7   *Despite our ever-growing:*
         U.S. Bureau of the Census. *Confectionery: 2006.* Current Industrial Reports, Table 1a, Summary of Manufacturers' Shipments of Confectionery Products: 1999 to 2006. Issued June 2007.

7   *And as our total:*
         USDA Economic Research Service. "U.S. Consumption of Caloric Sweeteners," in "Sugar and Sweeteners Yearbook Tables." http://www.ers.usda.gov/Briefing/Sugar/data.htm.

7   *$12 billion:*
         Packaged Facts, a division of MarketResearch.com. "The U.S. Market for Sweet Baked Goods," November 2005.

8   *Naomi Moriyama, author of:*
         Naomi Moriyama and William Doyle, *Japanese Women Don't Get Fat or Old* (New York: Delta, 2006), 222.

8   *the Persians discovered:*
         "Cultivation of Sugar in Persia," *Science* 14, no. 338 (July 26, 1889): 62.

9   *In 632:*
         Andrew M. Watson, "The Arab Agricultural Revolution and Its Diffusion," *Journal of Economic History* 34, no. 1 (March 1974): 8–35.

9   *It wasn't long:*
Mintz's *(Sweetness and Power)* reviews of the circumstances, particularly on pages 38–39, and conversations with James McWilliams about his work in *A Revolution in Eating: How the Quest for Food Shaped America* (New York: Columbia University Press, 2005), provided great insight too. Also helpful: Deerr, *The History of Sugar,* vol. 1, 146–49.

10   *the royal help:*
Jack Goody, *Food and Love: A Culinary History of East and West* (London and New York: Verso, 1998), 139.

10   *Among the newly:*
Andrew Smith, professor of food history at The New School, was immensely helpful in providing me the basic foundations of culinary history. Also: *The Oxford Companion to American Food and Drink* (New York: Oxford University Press, 2007), which Smith edited, and *The Encyclopedia of Junk Food and Snack Food* (Westport, Conn.: Greenwood Press, 2006), which Smith wrote.

10   *Certain parts of China had:*
E. N. Anderson, *Food in China* (New Haven and London: Yale University Press), 178. Subsequent e-mail and phone correspondence with Anderson provided valuable insight.

10   *For the nomadic:*
Charles Perry, "The Taste for Layered Bread Among the Nomadic Turks and the Central Asian Origins of Baklava," in *A Taste of Thyme: Culinary Cultures of the Middle East,* Sami Zubaida and Richard Tapper, eds. (New York: Tauris Parke Paperbacks, 2000), 89–90.

Chapter One: Sweet Enough for You?

16   *The first paper:*
"Six in Ten 'Tasteblind' to Bitter Chemical," *Science News Letter,* April 18, 1931.

18   *Bartoshuk came up:*
Linda M. Bartoshuk et al., "Differences in Our Sensory Worlds: Invalid Comparisons with Labeled Scales," *Current Directions in*

Psychological Science 14, no. 3 (June 2005): 122–25. Also helpful: Bartoshuk, "Comparing Sensory Experiences Across Individuals: Recent Psychophysical Advances Illuminate Genetic Variation in Taste Perception," *Chemical Senses* 25 (2000): 447–60.

18   *With the discovery:*
Bartoshuk kindly spent hours of phone, e-mail, and in-person to explain issues relevant to tasting. I also found these papers valuable for a basic understanding: Linda M. Bartoshuk et al., "From Psychophysics to the Clinic: Missteps and Advances," *Food Quality and Preference* 15 (2004): 617–32; Bartoshuk, "Sweetness: History, Preference, and Genetic Variability," *Food Technology* 45 (November 1991): 108, 110, 112–13; and David V. Smith and Robert F. Margolskee, "Making Sense of Taste," *Scientific American,* March 2001.

18   *Alcohol drinkers are:*
S. A. Lanier et al., "Sweet and Bitter Tastes of Alcoholic Beverages Mediate Alcohol Intake in Of-Age Undergraduates," *Physiology & Behavior* 83 (2005): 821–31; Valerie B. Duffy, "Bitter Receptor Gene (TAS2R38), 6-n-Propylthiouracil (PROP) Bitterness and Alcohol Intake," *Alcoholism: Clinical and Experimental Research* 28, no. 11 (November 2004): 1629–37; and J. M. Hall et al., "PTC Taste Blindness and the Taste of Caffeine," *Nature* 253 (1975), 442–43.

19   *Oddly, people with:*
D. Whissell-Buechy and Christopher Wills, "Male and Female Correlations for Taster (PTC) Phenotypes and Rate of Adolescent Development," *Annals of Human Biology* 16, no. 2 (1989): 131–46.

22   *poor English translation:*
E. Boring, *Sensation and Perception in the History of Experimental Psychology* (New York: Academic Press, 1942).

22   *written in German:*
D. P. Hanig, "Zur Psychophysik des Geschmacksinnes," *Philosophische Studien* 17 (1901), 576–623.

23   *the idea of opposites:*
Aristotle, *De Anima,* R. D. Hicks, trans. (Amherst, N.Y.: Prometheus Books, 1991), 65.

27   *One experiment found:*

For a discussion on the effects of age and disease on taste and smell, I found helpful an article by Kristin A. Seiberling, M.D., and David B. Conley: "Aging and Olfactory and Taste Function," *Oto-laryngologic Clinics of North America* 37 (2004): 1209–28. Bartoshuk et al. discuss taste damage in "Taste Damage: Previously Unsuspected Consequences," *Chemical Senses* 30, supp. 1 (2005): 1218–19.

27   *bit of a trickster:*

Bartoshuk seemed to have an especially good time exploring these topics. A few papers she first-authored: "Sweet Taste of Water Induced by Artichoke (*Cynara scolymus*)," *Science* 178 (1972): 988–90; "Taste Illusions: Some Demonstrations," *Annals of the New York Academy of Sciences* 237 (1974): 279–85; "Sweet Taste Induced by Miracle Fruit (*Synsepalum dulcificum*)," *Physiology & Behavior* 12 (1974): 449–56; "Sweet Taste of Dilute NaCl: Psychophysical Evidence for a Sweet Stimulus," *Physiology & Behavior* 21 (1978): 609–13.

Chapter Two: The Myth of the Refined Palate

31   *As the rumor goes:*

John Doherty and John Harrison, *The Waldorf-Astoria Cookbook* (New York: Bullfinch, 2006), 222–23.

31   *It probably started out:*

Check out http://whatscookingamerica.net and click on "Food History."

31   *chocolate layer cake:*

Greg Patent, *Baking in America: Traditional and Contemporary Favorites from the Past 200 Years* (Boston: Houghton Mifflin, 2002), 278.

33   *a term Pierre Bourdieu:*

Pierre Bourdieu, *Distinction: A Social Critique of the Judgement of Taste,* Richard Nice, trans. (Cambridge, Mass.: Harvard University Press, 1984), 44.

34   *early sweet tooth:*

Publication date, as of this writing, is still to be determined. An interesting discussion of sweetness and development can be found in

Gary Beauchamp and Beverly J. Cowart's "Development of Sweet Taste," in *Sweetness,* John Dobbing, ed. (London: Springer-Verlag, 1986), 134.

35 *some 11,000 years:*
Jared Diamond, *Guns, Germs, and Steel: The Fates of Human Societies* (New York: Norton, 1999), 115.

36 *sweet isn't outright rejected:*
Mintz, *Sweetness and Power,* 17.

36 *We all start:*
Martin Witt and Klaus Reutter, "Scanning Electron Microscopical Studies of Developing Gustatory Papillae in Humans," *Chemical Senses* 22, no. 6 (December 1999): 601–12.

38 *mothers drank carrot juice:*
Julie A. Mennella et al., "Prenatal and Postnatal Flavor Learning by Human Infants," *Pediatrics* 107 (June 2001): e88.

38 *infant formula:*
Julie A. Mennella et al., "Understanding the Origin of Flavor Preferences," *Chemical Senses* 30 (2005): 1242–43.

42 *Immanuel Kant:*
Immanuel Kant, *Anthropology from a Pragmatic Point of View* (New York: Cambridge University Press, 2006), 178–82.

43 *Cold Stone Creamery:*
"Cold Stone Creamery Launches in Japan," *Ice Cream Reporter,* November 20, 2005.

45 *By medieval times:*
Sidney Mintz, *Tasting Food, Tasting Freedom* (Boston: Beacon Press, 1996), 55.

45 *At the turn:*
Mazumdar, *Sugar and Society,* 45.

45 *It was more prized:*
Ibid., 28.

45 *During the eighth century:*
Ibid.

45   *quince jams and almond-stuffed:*
Jack Goody, *Cooking, Cuisine and Class: A Study in Comparative Sociology* (Cambridge and New York: Cambridge University Press, 1996), 127.

46   *industrialized sugar refinery:*
Maguelonne Toussaint-Samat, *History of Food,* Anthea Bell, trans. (Malden, Mass.: Blackwell Publishers, 2000), 553.

46   *an eleventh-century sultan:*
Nichola Fletcher, *Charlemagne's Tablecloth: A Piquant History of Feasting* (New York: St. Martin's Press, 2004), 12.

46   *and even honey:*
Mintz, *Sweetness and Power,* 85.

46   *One preparation of:*
Ken Albala, *The Banquet* (Urbana and Chicago: University of Illinois Press, 2007), 38.

47   *most important branch:*
Anne Willan, *Great Cooks and Their Recipes, from Taillevent to Escoffier* (London: Pavillon Books, 1995), 143.

47   *Between 1700 and:*
Mintz, *Sweetness and Power,* 67.

47   *sugar consumption rose:*
Wendy A. Woloson, *Refined Tastes: Sugar, Confectionery, and Consumers in Nineteenth-Century America* (Baltimore, Md.: Johns Hopkins University Press, 2002), 6.

48   *extracted from sugar beets:*
For helpful information about the history and science of making sugar from beets, check out the SKIL site (www.sucrose.com) and American Sugar Beet Growers Association site (www.americansug arbeet.org). Also Goody, *Cooking, Cuisine and Class,* 155; and Toussaint-Samat, *History of Food,* 560.

48   *In 1855:*
Woloson, *Refined Tastes,* 27.

48   *the layer cake:*
From Alice Ross and Angie Mosier, and insights from Patent's *Baking in America*; Susan Williams's *Savory Suppers and Fashionable Feasts: Dining in Victorian America* (New York: Knopf, 1985); and Nicola Humble's introductory remarks in the Oxford World's Classics 2000 edition of *Mrs. Beeton's Book of Household Management* (see following note); and Harvey Levenstein's *Revolution at the Table: The Transformation of the American Diet* (Berkeley and Los Angeles: University of California Press, 2003).

49   *As Isabella Beeton:*
Isabella Beeton, *Mrs. Beeton's Book of Household Management*, Nicola Humble, ed. (New York: Oxford University Press, 2000), 33.

49   *"Active snobbery":*
Beeton, *Household Management*, xxi. Also helpful: Levenstein, *Revolution at the Table*, 10–22.

50   *to make sure:*
Women of the First Congregational Church of Marysville, Ohio, *Centennial Buckeye Cookbook*, Andrew F. Smith, ed., originally published in 1876 (Columbus: Ohio State University Press, 2000), 49.

50   *"the beauty of":*
Beeton, *Household Management*, 303.

50   *eight sketches:*
Ibid., 314–15.

50   *2 million:*
Ibid., vii.

51   *"urban" foods:*
Harvey Levenstein, *Paradox of Plenty: A Social History of Eating in Modern America*, rev. ed. (Berkeley and Los Angeles: University of California Press, 2003), 27.

Chapter Three: The Real Taste of Strawberry

58   *By the turn:*
Interviews with Gascon and Sobel provided great insight on the

evolution of the taste industry. Also helpful: Woloson, *Refined Tastes,* chapter 2.

62   *So while sales:*
Mintel International Group, "Cookies and Cookie Bars—US—August 2006."

62   *thick, chewy, premium sort:*
Mintel International Group, "Just Dessert—December 2006."

64   *The mango is said:*
Check out the official website for the Mango Association, www.mad4mango.com.

65   *38 million Americans:*
U.S. Department of Commerce, Office of Travel & Tourism.

66   *35 million:*
2005 U.S. Census.

67   *food-science consultant:*
Mary Ellen Camire, University of Maine professor of food science and human nutrition, was the first to point out to me the importance of sugar in smoothies. She has since explored fat in frozen desserts. Check out her "Frozen Wild Blueberry–Tofu–Soy Milk Desserts," *Journal of Food Science* 71, no. 2 (2006): S119–S123.

70   *a group of monkeys:*
Elisabeth Rozin and Paul Rozin, "Culinary Themes and Variations," in *The Taste Culture Reader: Experiencing Food and Drink,* Carolyn Korsmeyer, ed. (New York: Berg, 2005), 36.

70   *In* American Cookery*:*
Amelia Simmons, *American Cookery* (Bedford, Mass.: Applewood Books), 53.

71   *Our current species:*
Deerr, *The History of Sugar,* 12.

72   *California can harvest:*
Statistics and general information from press materials and conversations with the marketing team at the California Strawberry Commission. (Check out www.calstrawberry.com.)

72   *99.6 pounds:*
        USDA Economic Research Service, "Fruit and Tree Nuts Year-
        book," October 2006, www.ers.usda.gov.

73   *$31.5 billion industry:*
        Produce Marketing Association (www.pma.com).

73   *They're attracting investors:*
        Katy McLaughlin, "New Fruits Get a Sugar Rush, *Wall Street Jour-
        nal,* June 3–4, 2006: 4.

74   *In a report:*
        JoAndrea Hoegg and Joseph W. Alba, "Taste Perception: More
        Than Meets the Tongue," *Journal of Consumer Research* 33 (March
        2007): 490–98.

74   *U.S. Army:*
        Brian Wansink, *Mindless Eating: Why We Eat More Than We Think*
        (New York: Bantam, 2006), 121.

Chapter Four: Always Room for Dessert

80   *the digestive system:*
        Allan Geliebter, a psychologist and research scientist at Colum-
        bia University College of Physicians and Surgeons, was very
        helpful and patient in explaining how all this works; so was
        Robert Lustig at UCSF. For a good basic overview, check out
        A.W. Logue, *The Psychology of Eating and Drinking* (New York:
        Brunner-Routledge, 2004), as well as a paper by Paul P. Bertrand
        and Rebecca L. Bertrand, "Teaching Basic Gastrointestinal Phys-
        iology Using Classic Papers by Dr. Walter B. Cannon," *Advances in
        Physiology Education* 31 (2007): 136–39, which can be found at
        www.physiology.org.

83   *allure of variety:*
        Barbara J. Rolls, "Pleasantness Changes and Food Intake in a Var-
        ied Four-Course Meal," *Appetite* 5 (1984): 337–48.

83   *Birds in the wild:*
        Barbara J. Rolls and Marion Hetherington, "The Role of Variety

in Eating and Body Weight Regulations," in *Handbook of the Psychophysiology of Human Eating,* R. Shepherd, ed. (Sussex, England: John Wiley & Son, 1989), 57–84.

83 *monkeys monitored:*
E. T. Rolls et al., "Neurophysical Analysis of Brain Stimulation Reward in the Monkey," *Brain Research* 194 (1980): 339–57.

84 *different varieties of sandwiches:*
Barbara J. Rolls et al., "Variety in a Meal Enhances Food Intake in Man," *Physiology & Behavior* 26 (1981): 215–21.

84 *less likely to grow tiresome:*
H. G. Schutz and F. J. Pilgrim, "A Field Study of Food Monotony," *Psychological Reports* 4 (1958): 559–65. Also Barbara J. Rolls, "Sweetness and Satiety" in *Sweetness,* John Dobbing, ed. (London: Springer-Verlag, 1987), 166–67.

85 *In his cookbook:*
Ludo Lefebvre, *Crave: The Feast of the Five Senses* (New York: Harper-Collins, 2005), 190.

86 *walnuts and pecans are best:*
Wayne Harley Brachman, *American Desserts* (New York: Clarkson Potter, 2003), 10.

86 *reverse contingency orders:*
Leann Birch at Penn State has written dozens of articles on this topic. Among them: L. Birch et al., "Learning to Overeat: Maternal Use of Restrictive Practices Promotes Girls' Eating in the Absence of Hunger," *American Journal of Clinical Nutrition* 78 (2003): 215–20. Also, E. Addessi et al., "Specific Social Influences on the Acceptance of Novel Foods in 2–5-Year-Old Children," *Appetite* 45 (2005): 264–71.

86 *when medical experts:*
Albala, *The Banquet,* 82.

87 *The Ancient Greeks:*
Andrew Dalby, *Siren Feasts: A History of Food and Gastronomy in Greece* (London: Taylor & Francis, 1997), 23.

88   *Japanese tea ceremonies:*
       The Urasenke Chanoyu Center in New York is a great resource
       for the culture of tea: www.urasenkeny.org.

88   *As Donald Keene:*
       Donald Keene, *Yoshimasa and the Silver Pavilion* (New York: Colum-
       bia University Press, 2006), 150.

88   *In the late Middle Ages:*
       Terrence Scully, *The Art of Cookery in the Middle Ages* (Woodbridge,
       Suffolk: The Boydell Press, 1995), 131. Also helpful: www
       .medievalcookery.com, a fascinating site run by period enthusiast
       Daniel Myers; Peter Brears, *Food & Cooking in 17th-Century Britain: His-*
       tory & Recipes (London: English Heritage, 1996), 25.

88   *"There is nothing":*
       Mintz, *Sweetness and Power,* 131.

89   *Henry IV's coronation:*
       Brears, *Food & Cooking,* 88, 132.

89   à la française:
       Margaret Visser, *The Rituals of Dinner: The Origins, Evolution, Eccentric-*
       ities, and Meaning of Table Manners (New York: Grove Weidenfeld,
       1991), 199–202. Visser gives an account about how the way we
       eat came to be in chapter 4, "Dinner Is Served," 137–295.

89   *While dessert is:*
       Marcy Norton, "Tasting Empire: Chocolate and the European In-
       ternalization of Mesoamerican Aesthetics," *The American Historical*
       Review 27 (June 2006). This essay was great at dispelling some of
       the myths regarding chocolate—including the fact that chocolate
       was sweetened only when the Europeans got their hands on it.
       I also discovered some interesting historical stories on the web-
       site of the Chocolate Manufacturers Association, http://www
       .chocolateusa.org/pdfs/Ch.2-History-of-Chocolate.pdf.

90   *first official cargo:*
       Sophie D. Coe and Michael D. Coe, *The True History of Chocolate*
       (London: Thames & Hudson, 1996), 133.

90   *From Spain and Portugal:*
       Ibid, 219.

90   *To celebrate the birthday:*
       Coe and Coe, *The True History of Chocolate,* 221.

90   *In a letter:*
       Maurice Lever, *Sade: A Biography,* Arthur Goldhammer, trans. (New
       York: Farrar, Straus & Giroux, 1993), 311.

90   *the Germans created:*
       Conversations with Walter Staib and Margaret Visser were help-
       ful in pointing out the influence of German sweets on American
       desserts. Also interesting, Staib's *Black Forest Cuisine: The Classic
       Blending of European Flavors* (Philadelphia: Running Press, 2006).

91   *Hannah Glasse instructed:*
       Hannah Glasse, *The Art of Cookery Made Plain and Easy* (Bedford,
       Mass.: Applewood Books, 1998), 162.

93   *James and Betty de Rothschild:*
       Ian Kelly, *Cooking for Kings: The Life of the First Celebrity Chef* (New
       York: Walker & Company, 2003), 23.

94   *For six weeks:*
       Brian Wansink, *Marketing Nutrition: Soy, Functional Foods, Biotechnology,
       and Obesity* (Urbana and Chicago: University of Illinois Press,
       2005), 38–40.

97   *"You will make":*
       Kelly, *Cooking for Kings,* 125. Also helpful: Peter Hayden, "The Fab-
       riques of Antonin Carême," *Garden History* 24, no. 1 (Summer
       1996): 39–44.

Chapter Five: Sweet Tooths Anonymous

101   *The National Institute:*
       http://www.drugabuse.gov/scienceofaddiction/addiction.html.

102   *Bart Hoebel, professor:*
       Bartley G. Hoebel, "Neural Systems for Reinforcement and

Inhibition of Behavior: Relevance to Eating, Addiction, and Depression," in *Well-being: Foundations of Hedonic Psychology*, E. Diener and N. Schwarz, eds. (New York: Russell Sage Foundation, 2003), 558–72.

103   *In another Hoebel:*
       P. Rada et al., "Daily Bingeing on Sugar Repeatedly Releases Dopamine in the Accumbens Shell, *Neuroscience* 134 (2005): 737–44.

104   *One study provided:*
       Willa Michener and Paul Rozin, "Pharmacological Versus Sensory Factors in the Satiation of Chocolate Craving," *Physiology & Behavior* 56 (1994): 419–22. Also worth checking out is Deborah Zellner's interesting article about how chocolate craving is cultural: "Food Liking and Craving: A Cross-Cultural Approach," *Appetite* 33 (1999): 61–70.

105   *One doctor at:*
       Mazumdar, *Sugar and Society*, 30.

105   Sylvester Graham:
       Sylvester Graham, Lectures on the Science of Human Life, 2nd English edition (London: Horsell and Shirrefs, 1854), 547.

106   *"We cry for":*
       C. W. Gesner, "Concerning Restaurants," *Harper's New Monthly Magazine* 32, issue 191 (April 1866): 591–94.

106   *In 1847, druggist:*
       Check out the Necco (New England Confectionery Company) candy website: http://www.necco.com/AboutUs/History.asp. For more on the burgeoning biscuit industry, see Goody, *Cooking, Cuisine and Class,* 155–56.

107   *"Although confectioners encouraged":*
       Woloson, *Refined Tastes*, 143–44.

108   *$22.54 billion worth:*
       "2006 State of the Vending Industry Report" from *Automatic Merchandiser Magazine,* http://www.amonline.com.

108   *The average area:*
       Food Marketing Institute, *Supermarket Facts, Industry Overview 2006,* http://www.fmi.org.

108   *There are 945,000:*
       National Restaurant Association, *Industry Fact Sheet,* http://www
       .restaurant.org/research/ind_glance.cfm.

109   *When Gene-Jack Wang asked:*
       Gene-Jack Wang et al., "Exposure to Appetitive Food Stimuli
       Markedly Activates the Human Brain," *NeuroImage* 21 (2004):
       1790–97.

109   *Marcia Pelchat:*
       Marcia Levin Pelchat et al., "Images of Desire: Food-Craving Ac-
       tivation During MRI," *NeuroImage* 23 (2004): 1486–93.

110   *With the help:*
       Susana Peciña et al., "Hedonic Hot Spots in the Brain," *The Neurosci-
       entist* 12, no. 6 (2006): 500–11. Also helpful: Kent C. Berridge,
       "Pleasures of the Brain," *Brain and Cognition* 52 (2003): 106–28.

111   *Carbohydrates, a category:*
       R. J. Wurtman and J. J. Wurtman, "Brain Serotonin, Carbohydrate-
       Ccraving, Obesity and Depression," *Obesity Research* 3 Suppl. 4
       (November 1995), 477S–480S.

112   *Fat seems to complicate:*
       L. Eckel et al., "Diet-Induced Hyperphagia in the Rat Is
       Influenced by Sex and Exercise," *American Journal of Physiology* 287
       (November 2004), R1080–R1085.

112   *In some children:*
       M. Y. Pepino and J. A. Mennella, "Sucrose-Induced Analgesia Is
       Related to Sweet Preferences in Children but Not Adults," *Pain*
       119 (2005), 210–18.

113   *scientifically measurable calming effect:*
       Yvonne M. Ulrich-Lai et al., "Daily Limited Access to Sweetened
       Drink Attenuates Hypothalamic-Pituitary-Adrenocortical Axis
       Stress Responses," *Endocrinology* 148, no. 4 (2007): 1823–34.

114   *ice-cream social:*
       Brian Wansink, "Ice Cream Illusions: Bowl Size, Spoon Size, and
       Self-Served Portion Sizes," *American Journal of Preventive Medicine* 31,
       no. 3 (September 2006): 240–43.

115   *77 percent more:*
         Brian Wansink et al., "Shape of Glass and Amount of Alcohol
         Poured: Comparative Study of Effect of Practice and Concentra-
         tion," *British Medical Journal* 331, no. 7531 (December 24, 2005):
         1512–14; "Bottoms Up! The Influence of Elongation and Pouring
         on Consumption Volume," *Journal of Consumer Research* 30, no. 3 (De-
         cember 2003): 455–63.

115   *thirty chocolate Kisses:*
         Brian Wansink et al., "How Visibility and Convenience Influence
         Candy Consumption," *Appetite* 38 (2002): 237–38. Also helpful:
         "Environmental Factors That Increase the Food Intake and Con-
         sumption Volume of Unknowing Consumers," *Annual Review of
         Nutrition* 24 (2004): 455–79.

Chapter Six: Does Sweet Make You Fat?

123   *He lists many reasons:*
         To get a good basis of how fat, fiber, and high-fructose corn syrup
         affect health, two papers are helpful: Robert H. Lustig, "Child-
         hood Obesity: Behavioral Aberration or Biochemical Drive?
         Reinterpreting the First Law of Thermodynamics," *Nature Clinical
         Practice/Endocrinology & Metabolism* 2, no. 8 (August 2006): 447–48;
         and Elvira Isganaitis and Robert H. Lustig, "Fast Food, Central
         Nervous System Insulin Resistance, and Obesity," *Arteriosclerosis,
         Thrombosis, Vascular Biology* 25 (December 2005): 2451–62.

124   *In the seventies, America:*
         See U.S. Department of Agriculture stats on http://www
         .indexmundi.com/en/commodities/agricultural/oil-palm/. Also di-
         rector of the Center for Science in the Public Interest Mark Jacob-
         son was particularly helpful in providing the facts from a health
         standpoint. You can read about the issue in the organization's Palm
         Oil Report, http://www.cspinet.org/palmoilreport/PalmOilReport
         .pdf. To hear the argument from the other side, check out an article
         by Yusof Basiron, from the Malaysian Palm Oil Council, "Palm
         Production Through Sustainable Plantations," *European Journal of Lipid*

Science Technology 109 (2007), 289–95. A lively, detailed account of how fat has changed in our diet is reported by Greg Critser, *Fat Land* (New York: Houghton Mifflin, 2003), 12–19.

125   *90 million homes own a microwave:*
Microwave facts provided by Association of Home Appliance Manufacturers and the Lemelson-MIT Program.

126   *$70-million-a-year lead:*
For Coca-Cola: Anne B. Fisher, "Peering Past Pepsico's Bad News," *Fortune,* November 14, 1983, 124.

126   *828 eight-ounce servings:*
"Special Issue: All-Channel Carbonated Soft Drink Performance in 2005," *Beverage Digest*, March 8, 2006.

126   *sweetener-laden foods:*
For an exhaustive list of sweetener content in foods, check out USDA Nutrient Data Laboratory, "USDA National Nutrient Database for Standard Reference, Release 18," www.nal.usda.gov.

126   *Worse, with cheaper:*
A good overview of how big our food has become can be found in Kelly D. Brownell's *Food Fight: The Inside Story of the Food Industry, America's Obesity Crisis, and What We Can Do About It* (New York: McGraw-Hill, 2004), 180–84. It even includes a photograph showing the transformation of the cute and curvy 8-ounce bottle of Coca-Cola into the current hefty 34-ounce guzzler.

129   *six more hours:*
John P. Robinson and Geoffrey Godbey, *Time for Life: The Surprising Ways American Use Time* (University Park, Penn.: Penn State University Press, 1999), 341.

129   *fifteen minutes or less:*
Clotaire Rapaille, *The Culture Code: An Ingenious Way to Understand Why People Around the World Live and Buy as They Do* (New York: Broadway, 2007), 103.

129   *One out of five:*
A. Elizabeth Sloan, "What, When, and Where America Eats: A State-of-the-Industry Report," *Food Technology,* January 2006, 19.

129   *Sixty-two percent:*
A survey done by American Dietetic Association and ConAgra
Foods Foundation Home Food Safety program and reported by
USA Today, September 30, 2004, http://www.usatoday.com/news/
health/2004-09-30-multitask-usat_x.htm.

129   *we spent 3,583:*
U.S. Bureau of the Census, Statistical Abstract, Information Communications, "Media Usage and Consumer Spending," 2007, 709.

130   *from 793 hours:*
Ibid., 709.

130   *Internet has shot:*
Ibid.

131   *Margaret Visser and her:*
Presented at "Feeding Desire: Dining as Spectacle," symposium at
the Cooper-Hewitt National Design Museum in New York City,
May 6, 2006.

131   *This face time:*
Will Goldfarb at the panel discussion "Classic Versus Avant-
Garde: The Direction of Desserts," French Culinary Institute's
International Culinary Theater, June 18, 2007.

133   *At the Ross School:*
"The School Lunch Test," *New York Times,* August 20, 2006. http://
www.nytimes.com/2006/08/20/magazine/20lunches.html?ex=
1184817600&en=b97216a676a092bc&ei=5070. Also helpful:
Ann Cooper and Lisa Holmes, *Lunch Lessons: Changing the Way We
Feed Our Children* (New York: Collins, 2006).

Chapter Seven: Let Them Eat Cake

137   *both articles:*
"Erika Kinetz, Candy-Colored Dreams," *New York Times,* January 1,
2006, http://select.nytimes.com/search/restricted/article?res=
FB0616FE3B540C728CDDA80894DE404482; Marian Burros
and Melanie Warner, "Bottlers Agree to a School Ban on Sweet

Drinks," *New York Times,* May 4, 2006, http://www.nytimes.com/
2006/05/04/health/04soda.html?ex=1184817600&en=
2ad5b2ff49a54672&ei=5070.

137   *obesity rates:*
      "Eating Well in Harlem: How Available Is Healthy Food? A Re-
      port from the East and Central Harlem District Public Health
      Office," New York City Department of Health and Mental Hy-
      giene, http://www.nyc.gov/html/doh/downloads/pdf/dpho/dpho
      -harlem-report2007.pdf.

141   *second-bestselling cookie:*
      A list of top-selling brands and vendors appears on the AIB In-
      ternational (formerly the American Institute of Baking) website
      www.aibonline.org/resources/statistics/2006cookies.htm.

141   *The yawning price gap:*
      Adam Drewnowski, "Poverty and Obesity: The Role of Energy
      Density and Energy Costs," *American Journal of Clinical Nutrition* 79
      (2004): 6–16.

142   *As one survey:*
      U.S. Bureau of Labor Statistics, 2007, "Consumer Expenditures
      in 2005."

143   *a farming journal:*
      George Stigler, "The Cost of Subsistence." *Journal of Farm Economics*
      27 (1945): 303–14.

143   *Thrifty Food Plan:*
      U.S. Department of Agriculture, "Thrifty Food Plan, 2006,"
      http://www.cnpp.usda.gov/Publications/FoodPlans/MiscPubs/
      TFP2006Report.pdf.

143   *Perhaps George Orwell:*
      Mintz, *Sweetness and Power,* 254. This is the passage that Drewnowski
      cited when he took down the book from his shelves.

143   *the highest quintile:*
      Adam Drewnowski, "Fat and Sugar: An Economic Analysis," *The
      Journal of Nutrition* 133 (2003): 838S–840S.

145   *Rebecca E. Lee:*
        The study itself is soon to be published; meantime, the following
        is helpful: Gail Regan, Rebecca Lee, et al., "Obesogenic Influences
        in Public Housing: A Mixed Method Analysis," *American Journal of
        Health Promotion* 20 (March 2006): 282–90.

147   *Sidney Mintz describes:*
        Sidney Mintz, "Quenching Homologous Thirsts," unpublished,
        1997.

149   *more "myopic":*
        Avner Offer, *The Challenge of Affluence: Self-Control and Well-Being in
        the United States and Britain Since 1950* (New York: Oxford University
        Press, 2006), 143.

150   *Into the '70s:*
        Levenstein, *Paradox of Plenty,* 191–93.

150   *American medicine has:*
        Peter N. Stearns, *Fat History: Bodies and Beauty in the Modern West*
        (New York and London: New York University Press, 2002), 43.

150   *New York University study:*
        Dalton Conley and Rebecca Glauber, "Gender, Body Mass and
        Economic Status," National Bureau of Economic Research
        (NBER), *Working Paper* No. 11343, May 25, 2005. Also helpful: Avner
        Offer's *The Challenge of Affluence,* 154–55, 166.

152   *As Harvey Levenstein:*
        Levenstein, *Paradox of Plenty,* 211.

152   *Packaged Facts:*
        Packaged Facts, a division of MarketResearch.com, "The U.S.
        Market for Sweet Baked Goods," November 2005, 15.

154   *It started when:*
        Levenstein, *Paradox of Plenty,* 180.

155   *oranges, apples, and bananas:*
        "Fruit and Tree Nuts Yearbook-Summary," Economic Research
        Service, U.S. Department of Architecture, October 2006.

155   *city-commissioned health survey:*
        "Eating Well in Harlem."

156 *National Cancer Institute:*
Cooper and Holmes, *Lunch Lessons,* 93.

Chapter Eight: Guilty Pleasures

159 *team of determined:*
Paul Rozin et al., "Attitudes to Food and the Role of Food in Life: Comparisons of Flemish Belgium, France, Japan and the United States," *Appetite* 33 (1999): 163–80.

162 *pounds of fresh blueberries:*
U.S. Highbush Blueberry Council, www.blueberry.org.

163 *"toxic food chain":*
Peter Applebome, "In a Fat Nation, Are Thin Mints on Thin Ice?" *New York Times,* February 21, 2007, B1.

163 *"empty calories":*
Christine Ammer, *The American Heritage of Dictionary of Idioms* (Boston and New York: Houghton Mifflin, 1997), 187.

163 Washington Post *letter:*
Pamela Labossiere, "More on Vending Foods," *Washington Post,* March 9, 1973, A27.

163 *Only 4 percent of the French:*
Rozin, "Attitudes to Food and the Role of Food in Life."

163 *42 percent:*
Obesity rates are available from the International Association for the Study of Obesity, www.iaso.org.

166 *11 million Africans:*
McWilliams, *A Revolution in Eating,* 29.

166 *In colonial Pennsylvania:*
Woloson, *Refined Tastes,* 23.

166 *George Fox:*
Ibid., 24.

166 *skyrocketed 400 percent:*
Ibid., 22.

166   *"Free" sugar:*
       Deerr provides a good overview of the movement in volume 2.
       Essentially it was debatable whether the sugar from India was in
       fact slave-free, 294–96.

167   *A few possible:*
       Howard M. Leichter, "Lifestyle Correctness and the New Secular
       Morality," in *Morality + Health*, Allan M. Brandt and Paul Rozin, eds.
       (London: Routledge, 1999), 369.

168   *Leichter suspects:*
       Ibid., 368. Further discussion on the impact of the frontier spirit
       on our attitudes toward our bodies can be found in Lynn Payer's
       *Medicine & Culture: Varieties of Treatment in the United States, England, West
       Germany, and France* (New York: Owl Books, 1996), 127.

168   *"the Golden Age of food faddism":*
       Levenstein, *Revolution at the Table*, 86.

169   *"The body housed":*
       James C. Whorton, *Crusaders for Fitness* (Princeton, N.J.: Princeton
       University Press, 1982), 31. Both Whorton and Levenstein's *Revo-
       lution at the Table* give an interesting overview of the health gurus of
       the day.

169   *Mary Mann:*
       Mary Tyler Peabody Mann, *Christianity in the Kitchen: A Physiological
       Cook Book* (Boston: Ticknor and Fields, 1861), 1–2.

170   *World hunger:*
       Daniel Sack, *Whitebread Protestants: Food and Religion in American Cul-
       ture* (New York: Palgrave Macmillan, 2000), 198.

171   *"Avoid sugar, I say":*
       John Yudkin, *Pure, White and Deadly: The Problem of Sugar* (London:
       Davis Poynter, 1972), 49.

172   *Meanwhile, high-sugar:*
       Amy Chozick and Miho Inada, "Tokyo ♥ New York Food," *Wall
       Street Journal*, April 21, 2006.

172   *When Paul Rozin and:*
       Paul Rozin, "The Ecology of Eating: Smaller Portion Sizes in

France Than in the United States Help Explain the French Paradox," *Psychological Science* 14, no. 5 (September 2003), 450–54. Also worth reading: "Food Is Fundamental, Fun, Frightening, and Far-Reaching," *Social Research* 66, 9–30.

173   *"the shape of the taste":*
      Wansink, *Mindless Eating*, 122.

174   *faith in fine things:*
      Rozin's most recent French data suggests that the French are more interested in quality and less in microvariety, and this interest extends beyond food.

174   *neurotic thinking: gastro-anomie:*
      Claude Fischler, *L'Homnivore: Le goût, la cuisine et le corps* (Paris: Odile Jacob, 1993), 212–16.

175   *The Japanese, who live:*
      A worldwide list of life expectancies is available from the Central Intelligence Agency's "World Factbook," www.cia.gov.

175   *Peter N. Stearns:*
      Peter N. Stearns, "Children and Weight Control: Priorities in the United States and France," in *Weighty Issues: Fatness and Thinness as Social Problems,* Jeffery Sobal and Donna Maurer, eds. (Hawthorne, N.Y.: Walter de Gruyter, 1999), 11–30.

176   *increasing number of school districts:*
      Sarah Kershaw, "Don't Even Think of Touching That Cupcake," *New York Times,* September 23, 2007; Marcelle S. Fischler, "New Attitude Means Smaller Cupcakes and No Candy," *New York Times,* October 8, 2006; Doug Thompson and Rob Moritz, "Senate Approves Impact Fees Bill; House OKs Candy in Schools Measure," *Arkansas News Bureau,* February 22, 2007; Susan Snyder, "Adding Rules to the Three R's," philly.com, September 11, 2007.

Chapter Nine: A More Perfect Sweetener

182   *Still, 48 percent of all households:*
      Mintel International Group, "Sugar and Sweeteners, U.S., June 2006."

183   *Tens of thousands of years ago:*
        Diamond, *Guns, Germs, and Steel,* 132.

184   *scientist at Johns Hopkins:*
        The story, in brief, is that in 1880, Ira Remsen, a scientist and then
        president of Johns Hopkins, was studying, among other things, the
        nature of sulfuric acids. In doing so, he had created various deriva-
        tives of coal tar. Another scientist, Constantine Fahlberg, a sugar
        analyst, was in town, and during his spare time was hanging out in
        Remsen's lab and tinkering with some materials. At one point he
        became distracted, his beaker bubbled over, and he got some of the
        substance on his hands. He forgot about the incident until he ate
        his lunch later that day, when he sensed a touch of sweetness in his
        sandwich. It turns out that the chemicals he was tinkering with
        were intensely sweet, and accidentally saccharin was born. For a
        lively telling of the story of saccharin, see Rich Cohen's *Sweet and
        Low: A Family Story* (New York: Farrar, Straus and Giroux, 2006).

185   *Determined dieters:*
        I've always wondered how diet soda drinkers develop a distaste
        for regular. Richard Doty, director of the Smell and Taste Center
        at the University of Pennsylvania, set me straight. He also edited
        Handbook of Olfaction and Gustation, 2nd edition (New York: Marcel
        Dekker, 2003).

187   *A 12-ounce can:*
        D. Eric Walters, "Aspartame, a Sweet-Tasting Dipeptide" on the
        University of Bristol's chemistry site, www.chm.bris.ac.uk. K.
        Wucherpfennig et al., "Alcohol: Actual, Total and Potential
        Methyl Alcohol of Fruit Juices," *Flüssiges Obst* 8 (1983), 348–54.

187   *Morando Soffritti:*
        "First Experimental Demonstration of the Multipotential Car-
        cinogenic Effects of Aspartame Administered in the Feed to
        Sprague-Dawley Rats," *Environmental Health Perspectives* 114, no. 3
        (March 2006): 379–85.

187   *acceptable daily intake:*
        Acceptable daily intake (ADI) is the maximum amount that the
        FDA considers safe to consume each day over a lifetime. The fig-

ure is set as one hundred times less than what might trigger a health problem. For ADI equivalents of common sweeteners, see http://www.mayoclinic.com/health/diabetes-diet/NU00592.

188 *"Misleading" and "flawed":*
Eyassu G. Abegaz, "Aspartame Not Linked to Cancer," *Environmental Health Perspectives* 115, no. 1 (January 2007): A4–A5.

188 FDA Consumer:
Check it out at http://www.fda.gov/fdac/406_toc.html.

190 *rats ingesting sucralose:*
Conversations with Susan Schiffman, a professor of psychology at Duke, turned me on to this information. She has also been researching neotame, a product from NutraSweet, so I didn't expect her to be a proponent of Splenda. She led me to the interesting details that can be found in the FDA papers: http://www.cfsan.fda.gov/~lrd/fr980403.html.

191 *In a survey study:*
David Benton, "Can Artificial Sweeteners Help Control Body Weight and Prevent Obesity?" *Nutrition Research Reviews* 18 (2005): 63–76.

192 *To underscore Benton's point:*
P. J. Royers et al., "Uncoupling Sweet Taste and Calories: Comparison of the Effects of Glucose and Three Intense Sweeteners on Hunger and Food Intake," *Physiology & Behavior* 43, no. 5 (1988): 547–52.

193 *Susie Swithers:*
Terry L. Davidson and Susan E. Swithers, "Food Viscosity Influences Caloric Intake Compensation and Body Weight in Rats," *Obesity Research,* vol. 13, no. 3 (March 2005): 537–44. Also T. L. Davidson and S. E. Swithers, "A Pavlovian approach to the problem of obesity," *International Journal of Obesity and Related Metabolic Disorders* 28 (2004): 933–35.

193 *For every study:*
A few studies I had in mind: M. J. Sigman-Grant, "Sensory and Nutritive Qualities of Food—Reported Use of Reduced-Sugar

Foods and Beverages Reflect High-Quality Diets," *Journal of Food Science* 70, no. 1 (January 2005): S42–S46; A. de la Hunty et al., "A Review of the Effectiveness of Aspartame in Helping with Weight Control," British Nutrition Foundation's *Nutrition Bulletin* 31, no. 2 (June 2006): 115–28.

196   *Splenda earned $212.3 million:*
Some helpful articles include Avery Johnson, "How Sweet It Isn't," *Wall Street Journal*, April 6, 2007, B1–B2; Lynnley Browning, "See You in Court, Sweetie," *New York Times*, April 6, 2007, C1–C4; "Suit Against Splenda Goes to Phila. Jury today," *Philadelphia Inquirer*, May 11, 2007; Lorraine Heller, "Sugar Industry and Splenda Embark on New Battle," FoodNavigator.com, November 7, 2006, http://www.foodnavigator-usa.com/news/ng.asp?n=71873-mcneil -tate-lyle-splenda-sucralose.

For *Philadelphia Inquirer* readers poll, check out http://www.philly .com/inquirer/polls/7459102.html?results=y.

200   *Sweetness and Sweeteners:*
The proceedings of the symposium are slated to be published in early 2008 as ACS Symposium Series 979, *Sweetness and Sweeteners: Biology, Chemistry, and Psychophysics,"* Deepthi K. WeeraSinghe and Grant E. DuBois, eds. (New York: Oxford University Press, 2008).

200   *the journal* Cell:
Greg Nelson et al., "Mammalian Sweet Taste Receptors," *Cell* 106, no. 3 (2001): 381–90.

201   *founders of Senomyx:*
Besides an interview with Mark Zoller, chief scientific officer, at the company, the website (www.senomyx.com) was helpful.

201   *"trick" the brain:*
Melanie Warner, "Food Companies Test Flavorings That Can Mimic Sugar, Salt or MSG," *New York Times*, April 6, 2005.

203   *stevia-based sweetener:*
Lauren Etter and Betsy McKay, "Coke, Cargill Aim for a Shake-up in Sweeteners," *Wall Street Journal*, May 31, 2007. Also helpful were

conversations with Ann Clark Tucker, director of media relations at Cargill.

Chapter Ten: And Good for You

208   *according to studies:*
M. E. Dinehart et al., "Bitter Taste Markers Explain Variability in Vegetable Sweetness, Bitterness and Intake," *Physiology & Behavior* 87, no. 2 (February 28, 2006): 304–13.

209   *bitter-receptor-taste genes:*
B. Bufe et al., "The Molecular Basis of Individual Differences in Phenylthiocarbamide and Propylthiouracil Bitterness Perception," *Current Biology* 15 (2005): 1–6.

209   *PROP tasters tend:*
Adam Drewnowski, "Genetic Taste Markers and Preferences," *Drug Metabolism and Disposition* 29, issue 4, part 2 (April 2001): 535–38.

210   *Galen recommended sugar:*
An interesting overview of Galen's philosophy can be found in Mark Grant's compilation of his work, *Galen on Food and Diet* (London and New York: Routledge, 2000).

210   *"of the apothecary":*
Deerr, *The History of Sugar,* 12.

210   *"like an apothecary":*
Jean Anthelme Brillat-Savarin, *The Physiology of Taste: Or, Meditations on Transcendental Gastronomy,* M.F.K. Fisher, trans. (Washington, D.C.: Counterpoint Press, 2000), 102.

210   *Sugar was thought:*
Mintz, *Sweetness and Power,* 105.

210   *Blended with pearls:*
Ibid., 107.

210   *Thomas Aquinas gave:*
Ibid., 99.

211   *Sugarcane juice is:*
        Mazumdar, *Sugar and Society*, 21–23.

211   *Back in medieval:*
        Check out the "Dietetics and Sociology of Fruit" section on the Me-
        dieval Gastronomy site, http://www.oldcook.com/en/medieval_
        gastronomy.htm.

212   *Mayan nobles:*
        Coe and Coe, *The True History of Chocolate*, 132–33.

212   *good-for-you compounds:*
        A few relevant studies: Chang Y. (Cy) Lee et al., "Cocoa Has
        More Phenolic Phytochemicals and a Higher Antioxidant Capac-
        ity Than Teas and Red Wine," *Journal of Agriculture and Food Chemistry*
        5, no. 25 (December 2003): 7292–95, Coe and Coe also describe
        the work of Hervé Robert, who writes in his 1990 book, *Les vertus
        thérapeutiques du chocolat*, that chocolate is an antidepressant and
        anti-stress agent (p. 31); K. A. Cooper et al., "Cocoa and Health:
        A Decade of Research," *British Journal of Nutrition* 99, no. 1 (January
        2008): 1–11; Carl L. Keene et al., "Cocoa Antioxidants and Car-
        diovascular Health," *American Journal of Clinical Nutrition* 81, no. 1
        (January 2005) 298S–303S; D. Taubert et al., "Effects of Low
        Habitual Cocoa Intake on Blood Pressure and Bioactive Nitric
        Oxide: A Randomized Controlled Trial," *Journal of the American
        Medical Association* 298, no. 1 (July 4, 2007): 49–60.

212   *Early research:*
        M. D. Basson et al., "Associations Between 6-n-Propylthiouracil
        (PROP) Bitterness and Colonic Neoplasms," *Digestive Diseases and
        Sciences* 50, no. 3 (March 2005): 483–89.

213   *In one study, Duffy:*
        J. E. Hayes and V. B. Duffy, "Revisiting Sugar-Fat Mixtures:
        Sweetness and Creaminess Vary with Phenotypic Markers of
        Oral Sensation," *Chemical Senses* 23, no. 3 (March 2007), 225–36.
        Also helpful: L. M. Bartoshuk, V. B. Duffy et al., "Psychophysics of
        Sweet and Fat Perception in Obesity: Problems, Solutions and

New Perspectives," Philosophical Transactions of the Royal Society of London, Series B, *Biological Sciences* 361, no. 1471 (July 2006), 1137–48.

213   *Non-tasters say they:*
S. A. Lanier et al., "Sweet and Bitter Tastes of Alcoholic Beverages Mediate Alcohol Intake in Of-Age Undergraduates," *Physiology & Behavior* 83, no. 5 (January 2005): 821–31.

215   *Never mind, either, that:*
These particular figures were cited in Kim Severson's article "Sugar Coated: We're Drowning in High-Fructose Corn Syrup. Do the Risks Go Beyond Our Waistline?" *San Francisco Chronicle,* February 18, 2004. Also check out "Sugar Content of Popular Food" on the Center for Science in the Public Interest website http://www.cspinet.org/reports/sugar/popsugar.html.

216   *a French experiment:*
Hervé This, *Molecular Gastronomy: Exploring the Science of Flavor* (New York and Chichester, West Sussex: Columbia University Press, 2006), 119–20.

218   *candied lettuce:*
Albala, *The Banquet,* 81.

218   *sliced turnips:*
Scully, *Art of Cookery,* 226.

218   *Bartolomeo Scappi:*
Albała, *The Banquet,* 78.

219   *Cristoforo di Messisbugo:*
Ibid., 60.

219   *Bartolomeo Stefani:*
Ibid., 54.

219   *Food anthropologists have:*
Elisabeth Rozin and Paul Rozin, "Culinary Themes and Variations," in *Taste Culture Reader: Experiencing Food and Drink,* Carolyn Korsmeyer, ed. (Oxford and New York: Berg, 2005), 34.

219   *In the cookbook:*
       Jeffrey Alford and Naomi Duguid, *Hot Sour Salty Sweet: A Culinary Journey Through Southeast Asia* (New York: Artisan, 2000), 76, 69.

220   *Chef Iacopo Falai:*
       Melissa Clark, "One Dessert, Many Flavors, Even Sweet," *New York Times,* May 3, 2006, F1.

Acknowledgments

I am grateful to all those who spent countless hours with me, inviting me into their world and making this project possible—this book is the result of many people who are as kind and generous as they are brilliant. A special thank-you goes to Linda Bartoshuk, whose enthusiasm for the science of taste is infectious, and who prompted me to think more seriously about my sweet tooth. And also to Adam Drewnowski, Sidney Mintz, Paul Rozin, and Brian Wansink, whose work fascinated me long before I even thought about writing a book; they are the ones who inspired me to ask more questions and who shaped the ideas explored here. They took time out of their busy lives not only to meet with me but to be tracked down again and again on the phone and by e-mail. I can only hope that I captured the essence of their work just as they'd like it; any errors found here are obviously my own.

This book would still be just an idea in my head if it weren't for my friend Sarah Deckey, who kept reminding me to write a proposal until I did. And it is thanks to her and her brother, Ben, that I found my agent, Larry Weissman, and his wife, Sascha, an incredibly creative, smart team who turned a small proposal into a book-worthy one; they are also fabulous cooks. Many thanks to my editors at *Life* magazine and *Fortune Small Business* for generously allowing me the time to put my thoughts on paper; to my editor, Lucinda Bartley, who provided intelligent and patient direction and kept me focused; to Stephanie Fletcher and Elisabeth Durkin for their tireless research help; and to my amazing friends who offered encouragement and advice. Finally I am deeply indebted to my family—my mother and father, Lana and Fusen, for inspiring me with their selfless love and support and their enthusiasm for food, both sweet and savory; my brother, Willis, for being my personal I.T. consultant and for his sharp feedback and suggestions; and, most of all, my wise and talented sister, Judy, for her thoughful ideas, insight, and guidance in pastries and in life.

Index